Jean-Roch Coignet

The narrative of Captain Coignet 1776-1850

Jean-Roch Coignet

The narrative of Captain Coignet 1776-1850

ISBN/EAN: 9783337135287

Printed in Europe, USA, Canada, Australia, Japan

Cover: Foto ©ninafisch / pixelio.de

More available books at **www.hansebooks.com**

"I took my spade and went to work in the garden." — Page 10.

OF

CAPTAIN COIGNET

(SOLDIER OF THE EMPIRE)

1776-1850

EDITED FROM THE ORIGINAL MANUSCRIPT

By LORÉDAN LARCHEY

TRANSLATED FROM THE FRENCH

By MRS. M. CAREY

NEW YORK
THOMAS Y. CROWELL & CO.
46 EAST FOURTEENTH STREET

PREFACE.

JEAN-ROCH COIGNET was pre-eminently what is called a thorough-going man. Whether as shepherd or wagoner, stable-boy or farm hand, soldier or captain, we find him always ready to do his best. Whether using a broom or drawing a sabre, he brings to bear all his mind, all his buoyancy of spirit, and all his pride. Consequently, the perusal of his life rests one as does the company of good reliable men, upon whose devotion one can always count.

It will be seen that his life was not without adventures, and that he knows how to relate them unusually well. One is not a story-teller at will. It is a natural gift, like the color-sense of the great masters, and without it a well-educated person will often find nothing to tell about a journey which an illiterate man so gifted will describe in the most eloquent manner. Our old captain was one of those who possessed this gift. He was uneducated, and he acknowledges the fact without hesitation. He did not know how to read or write until he was thirty-five years old. It was with great difficulty that, at the age of seventy-two, he traced the big schoolboy characters which cover the nine blank-books of his manuscript.

How could he, at seventy-two, remember so many minute details? The fact is less surprising than it appears: in the first place, the memory of early years becomes more vivid as age increases, and in the second place, Coignet had related his memories all his life long before writing them. Just so the bards of Homer recited his "Iliad."

Are Coignet's memorials valuable as a book of history? I do not go to them any more than to the "Iliad" to verify facts, as we say. I do not even stop to discuss or rectify their statements. Their interest is altogether of another kind. As is the case with all those who do the fighting, our soldier knew not how to give a detailed account of the operations of an army; but he gives us what we could never learn from the exact report of the chief of staff. From him you get the face of the combatant, the incidents of the march, the color of the battle-field, the unforeseen action, the hot work of the fight,— everything that is spirited, picturesque, or specially exciting.

We know the whole story, doubtless, but how much better we comprehend it here, when we see the decorations and the actors! We see them at Montebello when, being for the first time under fire, our hero stoops before the volley of grape-shot, and condemns his weakness immediately by answering, "I will not," to the sergeant-major, who cries, "Don't duck your head." We find them at Marengo, when, thrown down and sabred, he had no chance to save his life but to cling, all bleeding as he was, to the tail of a dragoon's horse till he could rejoin his demi-brigade, pick up a gun, and fire even better than before; in the icy bogs of Poland, where he was obliged to take hold of each leg with both hands, and pull it out of the mud in order to take a step forward; at Essling, when the Austrian cannonade made the bear-skin caps of the old guard fly about, and dashed around pieces of flesh with such force that many were knocked down by them; on the road to Witepsk, when, with only the formality of drawing lots, we see seventy marauders shot, offered up as a last sacrifice to the expiring discipline of the grand army; at Mainz, during the horrors of the typhus fever, the final scourge of the retreat, when it was necessary to bring out the cannon to force the convicts to cord-up the piles of dead bodies on foraging wagons, and afterwards dump the terrible load into one great pit. By the side of these black shadows we find bright lights, charming pictures of rural life, amusing scenes of bivouac, reflections no less amusing upon the countries traversed, and infinitely precious details of the relations of the chiefs with their soldiers. Particularly does he show what a chief may get out of our troops, when he knows how to win their esteem. The value of the office depends upon the man who fills it; and when the man is worthless, French indiscipline leaps at one bound to the greatest excess.

For this reason the officers risk their persons in every danger, keep a constant watch over their soldiers, and associate freely with them without fear of losing their respect. At Mount St. Bernard they tear up their clothing in hitching themselves to the cannon in the difficult passes. If a trooper does a brave act, they embrace him heartily, and make him drink from their cups. Courage not less than rank is the officer's distinction. At critical moments generals are seen to take the position of sharpshooters, and to rally fugitives under fire of the enemy. Dorsenne, knocked down by the explosion of a shell in the midst of his grenadiers, immediately rises, and cries out, "Your general is not hurt. Depend upon him, he will die at his post." Though he could not stand upright, as Dorsenne did, that colonel commanding the celebrated battery at Wagram was none the less great, who, though wounded early in the morning, had himself borne in an ambulance till evening, and remained at the head of his forces, though unable to sit up. "He commanded sitting up in bed," says Coignet, in six words that are worth as much as a picture.

At Kowno, Coignet sees Ney snatch a gun, and face the enemy with five men. At Brienne, Prince Berthier charges four Cossacks, and retakes a cannon from them. At Montereau, Marshal Lefebvre rides at a gallop over a broken bridge, and sabres a rear-guard with no following but his staff officers. With such examples before them, it is easy to believe that the soldiers did not remain behind. Thus, at the rout of the Mincio, the sight of a single horseman remaining alone at his post as sharpshooter suffices to rally his division. The grenadiers at Essling and Wagram contend for the honor of dying as voluntary cannoneers at an untenable post. At Austerlitz a Mameluke, who had already captured two flags in a cavalry fight, dashes in a third time, and is seen no more. Nor must we forget that quartermaster who, having his leg broken on the field of Eylau, walks off alone to the ambulance with two guns for crutches, saying that with his three pairs of boots he would have enough to last a long time. We recognize this as mere facetiousness; but at the point when the gayest-hearted can laugh no longer, facetiousness becomes heroism.

Is all this really true? they ask, who do not feel within themselves either the desire or the power to do so much. I have not seen it any more than they; but I do know very well that Coignet is a story-teller of the first order; that he has the gift of style without knowing it. I have always observed that any one who possesses this merit is sure to possess two others: that of feeling intensely, and that of expressing his feelings with absolute sincerity. I have also often remarked that absolute truthfulness will crown as an author many a writer who would fall below mediocrity if asked to lie; that is, to write a work of fiction.

I do not feel that Coignet has invented anything. He was not capable of it. But did this Coignet really ever exist? I know that this question also has been asked. Certainly, it is possible to doubt every thing, and to believe that I have taken the trouble to fabricate an original manuscript. That also has been said to me. They who consider fiction more powerful than truth, not suspecting that the richest imagination will always fall short of the unforeseen reality, will continue to have eyes that see not.

Let these sceptics take the road to Auxerre. Let them go to the municipal library, and question my obliging colleague Molard, to whom I owe the chance of obtaining the autograph manuscript. Let them see the last possessor of it, M. Lorin; let them demand an interview with M. Henri Monceau, who gave me two portraits of Captain Coignet, and who also afterwards sent me an extract from his will, dated Nov. 2, 1858, and written in the office of Maitre Limosin. At Paris, I refer them to the offices of the minister of war and the chancellor of the Legion of Honor, and thence obtained duplicates of Coignet's record of service and his commissions. Last May I saw again the Café Milon and that grocery at the corner of the Rue des Belles-Filles, where the captain, retired on half-pay, went on an errand to grind his pound of coffee, in order to make his offer of marriage with more delicacy. I had for my guide M. Monceaux, who knew Coignet as, indeed, he knows everybody and everything in old Auxerre. He could tell many things about him to those who doubt.

Proof is, therefore, abundant. There is no room for them here, for an illustrated book does not admit of the expansion or the completeness of apparatus which are usual in the publication of a historical document. The text of our first edition has not been changed; but it has been reduced so as to make an edition suitable for general readers. As a compensation for this, the illustrations, by a popular artist, add greatly to the attractions of the new book. Like ourselves, fascinated by the adventures of the brave Jean-Roch, M. Le Blant has identified himself with his hero. His pictures have the charm of truthfulness, and I add my thanks for them to those of the public.

LORÈDAN LARCHEY.

PARIS, August 30, 1887.

TABLE OF CONTENTS.

FIRST NOTE-BOOK.

MY CHILDHOOD. — I AM BY TURNS SHEPHERD, WAGONER, AND STABLE-BOY. — I LEAVE MY NATIVE VILLAGE A SECOND TIME. — I ENTER THE SERVICE OF M. POTIER 1

SECOND NOTE-BOOK.

DEPARTURE FOR THE ARMY. — MY MILITARY LIFE UP TO THE BATTLE OF MONTEBELLO 51

THIRD NOTE-BOOK.

THE BATTLE OF MARENGO. — EXCURSION INTO SPAIN . . . 71

FOURTH NOTE-BOOK.

MY DECORATION. — I AM POISONED. — RETURN TO MY COUNTRY. — THE CAMP OF BOULOGNE AND THE FIRST AUSTRIAN CAMPAIGN 101

FIFTH NOTE-BOOK.

PRUSSIAN AND POLISH CAMPAIGNS. — CONFERENCE AT TILSIT. — I AM MADE CORPORAL. — SPANISH AND AUSTRIAN CAMPAIGNS. — I AM APPOINTED SERGEANT 130

SIXTH NOTE-BOOK.

RE-ENTRANCE INTO FRANCE. — THE FESTIVITIES OF THE IMPERIAL MARRIAGE. — I DO THE DUTIES OF SERGEANT-INSTRUCTOR, MESS-CHIEF, AND BAGGAGE-MASTER 183

SEVENTH NOTE-BOOK.

THE RUSSIAN CAMPAIGN. — I AM APPOINTED LIEUTENANT ON THE MINOR IMPERIAL STAFF. — THE RETREAT FROM MOSCOW, 203

EIGHTH NOTE-BOOK.

I AM APPOINTED CAPTAIN. — CAMPAIGNS OF 1813 AND 1814. — THE FAREWELLS AT FONTAINEBLEAU. — MY VISIT TO COULOMMIERS 245

NINTH NOTE-BOOK.

ON HALF-PAY. — THE HUNDRED DAYS. — TEN YEARS OF SUPERINTENDENCE. — MY MARRIAGE. — THE REVOLUTION OF 1830. — I AM APPOINTED AN OFFICER IN THE LEGION OF HONOR . 272

DOCUMENTARY EXTRACTS.

STATEMENT OF THE MILITARY SERVICES OF COIGNET (JEAN-ROCH). FAC-SIMILE OF A PAGE OF THE NOTE-BOOKS OF CAPTAIN COIGNET 315

THE
NARRATIVE OF CAPTAIN COIGNET.

FIRST NOTE-BOOK.

MY CHILDHOOD. — I AM BY TURNS SHEPHERD, WAGONER, AND STABLE-BOY. — I LEAVE MY NATIVE VILLAGE A SECOND TIME. — I ENTER THE SERVICE OF M. POTIER.

I was born at Druyes-les-Belles-Fontaines, in the Department of the Yonne, August 16, 1776.

My father had three wives. The first left two daughters; the second, four children, — a girl and three boys. The youngest was six years old, my sister seven, I was eight, and my eldest brother nine, when we had the misfortune to lose our dear mother. My father married again the third time. He married his servant, who bore him seven children. She was eighteen years old, and was called a beauty. This stepmother ruled everything. We poor little orphans were beaten night and day. She choked us to give us a good color. Every day, when my father returned from hunting, he would ask, "My dear, where are the children?" and my stepmother answered, "They are asleep."

Every day it was the same thing. We never saw our father. She took every means to prevent our finding an opportunity to complain. However, her vigilance was at fault one morning, and my father found my brother and me with tears on our cheeks. "What is the matter?" he asked. "We are dying of hunger. She beats us every day."—"Come with me. I will see about this."

The result of this information was terrible. The whippings did not cease, and the bread was curtailed. At last, not being able to stand it any longer, my elder brother took me by the hand and said, "If you are willing, we will go away. Let us each take a shirt, and say good-by to no one."

Early in the morning we set out, and went to Étais, a place about an hour's walk from our home. It was the day of a fair. My brother put a bunch of oak leaves in my little hat, and hired me out for a shepherd. I earned twenty-four francs a year, and a pair of wooden shoes.

I went to a village called Charnois. It was surrounded by a forest. I served as a watch-dog for the shepherdess. "Go yonder," said the woman to me. As I was going along the edge of the wood so as to keep the sheep away from it, a big wolf ran out, drove the sheep back, and seized upon one of the finest in the flock. I had never had any experience with such a beast. The shepherdess screamed, and told me to run. I hastened to the spot. The wolf could not throw the sheep on his back, so I had time to catch hold of its hind feet, and the wolf pulled one way and I the other.

But Providence came to my assistance. Two enormous dogs, wearing iron collars, rushed out, and in a moment the wolf was killed. Imagine my joy at having saved my sheep, and seeing the beast stretched dead upon the ground.

I served the shepherdess as watch-dog for a year. From there I went to the fair at Entrains. I hired myself out, for thirty francs, a blouse, and a pair of wooden shoes. to two old farmers of Les Bardins, near Menon, who sold wood on the wharves, and who made from twelve to fifteen hundred francs by my labor.

They had twelve head of cattle, of which six were oxen. In the winter I threshed in the barn, and slept on the straw. I became covered with vermin, and was perfectly wretched.

On the first of May I began hauling wood to the wharves with my three wagons, and always returned to the fields. Every evening my master came and brought me my piece of bread and an omelet made of two eggs cooked with leeks and hemp-seed oil. I only went to the house on Martinmas Day, when they did me the honor to give me a bit of salt pork.

In fine weather I slept in the beautiful wood belonging to Madame de Damas. I had my favorite, the gentlest of my six oxen. As soon as he lay down for the night I was beside him.

First I pulled off my sabots, and then I poked my feet under his hind legs and put my head down on his neck.

But about two o'clock in the morning my six oxen arose without noise, and my comrade got up without my knowing it. Then the poor herdsman was left on the ground. Not knowing where to find my oxen in the darkness, I put on my wooden shoes and listened. I wandered along the edge of the young wood, torn by briers, which made the blood run down into my sabots. I cried, for my ankles were cut to the bone. Often, on my way, I used to encounter wolves, with eyes shining like sparks, but my courage never abandoned me.

At last I would find my six oxen, then I would make the sign of the cross. How glad I was! I led the deserters back to my three wagons, which were loaded with cord-wood, and then waited till my master came, to hitch up and set off for the wharf. Then I returned to the pasture, and the master left me there in the evening. I received my piece of bread, and always the two eggs cooked with leeks and hemp-seed oil. And this happened every day for three years. The pot was empty under the kneading-trough.[1] But the worst of it was the vermin that had taken possession of me.

Not being able to endure it any longer, in spite of all possible entreaties, I left the village. I went back to my native place to see if they would recognize me, but no one remembered the lost child. Four years of absence had made a great change in me, and no one any longer knew me.

I reached Druyes on Sunday; I went to see its beautiful fountains which flowed near my father's garden. I began to cry, but after a moment's struggle with my grief, I determined what to do. I washed my face in the clear water where formerly I had walked with my brothers and sisters.

At last the hour sounded for mass. I went to the church, my little handkerchief in my hand, for my heart was swelling. But I held out. I went to mass, and knelt down. I said my little prayer looking down. No one paid any attention to me. However I heard a woman say, "There is a little Morvandian who prays earnestly to the good God." I was so changed that no one knew me, but I knew everybody. I spoke to no one; when mass was over I went out of the church. I had at once recognized my father who sung among the choristers; little did he know that one of his children whom he had abandoned was so near him.

I had walked three leagues, and was very hungry when I left the church after mass. I went to the house of my half-sister, the child of the first marriage, who kept an inn; I asked her for something to eat.

"What do you want for dinner, boy?"

---

[1] *i.e.*, bread took the place of soup.

"Half a bottle of wine and a little meat and bread, madame, if you please."

A bit of stew was brought to me; I ate like an ogre, and got into a corner so I could see all the country people who came in doing the same. When I had finished my dinner I asked, "How much do I owe you, madame?"—"Fifteen sous, my boy."—"There they are, madame."—"You are from Morvan, are you not, child?"—"Yes, madame, I have come to try to find a place."

She called her husband. "Granger," said she, "here is a little boy who wants to hire himself out."—"How old are you?"—"Twelve, sir."—"Where do you come from?"—"From Menon."—"Ah, you are from Morvan?"—"Yes, sir."—"Do you know how to thresh in the barn?"—"Yes, sir."—"Have you worked at it already?"—"Four years, sir."—"How much do you ask by the year?"—"In our country, sir, we are paid in grain and money."—"Very well, if you like, you shall stay here, you shall be the stable-boy; all the tips shall be yours. Are you accustomed to sleep on the straw?"—"Yes, sir."—"If you suit me I will give you a louis a year."—"That is sufficient, I will stay; shall I pay for my dinner?"—"No," said he, "I am going to set you to work."

He took me into the garden, which I had known long before he had, and in which I had enjoyed all my childish frolics. I was the most boisterous one in the neighborhood, and my companions used to throw stones at me and call me "red head." I always came out best, being never afraid of blows; our stepmother had accustomed us to them. I remember once my nose was dirty; she took hold of it with the tweezers to wipe it, and was wicked enough to hurt me. "I will pull it off," she said. Consequently the tweezers were thrown into the well.

My brother-in-law, then, took me into his garden and gave me a spade. I worked a quarter of an hour; then he said, "Well done; but that's enough; we don't work on Sunday."—"Well," said my sister, "what shall he do?"—"He shall wait upon the table; go bring some wine from the cellar." I brought a basket of bottles and handed some to each one. I ran about like a young partridge.

In the evening they gave me some bread and cheese. At ten o'clock, my brother-in-law took me to the barn to sleep, and said, "You must get up early so as to thresh the grain, then put the bread into the oven and clean the stables nicely." — "All right, it shall all be done."

I bade my master good-night and rolled myself up in the straw. Imagine how I cried! If any one could have seen me he would have found my eyes as red as a rabbit's, so great was my mortification at the idea of being a servant in my sister's house and that at my father's door.

I awoke easily; there was nothing to do but crawl out of my hole and give myself a shake. I set to work to thresh the grain so as to make the bread by eight o'clock; then I went into the stable and put every thing in order, and at nine o'clock I saw my master appear. "Well, Jean, how does the work come on?" — "Not badly, sir." — "Let us see the barn. Your work is well done," said he; "these bundles of straw are well made." — "Ah, sir, at Menon I threshed the whole winter." — "Come along, my boy, come to breakfast."

At last with a swelling heart I went into the house of that sister whom my mother had raised as her own child. I took off my hat. "Wife," said he, "here is a little boy who works well, we must give him some breakfast." They gave me some bread and cheese and a glass of wine. My brother-in-law said, "You must make some soup for him." — "Very well, I will to-morrow; I got up too late this morning."

The next day I set to work, and at the regular hour I had my meal. Ah! what a surprise; I found an onion soup and some cheese with a bottle of wine. "Do not be bashful, my boy," said the master; "you are to spade in the garden." — "Yes, sir."

At nine o'clock I started off to my work with my spade on my shoulder. What was my surprise to see my father watering his cabbages! He looked at me; I took off my hat, my heart was bursting, but I tried to be brave. He spoke to me, asking, "Are you living with my son-in-law?" — "Yes, sir; so he is your son-in-law?" — "Yes, my boy. Where do you come from?" — "From Morvan." — "From what town?" — "From

Menon; I worked in the village of Les Bardins." — "Ah! I am well acquainted with all that country. Do you know the village of the Coignets?" — "Yes, sir; oh! yes." — "Well, it was built by my ancestors." — "Indeed, sir!" — "Have you seen the splendid forests which belong to Madame de Damas?" — "I know them well. I kept my master's oxen there for three years; every night in summer I slept under the fine old oaks." — "But, my boy, you will be happier with

my daughter." — "I hope so." — "What is your name?" — "Jean." — "And your father's?" — "In his neighborhood they call him 'The lover.' I don't know if that is his real name." — "Has he any children?" — "There are four of us." — "What does your father do?" — "He hunts in the woods;[1] there is much game thereabout, any number of stags and hinds and deer. And as for wolves, it is full of them; sometimes I was very much afraid of them. Oh! I suffered too much, so

---

[1] There was some malice in these replies, for Coignet's father was not famous either for his conjugal fidelity or for his respect for the game laws.

I came away." — "You did right, my boy; work away, you will be happy with my son-in-law."

One day some travellers came in two carriages. I put their horses in the stable, and the next day I got a franc for a tip. How pleased I was! I was sent to the cellar to rinse some bottles, and I did it well. After that the little stable-boy was set at all sorts of work; they made me trot around. It was, "Jean, come here," and "Jean, go there;" I waited on the table, I did duty in the cellar, the stable, the barn, and the garden. I often saw my father and said, "Good morning, M. Coignet." (I could not forget that name, it was graven on my heart.) "Good morning, Jean; are you getting tired, my boy?" — "No, sir, not at all."

Best of all, I earned money every day. At the end of two months I got entirely rid of the vermin, and was really clean. My Sunday fees and the stable fees together amounted to six francs a week. This life lasted three months, during which, to my great grief, I had heard nothing of my two younger brothers and my sister.

Every day I saw two of the companions of my infancy who lived next door. I spoke to them; the younger of the two came to see me. I was spading, and my father was in the garden. "Good morning, M. Coignet," said young Allard to him. "Ah! that you, Tiline?" That was my companion's name. And my father went away.

Then we entered into conversation. "You came from some distance away, didn't you?" said he to me. "I came from Morvan." — "Is Morvan very far?" — "Oh, no; only five leagues. M. Coignet knows all about my country. There is a village near us called the village of the Coignets." — "Ah, that wicked man has lost four of his children. We grieved for them, my brother and I, they were such jolly companions.[1] We were always together. They lost their mother when they were very young, and they were so unfortunate as to have a

---

[1] Four years spent in the woods must indeed have changed our hero, if none of his family could recognize him. But it must be observed that in the country, and particularly in a family where there are a lot of little children, and where the parents are not affectionate, the child's face is not so impressed upon the memory as in the city. Then, also, from eight to twelve years a child changes very much.

stepmother who beat them every day. They used to come to our house, and we gave them some bread, for they had had nothing to eat, and were crying. That grieved us very much. We used to take bread in our pockets and carry it out to divide between them. It was pitiful to see how they devoured it. One day my brother said to me, 'Come, let us go to see the little Coignets, and take them some bread.' To our surprise, we found that the two elder ones had gone away, and no one could find them. The next day there was no news of them. We told our father about it, and he said, 'Poor children, they were so unhappy: always getting beaten!' I asked the little one and his sister where their two brothers were. They answered that they had gone away. 'But where?'—'Ah, I cannot tell.' My father went over to inquire of Coignet, their father. 'I hear that your boys have gone away?' He answered, 'I believe that they have gone to see some relatives near the Alouettes mountains. They are little runaways. I shall thrash them when they come back.'"

But this was not all. Here is what I afterwards learned. There were little Alexander and Marianne still left to stand in this wicked woman's way. She was anxious to lose no time in getting rid of them, and one fine day, when my father was in the country, she called the two poor little ones down, and late in the evening she took them by the hand and led them as far as she could into the forest of Druyes, where she left them, saying she would return. But she never went back; she abandoned them to the mercy of the good Lord. Think of their wretchedness, those poor little things in the midst of the forest, in the dark, with nothing to eat, and not knowing how to find the way out! They remained three days in this pitiful situation, living upon wild fruits, crying and calling for help. At last God sent them a liberator. He was known as Father Thibault, a miller of Beauvoir. I knew him afterwards, in 1804.

My two companions next told me that the two youngest were no longer at home. "Poor little things!" said they, "nobody knows what has become of them. Every one talks about father Coignet and his wife." This story brought the tears to my eyes. "You are crying," said they. "It is very painful to hear such tales as this." — "Bless me! they got beaten every day, and their father has never tried to find them."

It was time, however, to stop talking, for I had heard all that I could bear. I returned to the barn, not knowing what I ought to do, whether or not I should rush into the house and overwhelm my father with reproaches, and attack that fury of a stepmother, who was the cause of all our misfortune. I turned the matter over in my little head, and concluded not to create a scandal. I took my spade, and went to work in the garden. I was greatly surprised to see my stepmother appear holding a little brat by the hand. I could not restrain myself at the sight of this horrible woman. I came very near betraying myself. I left the garden as she approached me, and sneaked out behind the stables to cry to my heart's content. I began to have a horror of the garden. Every time I went there I found either my father or my mother, whom I wished to avoid as much as possible. Many a time I was tempted to creep through the fence which separated the two gardens, and strike the mother and her child a blow over the head with my spade. But God restrained me, and I escaped.

Now the scene changes. Providence came to my assistance. Two horse-traders came to spend the night at M. Bomain's (he kept the large inn), but the host and hostess were having a fight with pitchforks, so the men came to my sister's. How glad I was to see two such fine gentlemen come to the house, and on such fine horses! What a godsend it was! "Little fellow," said they, "put our horses in the stable and give them some bran." — "Very well, gentlemen; it shall be attended to."

Then they went into the house and ordered a good supper, and after that they came to the stable to see their nags, which were well groomed, and standing up to their bellies in straw. "All right, my little boy, we are quite satisfied."

The smaller one said to me, "My young man, could you go with us to-morrow to show us the road to Entrains? We are going to the fair, but our horses must be ready at three o'clock in the morning." — "Very well, gentlemen; I promise you they shall be ready." — "It is three leagues off, is it not?"

— "Yes, gentlemen, but you must ask madame's permission for me to go with you." — "That is so. We will ask it of her."

I gave some oats and hay to the horses while the gentlemen stood there, and then they went to bed, so as to get up at three o'clock in the morning to go to the fair at Entrains, which is called Les Brandons. At two o'clock the horses were saddled. I went to waken the gentlemen, and told them their nags were ready.

I saw on the table two pistols and a watch; they made it strike. "Half-past two! Very well, little fellow. Give them some oats, and we will set out. Tell madame that we should like to have some boiled eggs for breakfast." I went to rouse my sister, who hurried as fast as possible. Then I returned to the stable to get my nags ready. The gentlemen came and mounted. "Madame, will you permit us to take your servant along to guide us through the wood?" — "Certainly, go with these gentlemen," said she.

So I started off. As soon as we had gotten out of sight the men dismounted, and getting on each side of me asked how much I earned a year. "I can tell you readily; some money, some shirts, a blouse, and a pair of sabots. Besides, I have some fees; I cannot tell exactly how much they amount to." — "Very well, is it worth a hundred francs to you?" — "Oh, yes, gentlemen." — "Since you seem to be an intelligent boy, if you will come with us, we will take you along with us, give you thirty sous a day, and buy you a horse and saddle. We will take you along as we come by on our return. If you get tired of us we will pay your way back." — "Gentlemen, I would like it very much, but you do not know anything about me, and neither do the people in the inn. So I will tell you my history. I am the brother of the tall woman at whose house you spent the night." — "It is not possible!" — "I swear it is true!"

"How did this happen?" — "If you will allow me I will explain it to you."

Then they came nearer to me; they took me by the arm. I assure you they were all attention. "Four years was lost. There were four of us children. The bad tr of our stepmother caused us to leave our father's house, and no one has recognized me. I am a servant in the house of my half-sister by a former marriage; you can assure yourself of the fact the next time you come by." And here I began to cry.

"Come, do not cry; we will write a line which you shall take to madame, who will send you to Auxerre for one of our horses which fell sick at the inn of M. Paquet, near the Temple Gate. Here is money and assignats to pay the veterinarian and inn-keeper; it amounts to thirty francs. Bring him slowly along, give him some bran at Courson, and do not mount him." — "No, gentlemen. But you must not speak of me to my sister." — "Make yourself easy, my little fellow. Take this note to her, and to-morrow you shall set out for Auxerre. Take good care of our horse. We shall be at Entrains for three days. When you see our horses coming, hold yourself in readiness. Take only a shirt in your pocket." — "All right."

I parted from these gentlemen with a beating heart. When I reached home they said, " You have been gone a long time." — "Yes, truly; those gentlemen took me a great distance. Here is a letter which they gave me for you, and money and assignats to go to Auxerre for a horse that is sick there." — "Well, they are pretty free." — "But here is the letter; that is your affair." He read the letter. "Very well, you must start at three o'clock in the morning; you will have to make fourteen leagues to-morrow."

That night I did not close my eyes; my little head was turned upside down by all that had just happened to me. I made my seven leagues in five hours, and at eight o'clock I reached the house of M. Paquet. I found my horse in good condition, presented my letter and was directed to the house of the veterinary, who gave me a receipt for his payment. Then I returned to the hotel, settled with M. Paquet, set off for Druyes, and reached home at seven o'clock exceedingly tired. To make fourteen leagues in one day was too much for a child of my age. However I groomed my horse, made him a good bed, and went to my supper. I put away the receipts and three francs remaining of the gentlemen's money, and then laid myself down in my straw. Oh, how I slept. I took only one long nap.

The next day I groomed my horse in the best possible manner and then went to breakfast. "You must go and thresh in the barn," said my brother-in-law. "Very well." I threshed until dinner-time, and then he said, "You must go and spade in the garden."

I went, and there I found my father and my stepmother. "Well, here you are, Jean." — "Yes, M. Coignet." — "You have come back from Auxerre?" — "Yes, sir." — "You walked fast. Did you go over the town?" — "No, sir, I did not have time to see much of it." — "That's true." As I was about to leave them I heard my stepmother say to my father, "Granger is very fortunate to have such an intelligent young fellow." — "He is indeed," said my father. "How old are you?" — "Twelve years, sir." — "Ah, I think you will make a fine man." — "I hope so." — "Continue as you have begun; every one is pleased with you." — "Thank you, sir."

Then I retired with a beating heart.

Every day I went into the garden to see if I could see the horses of the merchants coming; they could be seen half a league off. At last on the eighth day, I saw on the great white road a large number of horses coming towards the town. Each man led only one horse; they were not yet put in pairs. There were forty-five of them, and perhaps more. I hastened at once to the house to get my best waistcoat, put on one shirt, and another in my pocket, and then I went quickly to the stable to saddle the gentlemen's horse.

I had scarcely finished when I saw all those beautiful horses go by, all of them dappled gray. I did not dare speak to those Morvandians, I was brimming over with joy. The last one had still not passed by when those gentlemen rode into the court yard with three horses. "Well, my little boy, how does our horse come on?" — "It is in splendid condition." — "We will dismount and take a look at him. Ah, he is entirely well. Give him to our boy to take him along; he has not yet gone by." The horses continued to go by. As their stud-groom passed: "Francis, take your nag, follow the horses."

My sister appeared, and the gentlemen bowed to her. "Madame, how much do we owe you for the feeding of our

horse?" — "Twelve francs, gentlemen." — "Here they are, madame." — "Do not forget the boy." — "We will attend to that."

My sister looked at me as I went out with the horse. "See here," said she, "you have on your Sunday clothes." — "So you see." — "Come, to whom are you speaking?" — "To you." — "What are you saying?" — "Yes, to you. You don't understand that your servant is your brother?" — "What?" — "That's just how it is. You are a bad sister. You allowed me and my little brothers and sister to go away. Do you not remember that my mother paid three hundred francs to have you learn the linen-draper's trade under Madame Morin?

You have no heart. My mother loved you as she did us, and you allowed us to go away."

At this my sister cried aloud. "Well, madame, is it true what this little boy says? If so, it was a cruel thing." — "Gentlemen, it was not I who let them go away and get lost, it was my father. Ah, the miserable man, he lost four of his children."

Hearing the cries and lamentations of my sister, the neighbors came running in to see me. "This is one of father Coignet's children. One of them is found." And my sister and I wept. One of the gentlemen who held me by the hand, said, "Don't cry, my little fellow, we will never abandon you."

My little companions came and embraced me. My father, who heard the hubbub, came in. All cried out, "Here is this M. Coignet who has lost his four children." And I said to the gentlemen, "That is my father, gentlemen." — "Here is one of your children, sir, and we are going to take him away with us." Then said I, "O heartless father, what have you done with my two brothers and my sister? Go find that wretch of a stepmother who beat us." — "That is so," they all cried out, "he is a bad father, and their stepmother is still worse."

Every one continued to crowd around me, but these gentlemen kept hold of my arm. "Come, let us mount," said M. Potier (the smaller of the two), "we have had enough of this. Let us go; get on your nag." Then all followed me out, crying, "Good-by, little fellow, a happy journey to you!" My little companions came and embraced me, and the scalding tears flowed down my cheeks as I said, "Good-by, my good friends."

The gentlemen placed me between them, and we rode along between two rows of people. The men took off their hats, and the women courtesied to the gentlemen. As for me, I cried, with my little hat in my hand.

"We will trot up the mountain," said the gentlemen. "Let us catch up with our horses. Come, little fellow, be brave!" We passed the horses as they were coming out of the wood, reached Conasom, and went to the great hotel of M. Raveneau, where I visited the stables and had all necessary preparations made for forty-nine horses. The gentlemen ordered supper for forty-five men, not including the masters.

On arriving, the horses were divided into groups of four, so as to pair them off the next day, and they were attached to two tethers. This was the first time that these horses had been placed side by side. It was time to give the gay beasts their hay and oats; I was afraid we should not be able to manage them, for they were rearing like mad creatures. I began to beat them; I did not leave them a moment, and the masters laughed as they saw me strike first one and then another. At seven o'clock the gentlemen came to look after and order supper for their men, who numbered forty-five; they paid them their day's wages, retaining as many of them as they needed for the next day, set a watch in the stables for the night, and took me away with them. "Let us go to supper," said they; "come with us, boy; we will come back and see them again after awhile."

To my astonishment I saw a table served as if for princes; soup, boiled beef, a duck cooked with turnips, a chicken, salad, dessert, and sealed wine. "Sit there between us and eat. What a brave boy you are!" The king was not happier than I. "See here," said M. Potier, "you must put a leg of chicken and some bread in a piece of paper to eat as you go along, for we shall not stop until bed-time. You will find boys at the inns who will hand each man a large glass of wine as he passes, without stopping him, and all will be paid for. You must keep behind as much as possible."

Next morning we divided the horses into groups of four, fastened them together with poles padded with straw (this took a good deal of time), and then started off. Every day I was treated just as I had been the first day. What a change in my condition! How glad I was to sleep in a good bed! The poor little orphan no longer slept in the straw. And I had a good supper every day. I regarded these gentlemen as messengers sent by God to help me.

We reached Nangis-en-Brie a week before the fair, and I

had time to become acquainted with my two masters. One was named M. Potier and the other M. Huzé. The latter was good-natured, witty, and polite; M. Potier was small and ugly. "If I could only live with M. Huzé," I thought. But I was mistaken; it was at the house of M. Potier that a happy fate awaited me.

On Friday I left Nangis for Coulommiers. At three o'clock I rode into the great court-yard, mounted on my pretty nag, as proud as a pacha with three queues. Madame came out and said, "Well, my boy, but is not your master coming this evening?" — "No, madame, he will not be here till to-morrow." — "Have your horse put in the stable, and you come with me." As I went in walking by madame's side, four big housemaids cried out, "Ah! there he is, there is the little Morvandian." This hurt my feelings, but with my little hat in my hand I followed madame. "Go away," said she, "let the child alone. Go to your work. Come, little fellow."

How beautiful she was, this Madame Potier! for it was in fact the wife of the little man concerning whom I had had misgivings. I did not know it till the next day. I was so astonished to see such a beautiful wife, and such an ugly husband.

"Come," she added, "you must eat something, and have a glass of wine, for we do not have supper till seven o'clock."

Then madame made me tell her all about our journey, and I also told her that all the horses were sold. "Are you pleased with your master?" — "Oh, madame, I am delighted." — "Well, I am very glad to hear it; my husband has written me that you are a very promising boy." — "Thank you, madame."

At seven in the evening, supper was served. That was Friday. I was called and told to seat myself at the table. I found before me a table served as if for a great feast, a service of silver, silver goblets, and two baskets of wine. I was surprised also to find twelve servants: a miller, wagoners, a farm-hand, milkmaid, chambermaid, baker-woman, and maid of all work. Six others had gone to Paris with wagons to take flour to the bakers; they went there for this purpose every week. Coulommiers is fifteen leagues from Paris. There were two dishes of matelote on the table. The feast seemed ordered to suit my especial taste.

A seat was given me beside a big, good-natured fellow, and madame asked him to help me. He gave me a piece of carp; I felt mortified to see my plate so full of fish. I could have

made two meals on the quantity he gave me. He saw that I ate very little, so he put a piece of bread in his pocket, and gave it to me when he came to the stable, saying, "You did not eat anything, you were too bashful." Ah! how I devoured it then, at my leisure, that nice piece of white bread! At nine o'clock, a big maid came to make a bed for me in the stable. I was comfortably lodged; a feather bed, a mattress, and nice white sheets. I felt very happy.

Next morning my big comrade took me to the dining-hall, where I breakfasted with my half bottle of wine, and cheese. *Mon Dieu*, what cheese it was! it was like cream. And Gonesse bread and native wine. I asked him what I should do. "Wait till madame gets up, she will tell you." — "Well, I will go and groom and water my nag, and clean out the stable." I was crazy to be at work. The stable-boy had gone to town, so I took advantage of the opportunity to clean out all the stables.

Madame came out and found me with my coat off, and a broom in my hand. "Who told you to do that?" — "No one, madame." — "Very well, but that is not your work; come with me. Each one has his special work to do in this house; but you have done this well. When my husband comes, he will tell you what you must do. Let us go into the garden; take this basket, we will gather some vegetables. Do you know how to spade?" — "Yes, madame." — "So much the better. I will have you spade in our garden sometimes, for at our house each one has his own work; they do not interfere with one another."

I went back to the house, and paid a visit to the mills of Chamois. On my return, I was surprised to find my two masters, who were looking for madame. "So, here you are, my dear," said Madame Potier to her ugly husband, for it was indeed the one to whom I had least desire to belong. He was, however, the superior man of the two, both in fortune and in heart. M. Huzé bade me good-morning and went away. I was sent for. "Wife," said my master, "here is a child whom I have brought you from Burgundy: he is a promising boy, and I can recommend him to you. I will tell you his history later." And there I stood, much abashed.

"Well," said he, "are you feeling blue, my boy? Come, let us go and see the horses." Then he showed me all the stables and mills. All the servants bade their master good-morning. He did not seem like a master, he was a father to every one. A disagreeable word never fell from his lips.

"To-morrow," said he to me, "we will go out on horseback, and I will show you my farms and the laborers. You must become acquainted with everything that belongs to me." I said to myself, "What is he going to do with me?" He spoke to his farm-hands and to all his workmen in the pleasantest manner. Then he said to me, "Come, let us go and see my meadows." And all the time he talked to me most kindly. "Pay attention to everything I show you, and to the landmarks, for I may send you sometimes to go the rounds among my farm-hands and other workmen, so as to inform me of what is going on." — "You may rest assured that I shall render you a faithful account of everything." — "I shall have to make you thoroughly acquainted with everything. You must always take your horse, for the distances are great." We had been out more than three hours, when he said, "Come, let us return to the house. To-morrow we will go somewhere else."

In this way he made me familiar with all the details of his business. We spent eight days in going from one place to another. The ninth day a terrible storm arose. Water came from every direction, and surrounded the house; no one could get out. The horses were all in the stables. Neither master nor miller could go out. I ran from one stable to the other, for the water was rising rapidly. At last I was obliged to paddle like a duck. The horses stood in it up to their haunches, but it still had not penetrated the house.

There were three pig-sties in which the pigs ran great risk of being drowned, as they were in the basement. M. Potier sent for me, and said, "Try to save the pigs." — "All right, I will go at once," said I. I plunged into the water. At first I thought it would be impossible to do it, but upon reaching the first door, I punched a hole, and the water helped me to open it. In a moment my six big pigs were out and swimming like ducks. I did the same thing to the two other sties, and thus saved all of the eighteen pigs. Every one in the house was looking at me from the windows. M. Potier, who did not lose sight of me for a moment, directed me all the time. "Is the small gate of the courtyard closed?" — "No, sir." — "Then the pigs will go through, they will follow the course of the waters."

FIRST NOTE-BOOK. 21

I set out to cross the courtyard, but the water was too strong for me; I was too late. One of the pigs was just going through the gate, borne on by the current. M. Potier, who saw that one pig had escaped me, ran to the corner of the house, and called to me, "Take your nag, and try to get ahead of him."

I ran to the stable, put a bridle on my nag, and dashed into the water to catch my deserter. M. Potier cried to me, "Carefully, bear to the right." But his words were lost. I went too far to the left. I plunged into a hole where lime had been slacked. With one bound my horse went in and then out of the hole. I could see nothing. Holding my horse firmly

with the right hand, I wiped off my face, and followed my pig which was going swiftly down the meadow. Finally, though I had a hard struggle with the water, I got ahead of my pig. When I got his snout turned towards the house, he went as I directed. On reaching the courtyard, I slipped off my horse, perfectly stiff with cold. My masters were waiting for me on the stairway, and the stout maids stared at the poor little orphan all dripping and pale as death. But I had saved my master's pig.

"Come, my dear," said my host and hostess, "come change your clothes." They took me into their beautiful chamber, where a bright fire was burning, and stripped me as naked as

I came into the world. "Drink," said they, "some of this warm wine." Then they wiped me dry as tenderly as if I had been their own child, and wrapped me in a blanket. M. Potier said to his wife, "My dear, if you would bring him one of my new shirts, he might try it on." — "Sure enough, the poor little fellow has only two of his own." — "Very well, we must give him half a dozen. See here, he must be rewarded for his good conduct. I shall make him a present of that pair of pantaloons and round waistcoat you had made for me. He shall be dressed entirely in a new suit." — "You are right, my dear. I shall be delighted." M. Potier added, "You shall be paid eighteen francs a month, and the fees, three francs a horse." — "Monsieur and madame, how much I thank you." — "You deserve the reward. Just suppose you had been drowned trying to save the pig!"

I imagined myself dressed like the master of the house. Lord, how proud I felt! I was no longer the little Morvandian. But as they were getting ready to dress me up, I said, "Master, I must not put on those clothes. I shall have to go back to my work. The horses and pigs must be cared for, and I should spoil them all." — "You are right, my child."

Then they went for some clothes belonging to their nephew, and soon I was dressed in a working suit. There was no one at the stables. The stable-boy had gone to town, and the millers would not set foot into the water. They gave me a large glass of Burgundy, well sweetened, and I waded in again. I gave the horses their hay. I stopped my pigs up in an empty stable. In order to accomplish this, I got a long pole, drove all my fat fellows before me, and finally got them under control. I am sure I must have paddled about in the water two hours that day. By the evening, the water had disappeared, and the wagoners came in from all directions. I returned to the house, changed all my clothes, and went immediately to bed. The sweet wine made me sleep. Next day I thought no more about it.

My master and mistress sent for me, took me into their chamber, and put an entirely new suit on me. After breakfast, M. Potier said to the stable-boy, "Saddle our nags."

Then we set off to see the large farmers, and buy grain. My master bought ten thousand francs worth, and they treated us as friends. Doubtless M. Potier had spoken to these farmers; for they paid me much attention, and I was seated at table next my master. I must say I had been much smartened up. I looked like a secretary. If they had only known that I did not know a letter in the alphabet! However, M. Potier's clothes served me as a passport with these gentlemen. All went well, and after dinner we started off at a gallop, and reached home at seven o'clock. I found that my place at table had been changed; my plate was beside M. Potier on the left, while madame's was on the right. Then the head miller was next to madame, who served to our masters first. I ought to observe that my master and mistress always sat at the end of the table. It was like a family table. We never said "thee" to any one, always "you." On Sunday the master asked, "Who wants his wages advanced?"

When all the servants were assembled, M. Potier said to them, "I have appointed this young man to take my orders to you. I shall give him the keys to the hay and oats. He is to distribute to all the teams." Every one looked at me, and I, knowing nothing of all this arrangement, was overcome with confusion, and could not look up. At last my master said to me, "Get ready to go to town with me;" I was glad to get away from the table.

M. Potier gave me his keys, saying, "I must be off, we are going to see some large wheat-barns. Say, are you satisfied with what I have done for you? My wife will take care of you." — "I will do everything I possibly can to please you." The next day, the bell rang to call me to give the order which I was to transmit to all the servants. The head man said to me, "What is it, sir?" — "I am not 'sir.' I am your good comrade; tell them all so. I am hired as you are. I do my work. I shall never abuse the confidence of my master and mistress, and I have need of your counsels." — "As I am the oldest one in the house, you can rely on me," he replied.

I can truly say that every one was pleasant to me. As I had charge of the distribution of the bran and oats an each one paid court to me so as to be sure of good measure. M. Potier scolded me when he found bran left in the troughs. "My horses are too fat; I must see to it that this does not happen again. They must not give them such big feeds."—"Tell me the quantity of bran and oats, and I will measure it out myself. They take their baskets and go to the mill to fill them. Hereafter not one of them shall step his foot there. Each man's feed shall be placed at his stalls."—"That is a good idea," said my master. When the wagoners and farm-hands returned, and found each man's feed measured out, they asked, "Who measured out our feed?"—"You got me a scolding. The master himself measured the bran and the oats, and told me to allow no other person to do it, and I shall see to it, you may be sure."

The next day two big farmers came to breakfast. M. Potier rang for me, and said, "Go to my cabinet, and bring me ten bags of money." I brought them. Good Lord, what piles of crowns there were in those bags! I stood hat in hand. "Jean," said he, "have the nags saddled. We shall go away with these gentlemen." And madame said, "Dress yourself neatly. Here is a handkerchief and a cravat." She was so good as to arrange my dress, and said, "Now go, my little fellow, you are all right."

How proud I was! I brought out my master's horse, and held the bridle. This flattered him, in presence of the gentlemen: he told me so afterwards. They all mounted and started off. I followed behind, plunged in my own little reflections. We went to a fine farm, where our horses were put in the stable, and I remained in the courtyard looking at the beautiful mows of wheat and hay. A servant came to call me to dinner. I excused myself with thanks. But the master of the house came and took me by the arm, and said to my master, "Have him placed near you at the table." I was not at my ease. After the first course, I rose from the table. "Where are you going?" said the host. "M. Potier has permitted me to retire."—"Then we excuse you."

I was flattered at being seated at a table so well appointed. I shall always remember it. After dinner, the farmer's wife invited me to see her dairy. I never saw anything so neat. There were spigots everywhere. "Every fortnight," said she, "I sell a wagon-load of cheeses. I have eighty cows." She took me into the dining-room to show me her cooking arrangements. Everything was bright and clean. The table and benches were all polished. Scarcely knowing what to say to this kind woman, I remarked, "I will tell Madame Potier of all that I have seen." — "We go to her house three times during the winter to dine and spend the evening. How pleasant M. and Madame Potier are in their own house!"

The gentlemen then came in, and I retired. M. Potier beckoned to me and put twenty-four sous in my hand. "Give that to the stable-boy; have the horses saddled, we must go." Our two nags were brought out. The handsome farmer's wife said to M. Potier, "Your servant's horse is beautiful. It would just suit me. If my husband were as gallant as he should be, he would buy it for me, for mine is very old." — "Very well," said the latter, "we will see about it. Do you want to try it? Have your saddle put on it, and get on. You can see how it goes."

The side-saddle was brought. I said, "Madame, he is very gentle, you can mount without fear."

So madame mounted, and started off at a trot, leading first with the right foot, and then with the left, saying, "He has an easy trot. Do, husband, make me a present of this nag." — "Well, M. Potier, she must have it," said her husband. "We will arrange it. How much will you take for it?" — "Three hundred francs." — "That's fair. There, wife, you

are satisfied; now you must give the boy his fee." — " I will
at once. Come here," said she to me. She put six francs in
my hand, and made me put my saddle on her old horse.
Then we started off at a good trot. What a happy day it had
been for me! M. Potier said to me, " I am very well pleased
with you." — "Thank you, sir. The lady showed me her
dairy and her kitchen arrangements. How nice it all was!
They are true friends; and the lady is not proud."

Next day, the old horse was sent for, and M. Potier said
to me, " You must take the one we brought from your
country. To-morrow we shall go and put the flour in bags.
We shall have to take a hundred bags to Paris. You must
hold the bushel measure. I will show you how. To-morrow
you must drink your wine without water. You must learn to
do everything. Here you will never do the work of a servant,
but I will teach you how to do various kinds of work. I
want you to know how everything is done."

The next morning, he introduced me to the miller, and said
to him, " Baptiste, here is Jean, I wish you to show him how
to handle the bushel measure. He will be at your disposal
whenever you need him, and you will find him always willing
to work." — " But, sir, is he strong enough to handle the
bushel measure ? " — " Do not fear, I will stand by and see to
that."

Then M. Potier took the bushel measure and showed me.
" This is the way," said he; and when I wanted to take the
measure in my own hands, " No," said he, " let me finish this
bag." Then I took hold of the measure, and handled it as if
it had been a feather. After I had filled my first bag, Baptiste
said to M. Potier, " We shall make a man of him." — " I will
help you," said my master. " That is unnecessary," said
Baptiste, " we two can manage it."

So I did my best, under the direction of this somewhat
stern man. We worked all day. How my sides ached! We
had only made fifty loads, and we were obliged to go at it
again the next morning. At last, however, we finished, and I
had done myself credit.

My master and mistress, perceiving some jealousy towards

"Look between the two ears of your lead horse, at the points I have showed you." — Page 27.

me on the part of the other servants, took advantage of my absence to relate to them my misfortunes. They told them that I had not been born to be a servant, and that my father was wealthy, and had lost four of his children. "I," said M. Potier, "found this one. The others are lost. I want him to learn how to do everything." — "I will show him how to handle the plough," said the head farm-hand. "Very well, I shall be obliged to you." — "I will take charge of him whenever you wish." — "Take him under your charge. I confide him to you. Do not let him fatigue himself: he is very energetic." — "Do not be anxious. I will show him how to sow grain, and I will give him my three horses."

That evening I came back after carrying invitations to three different places, and brought back the replies. When I came to the table, my master and mistress asked me a good many questions about the persons to whom I had taken the invitations. I told them that everywhere refreshments had been offered me, but that I had not accepted anything. I saw all the servants looking at me.

The head farm-hand said at the table, "Jean, if you wish, I will take you with me to-morrow, and I will show you how to make a furrow with my plough." — "Ah, you are very kind, Father Pron" (that was the good man's name); "if monsieur will permit me, I will go with you." — "No," said M. Potier, "we will go together."

As we went along, my master told me that this good man had offered of his own accord to teach me to plough, and he added, "You must take advantage of his offer, for he is the best ploughman in the country." When we arrived, my master said to him, "Here is your pupil: try to make a good farm-hand of him." — "I will take charge of him, sir." — "Come, let us see, show him how to make the first furrow." Then Father Pron harnessed up his plough, putting his three horses in a line, one before another, and made me take note of certain distant points, and other points intermediate. Then he said to me, "Look between the two ears of your lead horse, at the points I have showed you; do not look at your plough, hold your reins tight, and keep your eye on your three points of sight. As soon as you pass by one of them, look to the next."

As soon as I reached the end of the field, I looked at my first furrow. It was straight. "That is very well," said M. Potier, "it does not waver. I am satisfied; that will do very well; go on." He had the kindness to stay with me two hours, and then took me back to the house, where madame was expecting him. "Well," said she, "how about the plough, how did he manage it?"—"Very well. I assure you, Pron is delighted with him; he will make a good farm-hand."—"So much the better, poor child."—"That was a good idea of Pron's showing him how to handle the plough. I shall have him taught how to sow grain. He shall begin by sowing vetch, and afterwards he can sow wheat."

The next day I perceived that all the servants were specially gracious to me. I did not understand the reason of this, but it was because they had heard my history from my master and mistress; every one had in consequence become a friend to me. M. Potier had seven children. I used to go to the boarding-schools for them, and take them back again. Those were holidays for me and for them. I was with them wherever they went, whether on foot or in the carriage. I settled all the little squabbles between the girls and their brothers.

One day M. Potier said to me, "We shall start to-morrow for the fair at Reims. I want some horses to sell in Paris. They must be well-matched, as they are for some of the peers of France.[1] They wish them to be well-trained, and four or five years old. You will have a chance to try your skill." He called his horse-trader and said to him, "I want you to go with me on horseback to-morrow morning to the fair at Reims. I want fifty horses. Here is a list of the sizes and colors. I don't need to say anything more to you, you know your business."

M. Huzé was notified to be ready to go with us, and told to take with him a servant to lead the horse which was to carry the valises. We started at noon, and reached Reims

---

[1] There were no peers then; but the sequel shows that he was speaking of the Directory, which was more or less known in the country districts.

three days before the fair. M. Potier's old groom scoured the country round for horses which might be suitable for our purposes, and returned with the description of thirty, upon which he had already paid an instalment. The old fellow said, "I think I have done well. I have a list of a hundred horses that I have spoken for, and I have taken down the names of their owners."

The fair lasted three days. There were in all fifty-eight horses. We had the pick of the fair. The gentlemen were well pleased with their trip; in

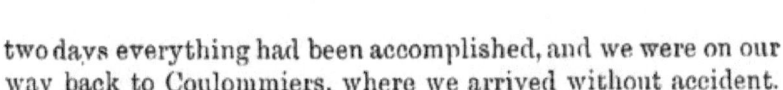

two days everything had been accomplished, and we were on our way back to Coulommiers, where we arrived without accident.

Then I was put to my wits' end to train all those horses. Two days after we reached home the training began; twenty horses a day were brought out with halters on their heads. How they reared! But at last they were conquered and made obedient. There was not a day of rest during the whole month of training. We trained them to pleasure-cars, to cabriolets, and under the saddle. How glad they were afterwards to stretch themselves on their straw! They slept like beggars who had their wallets full of bread. We took them to the fields, where at first they were ill at ease in the ploughed ground. I rode first one and then another, and was very strict with all those gay creatures. I punished the unruly, and petted the gentle ones. This training lasted two months without intermission. At the end of that time I was worn out; my lungs were affected, I spit blood, but I had acquitted myself with honor.

M. Potier wrote to those distinguished personages in Paris that their horses were ready. Instead of returning an answer by letter, they came themselves, in beautiful open carriages, with servants in livery. Their horses were put in the stables, and M. Potier, hat in hand, led them to the dining-hall, and madame appeared. What a fine manner she had! Those portly gentlemen arose and bowed to her. She retired, and ordered refreshments. She asked if the gentlemen would do her the honor to dine with her, and they replied that they would do so with pleasure. The dinner was magnificent. M. Potier called me to him and said, "Tell all the grooms to have the horses ready. I shall bring these gentlemen to look at them." I gave the orders, and everything was in readiness. The gentlemen wished to look over the establishment, with which they were charmed, and then went to the stables to have the horses brought out. "There they are," said M. Potier, "all in a row. Bring them out."

They called for number one, with snaffle-bridle and blanket. The horse was handed over to me, and I made him trot. "Mount him," said the gentlemen. I made him walk a few paces. holding him by the bridle, and then getting a good hold, I sprang on his back so quickly that they scarcely saw me mount. I made him trot, and then presented him before the gentlemen. who praised him, saying, "Very good." — "Number two," said my master. The horse was brought to me. "Mount him," said the gentlemen, "walk, trot. That will do. Bring another."

And so on, till they had seen twelve. They asked me, "Are they all as well trained as these twelve?"—"I assure you they are."—"That will do, then. This young man rides well."—"He is pretty plucky," said my master. "To-morrow we will hitch them to the pleasure-car. Have you suitable harness?"—"Everything is at hand."—"Well, we have had enough for to-day. We should like to see the town."—"Would you like to have us put the horses to your carriage?"—"Yes, that would be better. We ask your permission to bring two friends back with us."—"Whatever is agreeable to you. Jean, put the horses to the open carriage."

Then they started off. My master was well pleased. "Jean," said he, "we will do a good job to-day; all goes well. You have done yourself credit. I want you to wait at table, so dress yourself with care. Go, consult my wife. You must go to the town for things I have ordered; have your hair dressed, and put on your Sunday clothes." I returned, well powdered. Madame explained my duties to me, and when the table was set, she went and made a magnificent toilet. How beautiful she was!

The gentlemen returned at six o'clock. There were six of them. My master received them hat in hand. "Well, sir, we have done as we said, we have brought you two guests."—"You are welcome, gentlemen." My master recognized the sub-prefect and the procureur of the Republic. They sat down to the table. Madame did the honors; nothing was wanting, neither I, with my napkin on my arm, nor the gentlemen's footmen, who stood behind their masters. They all ate without speaking during the first course. One of the footmen acted as carver, and gave us the meats already cut up, which we handed to the gentlemen, and which they often refused. For the second course, there was an enormous pike and delicious crabs. "Ah, madame," said one of the guests, "this is a great rarity."—"It is indeed," said all of them. But the prefect added, "M. Potier has a splendid pond. He gets magnificent eels from it." And thus the praises resounded on all sides. The champagne came on; every one became lively. My master said, "I laid in a little stock of it as I came through Épernay." — "It is perfect," said the sub-prefect.

When the dessert was brought in, the servants were sent out of the room, and madame asked permission to withdraw for a moment. "Certainly, madame," they replied. Madame gave her orders, and then said to her husband, "Would these gentlemen like some punch to finish the evening?" — "That would go very well indeed." The sub-prefect said, "I beg that you will use my house as a stopping-place; and I invite you and your husband, madame, to be so kind as to dine with me. To-morrow we will come to see your beautiful horses."

The gentlemen came at noon to see them harnessed up. Everything was ready. They looked on, following the list. "Take both the pleasure-car and the open carriage, that will save time. Lead the horses out by fours." We soon had them hitched up. I drove the pleasure-car, and the head groom the open carriage. "Drive around in front of the house, so we can see you." — "They are very handsome," said the gentlemen. "Are they all as well broken as these four?" — "Yes, gentlemen," answered M. Potier. "Would you like to see a very beautiful horse? If so, I will show you one I went wild over at Reims." — "Let us see him." — "Jean, go bring him." He was all ready. I brought him out before the gentlemen. "Ah!" they exclaimed, "how handsome he is. Make him mount him."

I said to the footman, "Take hold of my foot, so I can spring up; he is too high." When I was on the back of this proud creature, I made him walk and trot, and then presented him. "Very well," said the master to his footman, "mount him, so I can see him better."

The young man was more skilful than I. How beautifully he managed him! "Lead him here; that will do." The footman presented him to his master, hat in hand. "Monsieur," said he, "his gaits are very easy." — "I have found an owner for him," said the peer of France. "He will suit the president of the Assembly; put him at the head of your list. All your horses are accepted. I will send you an order when I wish you to start for Paris. Come with them yourself, and this young man will accompany you as guide. If he would like to enter my service, I will employ him." — "Thank you, sir, but I will not leave my master." — "Very well, I will give you your fee." They got into their carriage, and bowing to my master and mistress drove off. "At six o'clock, without fail," called out the sub-prefect. My master ordered the carriage to be ready at five o'clock. "Jean," said he, "dress yourself, you are to drive."

My master and mistress were received with cordiality by all the gentlemen. All the town authorities dined with them that day, and my mistress's seat was beside the host. The party was kept up till midnight, and the next day they set out for Paris. M. Potier received an order to start on Friday so as to reach the École Militaire on Sunday, where they would meet him at noon precisely, and receive the horses. My master informed M. Huzé that all the horses had been sold. "Can it be possible!" said he.

We set out next day at six o'clock with ninety-three horses and a wagon-load of bran for the journey. I led the handsome horse alone. At ten o'clock we reached the École Militaire, where we found an aide-de-camp and equerries. We fed and groomed the horses, and blackened their feet nicely. At noon all was in readiness.

The aide-de-camp made provision for our breakfast, and set a guard of the servants. M. Huzé breakfasted with the aide-de-camp, and my master went off to inform the noble gentlemen that their horses were ready. At two o'clock precisely, all those portly fellows descended from their carriages and went to look at the horses, ordering them out in sets of four. "Those are handsome horses," said the president, "now you can renew your supply for the carriages. Where is the one you spoke to me about? Have him brought out."

I brought him to the aide-de-camp, who mounted the proud-looking animal, put him through his gaits, and took him to the president. "That's a fine horse," said he, "take him back." The aide-de-camp then retired with M. Potier and M. Huzé to provide for our dinner, and meantime men were sent to groom the horses, a man for every four horses.

The gentlemen sold twenty of their own horses to my master at the price fixed by the horse-traders. After this splendid transaction was completed, he sent me back with the gentlemen's fine carriage horses. M. Potier and M. Huzé remained a week in Paris settling up their accounts. They were invited to the house of the great peer of France who had been entertained at Coulommiers. In order to assist the gentlemen in choosing their teams from among the new horses, it was decided that each should draw by lot, four at a time, and that each should fee the servants.

These gentlemen were so pleased with the fair dealing

of my master that the president spoke of him to the minister of war. The latter sent for M. Potier to offer him an order of two hundred horses for the artillery service. "There is the price and the size. How soon could you furnish them?"— "I can deliver them in two months, sir."—"I can assure you they are very strict as to what horses are received. Those which are rejected will be left on your hands."—"That is all right, you have warned me."—"They will be received at the École Militaire. You know the age: from four to five years, and no stallions. Are you able to advance the money for the purchase?"—"Yes, sir."—"Where will you get them?"—"From Normandy and the Lower Rhine."—"Ah! very well, that is a good stock."

M. Potier arrived at Coulommiers in excellent spirits, and found his twenty horses in the best possible condition. "I should not know them," said he. "We must take them to the fair at Nangis, we shall be able to sell them. They were bought for a mere song, and we can make fifty per cent on them. Have them ready to-morrow, and we will be ready at six o'clock. There is no time to lose. We shall have to go to Normandy; I have taken an order from the minister of war."

The fair at Nangis was a success, and the horses were all sold. M. Potier said, "I have doubled my money." Four days after, he set out for Caen in Normandy, where he made some of his purchases. He sent them home, and we went on to Colmar, where he made more good bargains, and at Strasbourg he bought all the rest that he needed. M. Huzé was commissioned to take all the horses home. My master went to Paris, and informed the minister that in a fortnight his horses would arrive. "Very well," said the minister, "have them brought direct to Paris, you will save much expense. Give orders at once to have them sent on; you have been very prompt. Give me notice, and lose no time."

M. Potier took the diligence, had the three hundred horses brought to Paris, and wrote to his wife to start me off for Saint Denis with a wagon-load of bran, as the horses would stop there four days to rest. I was fortunate enough to arrive first at Saint Denis, and had everything ready for them. We had time in the four days to put new shoes on all the horses, and when we reached the École Militaire, they looked as fresh as if they had just stepped out of a bandbox.

The load of bran was well paid for. All the horses were received. I was four hours trotting them out before the artillery officers, inspectors, and a general, but I got no fee for myself. I was greatly disappointed at this. My master said to me, "You shall lose nothing by it. I will make you a present of a watch." Accordingly, he gave me a beautiful one, and also two hundred francs for the horses of the representatives, and two louis for the handsomest horse. What a fortune it was for me! When I reached home I gave all my money to my mistress, and the next Sunday she made me a present of six cravats. My master said, "My two trips have been worth thirty thousand francs to me." He had also disposed of five hundred bags of flour.

We resumed our usual employments. I grew strong and intelligent. I rode the most fiery horses and broke them in. I also did more ploughing, and made my farm-hand master a present of a blouse beautifully embroidered on the collar, with which he was much pleased. At sixteen I could lift a bag like a man. At eighteen I could lift a bag weighing three hundred and twenty-five. Nothing daunted me, but the position of a servant began to be exceedingly distasteful to me. My thoughts turned towards a soldier's life. I often saw fine-looking soldiers with long sabres and handsome plumes, and the sight of them would set my little head working all night. Afterwards I would reproach myself, — I who was so fortunate already. Those soldiers had turned my head. I cursed them. Then the love of work would resume its power over me, and I would think no more about them.

The farmers came from every direction to deliver the grain sold to M. Potier. Each farmer had a sample of his wheat at the house. "Jean," my master would say, "go, bring me ten money-bags." How many bags of a thousand francs went out of that cabinet of his! This went on till Christmas came.

I used up a big pile of a hundred bags in two months. Then my master said to his wife, "Write your invitations for this day week. I am going to Paris. I am going in the open carriage. We shall go and see our children, and Jean will bring some empty sacks, for there is a great deal of money due me. We will return Saturday, and on Sunday you can give your grand dinner." — "You must bring me some salt-water fish," said my mistress, "and whatever you wish for two dishes of meat, and some oysters." — "Very well, madame."

The money had all been received and well invested by Thursday. "See what good luck you have brought me," said my master. "All our business is transacted satisfactorily. We will make our purchases, and start for home to-morrow."

We arrived at five o'clock. My mistress was delighted that we came so early. The next day at five o'clock open carriages and jaunting-cars came in from every direction. I did not know which to attend to first. "Jean, go to town and bring M. and Madame Brodart and their daughter." — "Jean, go back again immediately for my son-in-law and my daughter." And I made the carriage spin along the road, with the horses always at a gallop. "Jean, you must wait on the table." And poor Jean was everywhere.

The party was magnificent, and my mistress put by a portion of the dainties for me. At eleven o'clock I was told to be ready to take everybody home. I began at midnight, and made three trips, which were worth eighteen francs to me. My master and mistress called me in to give me something to drink. "Take a good glass of our own wine and a bit of cake; we are much pleased with you." — "Ah, I have put his portion aside," said madame. The next day I received my good things, which I divided with my comrades; and I took the bushel measure, and went with the miller to Paris to bag flour for eight days. And so I learned to do all sorts of things.

My mistress begged me to pay great attention to her garden. At first I made her a pretty arbor at the bottom of it, in front of the gate, and laid off two beautiful flower-beds. I dug a walk four inches deep, so as to set off my beds, and replaced the earth I dug out with sand.

My master and mistress came out to see me. "Well, Jean," said my master, "are you going to make us a road in our garden?" — "No, sir, but a fine walk." — "You cannot do that all alone, I will call the gardener." — "But, sir, the worst part is done." — "What do you mean by that?" — "See the three lines I have made, and the sticks I have driven down; that is the middle of my walk." — "You have taken all my wagon lines." — "I could not make a straight line without them." — "That is a fact." — "At the last stick near the arbor, I shall make a basket for madame." — "Ah! that is a good thought, Jean. It is an excellent idea to make me a basket." — "I must have some box to plant along the walk, and a great deal of sand, and some plank to make benches in madame's arbor." — "And what will you make for your master?" — "The master will sit beside the mistress." — "Well, go to work; but, Jean, where will you get the sand?" — "I have found it, sir." — "Where?" — "Under the little bridge near the place where the horses go to water. I have just been there, and I found it three feet deep." — "You will have to draw it up." — "No, sir; we can load up under the bridge this summer; you know that all the bend of the river is dry, and we can drive out by the watering-place." — "That is so." — "We shall need about twenty loads. You see the walk is eight feet wide." — "Wife," said my master, "call your gardener, for Jean is going to make a road in your garden." — "Please, madame, will you send me some box and rose-bushes to plant along the walk?"

The gardener came at evening, and madame brought him into the garden and said, "Jean, come and show your work." The gardener was surprised. "Well," said she, "what do you think of Jean's idea?" — "Why, madame, it is beautifully laid out. You can walk four abreast on the walk, and the children will not tread on the borders." — "Very true," said she. "But you come to-morrow, for he will kill himself. He took it into his head to do this to please me." — "Madame, he has much taste. It is very well designed. We will make you a beautiful garden. We must have forty tall rose-trees, and some box for the walk and the basket. Your garden will be finished in a fortnight. The sand is so convenient." — "But do not leave Jean to work alone. He will hurry so that he will make himself ill." — "I know it, I will take care of him." — "Be sure you do, for I found him with his shirt all wet with perspiration."

Then madame went away, and the gardener said to me, "I

"There were only four suitable horses to be found in the neighborhood." — Page 41.

like the way you have begun your work. We will arrange a little surprise for her in front of the arbor. Let us make four side beds, and plant four Persian lilacs in them, and honeysuckle all around, and paint the benches green. That will be lovely. We must ask madame not to come out to see her garden for eight days." So that evening I told her that the gardener said she would please not come out to see her garden for eight days. "Well," said M. Potier, "I am going to Paris to dispose of some flour and see our children." — "Ah, that is very good of you." — "I shall return on Saturday, and I will see this tomfoolery of Jean and the gardener, after I have found out whether my big representative is pleased with his horses or not."

He returned satisfied with the reception given him by the representative, who said to him, "I am coming with my wife to see you in the spring. I have spoken to her of your lady, and she desires to make her acquaintance." — "I hope you will let us know beforehand." — "I will do so; we must not surprise madame, who entertains so well."

My master and mistress returned, and were surprised to see the great walk finished. "Oh, it is lovely; I am delighted; it is beautifully done. One can walk about and sit down. See these nice benches. Jean will ruin us with his fancies." — "Do not say a word to him for a week, until he has finished my garden. Pray do not. I wish to have it gravelled." — "Well, we will give Jean a surprise; we will turn off the water which flows under the little bridge, and he can get as much gravel as he likes. He shall not always be the smartest." — "He will laugh," said madame.

At the end of the week the garden was finished, and I went in to say, "Master and mistress, your garden is finished. You can come out and see it. Ah! if I only had some gravel it would be beautiful." — "Well, Jean, you shall have some to-morrow; my husband has turned the water on to the other side of the bridge, and left the gravel dry. To-morrow you shall have two carts and some men to load them; you will only have the trouble of putting it on the walk." — "Ah, madame, that finishes it. In four days all will be completed."

My master and mistress watched us from the windows without coming out. The gardener went and told them that all was done. "Come, wife, let us go out and see it." There I stood beside the gate, hat in hand, with my rake on my shoulder. M. Potier took me by the arm, and patted me on the shoulder; "Jean," said he. "you have made your mistress happy, and I am very glad. This looks much better than the grass which was here before." — "It is beautiful," said madame. "If your fashionable people from Paris come to see you, you can bring them out to walk around." — "You shall see no more grass in your walks."

I continued to work in the mill, I ploughed. I did everything, and especially I trained horses. My master received a letter from Paris ordering him to come at once to the representative at the Luxembourg on business. "Jean, my boy, we must start for Paris to-morrow morning. I think they want some horses." — "If that is so, it will pay for our tomfoolery of a flower-garden." We set out at five o'clock; at eleven we were in Paris. My master went to the address given: the chief of the Directory[1] said to him, "We want twenty horses of first-rate size, all entirely black, without a spot. The price will be forty-five louis. Where can you get them?" — "In the Pays de Caux and at the fair at Beaucaire. I always go there for horses of that size." — "Very well, go at once. When can you deliver them?" — "I must have three months, and I cannot guarantee to be ready even then; horses of that size are hard to find."

[1] That is to say, some principal functionary of the administration of the Directory.

We were soon back again at Coulommiers, and my master said, "We must start for Normandy, and we will return by way of Beaucaire, so as to attend the fair. I will have François come to me at once, so I may give him my orders, and will tell my wife that we are going." We went first to Caen, where several horses were offered us. There were only four suitable horses to be found in the whole neighborhood, and they asked fifty louis for them. "Very well," said my master, "take them to the fair; we will see about it." We visited the whole Pays de Caux, found magnificent farms, and a fine breed of horses, and selected four very handsome ones. The fair at Caen was well suited to our purposes. My master bought six superb horses, but we needed ten more. The people of the Pays de Caux are extremely handsome, particularly the women, with their great beautiful high head-dresses. The little women even look tall, for their bonnets are almost a foot high, and this makes their faces seem small. Both the people and the animals are magnificent.

Then we set out for Beaucaire, where we found ten horses. I had never seen such splendid fairs; strangers from all over the world were there. The city is built in a plain, and we found cafés, restaurant-keepers, and everything in the best style. Millions are employed in business there, and the fair lasts six weeks. My master's purchases being completed, we started on our return, having first collected the horses, and sent them on to Coulommiers. This was a long trip; we had been two months away from home. How glad madame would be to see us again!

My master said to me, "I must make a purchase for the horses. I shall have blankets and ear-pieces made for them; that will set them off. We will have them made of striped stuff. Go at once to M. Brodart. It is a necessary expense toward presenting them properly." In a week all was done. I was proud to see my fine horses adorned with such beautiful blankets. Then M. Potier set out at once for Paris, rendered the representative [1] an account of his purchase, and informed

---

[1] All these appellations of chief of the Directory, representative, peer of France, portly fellows, etc., in the mind of honest Coignet referred only to one person.

him that the twenty horses were at his house, and if my lord wished to see them he could do so. "Are they handsome?" said he. "We will come to your house on Sunday at two o'clock. There will be four of us, one of my friends and his wife and mine; tell Madame Potier that I shall bring two ladies with me."

At two o'clock their handsome post-chaise stood before our door. My master and mistress received them, and conducted them immediately to the dining-hall, where a superb collation was served. The ladies were delighted with madame's kind reception. M. Potier had invited some friends of the representative. The dinner was elegant. Madame pleased the ladies by asking them to take a walk in her garden, and the gentlemen went to take a look at the fine horses. The blankets had a wonderful effect. "Your horses are extremely handsome, their height is superb; our guards will be well mounted. I thank you very much, and I will write at once to the president of the Directory. They will be received at the Luxembourg. You can send them on in the next twenty-four hours. Two days of rest will be sufficient to put them in condition to be presented for examination; our gentlemen will be satisfied when they see them. Leave their blankets on them, they look well with them on, and you shall be paid for them in addition. How much did they cost you?" — "Four hundred francs." — "Very well, you shall be paid for all. Bring them out, so we can see them outside. They are finer than the horses of our grenadiers, these will do for the non-commissioned officers; they are splendid animals. Send them off to-morrow; it will take three days for the trip and two days for rest. I shall be in Paris in time to present them to the officers."

We reached the Luxembourg on the fourth day, and found all in readiness to receive us. The fine-looking non-commissioned officers and grenadiers surrounded us, took our horses, and put them in what seemed to me a palace. I had never seen such grand stables. M. Potier had us take off their blankets in order to groom them, and the grenadiers took charge of them. "You can leave them to our care," said an officer, "we will attend to them; you can put the blankets on again afterwards."

The next day M. Potier received an order to present his horses at one o'clock in the beautiful chestnut avenue in the garden. At two o'clock about twenty men arrived, who admired our horses and made them show their gaits. An officer came up to me and said, "Young man, I hear that you know how to ride." — "A little, sir." — "Well, let us see; mount the first one there. That will do." Then he took me to one of the quartermasters, and said to him, "Give your horse to this young fellow, and let him ride him." — "Thanks," said I to him. I was delighted. I started off at first at a walk; then my master said, "Trot," and I came back at a trot. "Go again at a gallop." I flew like the wind.

I drew my horse up before the gentlemen with all four of his feet in line. "How handsome that horse is," they said. "They are all equally so," said M. Potier. "If you wish, my boy will show them all for you." They consulted together for a moment, and then pointing out a horse which had seemed frightened, they had me called. "Young man," said the representative who had seen me at Coulommiers, "show this horse to these gentlemen; mount!"

I made him trot, leading from each foot, and then galloped off as before. I brought him back, and they said, "He rides well. He is bold, your young man." M. Potier said to them, "It was he who trained my lord the President's handsome horse; no one could ride him; he had to be led even on a level road; and he made him as gentle as a lamb." The President said to one of the officers, "Give this young man a louis for the horse he trained for me, and a hundred francs for these others: he ought to be encouraged." The officer said to the guards, "See how this boy manages a horse." I was handsomely feed by every one, and the soldiers shook hands with me, saying, "It is a pleasure to see you on horseback." — "Oh," said I, "I make them mind me. I punish the unruly and pet the gentle ones; they are obliged to yield to me."

Finally, M. Potier got through showing all of his twenty

horses, which were all accepted, with their blankets as a separate item, and all the expenses of the journey were also defrayed. "Without that," said M. Potier to them, "I should lose by the transaction." They answered him, "We have perfect confidence in you; the relays of horses which you have furnished us leave nothing to be desired." — "Thank you, gentlemen," said M. Potier. — "Make out three bills. They will make you three drafts, which will be paid you at the treasury. They will be signed by the treasurer of the government, and will be paid at sight. Meanwhile, I appoint you to receive six hundred horses which are coming from Germany, suitable for chasseurs and hussars. Do you accept this? You will receive them within eight or ten days. The fees will be three francs a horse, and this includes the services of your boy, who will ride them all, and be specially strict in training the German horses. You will receive notice as soon as they arrive." — "You may rely upon me." — "The officers will be there to receive their horses."

M. Potier concluded his transactions, and we set out for Coulommiers, where he was heartily welcomed after this long absence of three months. All home affairs had been conducted as the master desired. "Well, my dear," said Madame Potier to her husband, "have you enjoyed your trip?" — "I was delighted with those gentlemen. Everything turned out as well as possible. Jean surpassed himself in skilfulness. Every one remarked upon him. He has been asked to come with me to receive six hundred horses for a cavalry supply, and has been appointed to train them. Those gentlemen all included him in the fees they allowed me. You can make him your present, he deserves it. He carried off the palm from the grenadiers of the Directory for the management of horses."

The next Sunday my mistress took me into the town and made me a present of a suit of clothes. "Send that to my husband, with the receipted bill." I was greatly flattered at this. M. Potier presented the package to me: "Here is the present which you have so well deserved. We must have his suit made immediately. To-morrow we will resume our work at the mill, and get a hundred bags of flour ready to send to Paris." The whole week was employed at the mill. On Sunday we reviewed our horses. My master and mistress went to dine in the town, and I entertained all the servants with an account of our travels, telling them of all I had seen in Paris. That evening I went for my master and mistress without their having ordered it. They were pleased at the attention, and I brought them home about midnight. The next day I received my suit of clothes, everything complete. "Come, Jean, we must see if they fit well." They took me into their chamber, and presided over my toilet, exclaiming, "No one would ever recognize you."— "See," said madame, "here are some cravats and pocket-handkerchiefs. I have bought you a trunk to hold all your things."— "Master and mistress, I am overwhelmed by your kindness."  On Sunday I dressed myself, and made my appearance before the household, looking as if I had just jumped out of a bandbox. All my companions stared at me from head to foot, and every one paid me compliments. I thanked them by a pressure of the hand, and I was ready to wait upon them all.

Thus the years passed away in pleasant though laborious

service, for I took part in everything, and watched over all the interests of the house. I thought constantly of my brothers and my sister, and especially of those two who had disappeared from home at so tender an age. I could not help shedding tears over the fate of those two poor little innocent ones, and often wondered what could have become of them. "Could that wicked woman have destroyed them?" This thought pursued me constantly, and I longed to go and satisfy myself, but dared not ask permission, lest I should lose my place. My presence was necessary at the house. I was obliged to be patient, and resign myself to fate. The years passed by without bringing me any tidings of them. My gay spirits suffered from this. I had no one to whom I could tell my troubles.

I did a great deal of farm work, in which I became very skilful, and was considered so by all. At twenty-one, I could take the place of instructor in ploughing and in driving an eight-horse team.

The orders came from Paris, and we were obliged to start at once for the École Militaire, where we found a general and the officers of the hussars and chasseurs. My master was appointed by the general to review the horses, and his nomination as inspector of the relay was confirmed. The next day, the horses, fifty in number, were brought to the Champ de Mars. I bought a pair of buckskin breeches and a broad belt to strengthen my loins. These cost me thirty francs.

My master walked around with the general, who had me called up: "You are the boy who has been appointed to ride the horses, are you? Well, let us see. I am hard to please." — "Make yourself easy, general," said M. Potier, "he knows his business." — "Very well, mount; the cavalry horses first." — "Let him alone; you will be quite satisfied with him. He is only very bashful." — "Very well, go on; begin with the one on the right, and go through them."

I mounted the first, and so quickly that no one had time to see me do it. The horse shied several times. I gave him two cuts with my whip under his breast, and made him wheel about, and soon got him under control. I led him off at a trot, and brought him back at a gallop. I began again at a walk, as it is the gait most necessary to the cavalry. Then I dismounted, and said to the officer, "Mark this horse number one; he is good." I said to the veterinarian, "Examine the mouths of all the horses, and particularly their teeth. I will look at them afterwards."

And so I went on. I divided them into three lots, and had them marked by the captain of chasseurs. When we came to the thirtieth, I asked for a glass of wine, which the general had them bring me, saying, "I have left you alone, young man. Tell me, why these different lots?" — "The first is for your officers, the second for your chasseurs, and the third is retired." — "How retired?" — "Well, general, I will explain. The four horses of the third lot have been done up, and ought not to be accepted without examination by an expert. See how strict I am. This is on your account. Now shall I go on with my examination?" — "Yes, I approve of your method, severe and just."

Thus I continued at this work all day long. I rode fifty horses: six of the first lot and four of the second were bad. There were forty left for the chasseurs. When the officers saw what I was doing, they took me by the hand, and said, "You understand your business; we shall not be cheated." — "There are," said I, "six perfect horses, they will do for the officers." The general sent for me to come to him as he stood with his aide-de-camp near M. Potier. "You have worked well. I watched you, and am satisfied with you. Go on as you have begun. You must be tired; to-morrow we will examine the horses for the hussars, and you will work in the same way. At eleven o'clock, remember." — "Very well, general." — "Do you know how to write?" — "No, general." "I am sorry for that. I would have taken you into my service." — "I thank you, sir. I shall not leave my master; he has brought me up." — "You are a faithful boy." Then he called the officers, and said to them, "Take charge of this young man. Let him dine with you, he works for your interest. Do not allow the contractors to speak to him, and bring him to my house at nine o'clock. The inspector will dine with me."

I was cordially received by all the officers. The dinner passed off very gayly. At nine o'clock we went to the general's house, and coffee was served. I received the kindest welcome possible from the general. "To-morrow," said he, "we will go and see the horses that you are to ride, and I will send one of the quartermasters, who rides well, to assist you. You will get through sooner." — "I will make him ride the mares." — "Why the mares?" — "General, the mares are better than the geldings; they are not so easily fatigued. I will examine them before he mounts them." — "I am pleased with your observation, let me tell you. I heartily approve." — "If your soldier is pleased with his mare, he shall put her in the first lot, and so on. I will do the same." — "Well, gentlemen, what do you think of all this? We have fallen into good hands, and we shall have no more of those worthless horses, which will not last six months." — "I can be deceived, but I will do my best." — "Come, then, gentlemen, to-morrow at eleven o'clock precisely."

We took leave of the general, and my master put me into a carriage to go back to our hotel. "Jean," said he, "the general is pleased with you, he is really delighted. Try to do a good day's work to-morrow. As there will be two of you, he will doubtless be able to receive a hundred horses. That will help us a great deal." — "I will do my best, sir." The next day at six o'clock, we received a visit from the captain of hussars, and my master said to him, "Do me the kindness to accept a cutlet and a cup of coffee. We are about to be off, the cab is ready." — "Let us hurry; the general is no jester." At half-past ten we were near the Champ de Mars, ready to examine the horses. My master said, "Have fifty horses ready." At eleven, the general arrived. We reviewed the horses, and rode them two at a time.

Those horses were splendid: I was delighted with them, and I said so to the general, who also was satisfied. Only two in a hundred were rejected. The poor horse-traders were not so mortified as they had been the day before. In this way we received a hundred horses a day, and in nine days all was done. I was highly commended by all the officers and by the general, who ordered thirty francs to be paid me for the ten rejected horses. I went with my master to thank the general, who said to us, "I have made a report of the care you have taken in the choice of the horses for the officers, and of the reform which you instituted. It was on this account that I gave the thirty francs as a reward to your young man." I thanked him, and we went to settle up our business; my master realized eighteen hundred francs from his trip, and we started the next day for Coulommiers. My master said to me, "We have done a first-rate piece of business, and every one is satisfied."

I said to him, "If ever I am a soldier, I will do my best to get into the hussars; they are so splendid." — "You must not think of that. We will see about it after a while; that shall be my business. I warn you that the life of a soldier is not all rose-color." — "I am sure of it, consequently I have not gone into it; if I ever leave you, it will be because I am obliged to." — "Very well, I am pleased to hear you say so."

We reached home on Saturday, and Sunday everybody had a holiday. My master did not worry about me. I returned to my usual duties, but one day I was summoned to the mairie. There they asked me my name and Christian names, my profession and age. I answered that I was named Jean-Roch Coignet, and was born in Druyes-les-Belles-Fontaines, in the Department of the Yonne. "How old are you?" — "I was born on the 16th of August, 1776." — "You can retire."

This set my head to throbbing. "What in the devil did they want with me? I had done nothing." I said this to my master and mistress, who replied, "They wish to enroll you for conscription." — "Am I then going to be a soldier?" "Not yet, but this is one of the preliminary steps. If you wish, we will procure you a substitute." — "Thank you, I will think about it." I was overwhelmed by this piece of news. I should have been willing to start at once, but I had all the time till the month of August for reflection. My head was at work night and day. I saw myself about to leave the house where I had passed so many happy days, with such a good master and mistress, and such kind companions.

Here I bring to a close the first part of my work, lest such details should grow tiresome. I am about to begin the history of my military career. Compared with that, my sorrowful early life was a bed of roses.

SECOND NOTE-BOOK.

DEPARTURE FOR THE ARMY. — MY MILITARY LIFE UP TO THE BATTLE OF MONTEBELLO.

On the sixth Fructidor, year VII., two gendarmes came and left with me a way-bill and an order to start for Fontainebleau the tenth Fructidor. I immediately made preparations for my departure. My master and mistress wished to procure me a substitute. I thanked them with tears in my eyes. "I promise you that I shall bring back a silver gun, or die." It was a sad leave-taking. I was overwhelmed with kindness by the whole household. They accompanied me to the end of the road, and bade me good-by with many embraces. With my little bundle under my arm, I reached Rozoy, the first military halting-place, where I spent the night. I took my billet, and presented it to my host, who took no notice of me whatever. Then I went out to buy something to make a stew, and the butcher gave it to me. I felt quite desolate when I saw that piece of meat in the palm of my hand. I gave it to my landlady, and asked her to have the kindness to have it cooked for me, and went to find some vegetables for her. At last I got my little stew, and by that time I had won the good graces of my hosts, who were willing to talk to me, but I took no fancy to them.

The next day I reached Fontainebleau, where some very unenthusiastic officers received us and put us in barracks which were in wretched condition. Our fine battalion was formed within a fortnight; it numbered eighteen hundred men. As there was no discipline, a revolution at once occurred, and half of them left and went home. The chief of battalion reported them at Paris, and each man was allowed fifteen days to rejoin his battalion, or else be regarded as a deserter, and punished accordingly. General Lefebvre was immediately sent to organize us. Companies were formed, and grenadiers selected. I belonged to this latter company, which numbered a hundred and twenty-five men, and we were uniformed at once. We received an entire outfit, and immediately began to drill twice a day. The stragglers were brought back by the gendarmes, and we were brought into order again.

Sunday was the *décadi*[1] for the whole battalion. We had to sing "La Victoire," and the officers flourished their sabres about; the church resounded with them. Then we cried out, "Vive la République!" Every evening, around the liberty-pole in the principal street, we had to sing, "Les aristocrates à la lanterne." It was very entertaining.

This sort of life had lasted nearly two months, when a report was circulated in the newspapers that General Bonaparte had landed, and was on his way to Paris, and that he was a great general. Our officers went crazy about it, because the chief of our battalion knew him, and the whole battalion was delighted to hear it. We were reviewed, and our clothing examined. We were made to carry and present arms and charge bayonets. They undertook to make soldiers of us in two months. We had callouses on our hands from beating them on the butt-ends of our guns. All day long we were under arms. Our officers took us by the collars and examined

---

[1] The *décadi* was the substitute for Sunday as the day of rest, but occurred only once in ten days. To sing "La Victoire" means here to sing the "Chant du Départ," which began with the words, "La victoire en chantant." . . .

our clothing; they took every precaution that we should be lacking in nothing.

At last a courier brought the information that Bonaparte would pass by Fontainebleau, and that he would spend the night there. We were kept under arms all day long, but he did not come. We were scarcely allowed time to eat. The bakers and innkeepers on the principal street did a good business. Videttes were placed in the wood, and every moment there was a cry of "*Aux armes,*" and every one rushed out on the balconies, but all for nothing, for Bonaparte did not arrive till midnight.

In the principal street of Fontainebleau, where he dismounted, he was delighted to see such a fine battalion. He called the officers around him, and gave them an order to set out for Courbevoie.[1] He got into his carriage again, and we, shouting "Vive Bonaparte," returned to our barracks to make up our knapsacks, wake up our washerwomen, and pay them off.

We slept at Corbeil. The inhabitants received us as if we had been natives of that country, and the next day we started for Courbevoie, where we found the barracks in the most destitute condition, not even straw to sleep on. We were obliged to get trellises from among the vines to warm ourselves and boil our pots.

We remained there only three days, as orders were sent us to go to the École Militaire, where we were put in rooms which had nothing in them but straw mattresses, and at least a hundred men in each room. Then a distribution of cartridges was made: three packages of fifteen cartridges each to each man, and three days after we were made to start for St. Cloud, where we saw cannons everywhere, and troopers wrapped in their cloaks. We were told that they were the *gros talons*,[2] that they came down on the enemy, in a charge,

---

[1] This visit must have been made, not on his return from Egypt, but a little before the Coup d'État, which was about a month later. At a time when soldiers did not read the newspapers, it is not astonishing that such mistakes were made. Some one told Coignet that the general was coming from Egypt, and he concluded that he had not been to Paris. Moreover, the order to depart must have been merely transmitted and not given by Bonaparte.

[2] Cuirassiers, so called because of their heavy boots. They were afterwards called "*gilets de fer*" (iron waistcoats), on account of their cuirasses.

like a thunderbolt, and that they were covered with iron. But this was not really so. They had only ugly three-cornered hats with two iron plates in the form of a cross in front. These men looked like big peasants, with horses so large they made the earth shake, and great sabres four feet long. These were our heavy cavalrymen, who afterwards became cuirassiers, and were called the "*gilets de fer.*" At last the regiment reached St. Cloud. The grenadiers of the Directory and of the Five Hundred were in line in the front court; a half-brigade of infantry was stationed near the great gate, and four companies of grenadiers behind the guard of the Directory.

Cries of "Vive Bonaparte" were heard on all sides, and he appeared. The drums beat a salute; he passed in front of the fine corps of grenadiers, saluted every one, ordered us into line of battle, and spoke to the officers. He was on foot, and wore a small hat and a short sword. He went up the steps alone. Suddenly we heard cries, and Bonaparte came out, drew his sword, and went up again with a platoon of grenadiers of the guard. Then the noise increased. Grenadiers were on the stairway and in the entrance. We saw stout gentlemen jumping out of the windows;[1] cloaks, fine hats, and plumes were thrown on the ground, and the grenadiers pulled the lace from the elegant cloaks.[2]

At three o'clock orders were sent us to start for Paris, but the grenadiers did not go with us. We were famishing. On our arrival brandy was distributed to us. The Parisians crowded around us to hear the news from St. Cloud. We could scarcely make our way through the streets to the Luxembourg, where we were quartered in a chapel at the entrance of the garden (we had to go up-stairs). To the left, after we mounted the stairs, was a great vaulted chamber, which they told us was the sacristy. Here they made us put up big kettles for four hundred soldiers. In front of the main building there were handsome linden trees; but the beautiful square in front of the palace was covered with the ruins of

---

[1] These "stout gentlemen" were the representatives of the nation.
[2] The mantle and plumed cap then formed a part of the parliamentary dress.

buildings. There was nothing left in this beautiful garden but the old chestnut trees, which are still there, and an outlet in the rear at the end of our chapel. It was pitiful to see that lovely garden utterly destroyed.

Then a fine-looking grenadier rode up with the chief of battalion, who ordered us under arms to receive M. Thomas (or Thomé) as lieutenant in the 96th half-brigade, and he also said to us, " My comrade and I saved General Bonaparte's life. The first time he entered the hall, two men rushed upon him with two daggers, and it was my comrade and I who parried the blows. Then the general went outside, and they cried, 'Outlaw him.' Whereupon he drew his sword, and ordered us to charge bayonets, and shouted, 'Clear the hall,' and called for his brother. All the web-footed creatures jumped out of the windows, and we were left masters of the hall." [1] He told us also that Josephine had given him a ring, worth full fifteen thousand francs, forbidding him to sell it, and saying she would attend to all his wants.

Our whole fine battalion was finally incorporated in the 96th half-brigade of the line, composed of old and experienced soldiers, and officers who were very strict. Our colonel was named M. Lepreux, a native of Paris, a good soldier, and kind to his officers. Our captain was named Merle, and he had all the qualities of a soldier. Strict, just, always present when rations were distributed to his grenadiers, on drill twice a day, strict in discipline; he was present at meal-times. He also taught us to shoot. We were at work every moment of our time. In three months our companies were able to go through the drill in presence of the First Consul.

I became very skilful in the use of arms. I was supple, and I had two good training masters who helped me on. They had examined me, and so had felt my belt-pockets; they therefore paid court to me. I paid for their drams. It was necessary to deal in this way with these drunkards. How-

---

[1] This story is a little *too* exact. The armed force was sent at the requisition of the president of the Assembly. But a boasting grenadier is not always a historian. His epithet of "web-footed" had reference, doubtless, to the bows of ribbon on their shoes.

ever, I had no reason to complain of them, for at the end of two months they put me to a severe test. They made me seek a quarrel, and that without pretext. "Come," said this swaggerer[1] to me, "draw your sabre, and I will spill a little of your blood." — "All right, we will see, you puppy." — "Find your second." — "I have none." Then my old master, who was in the plot, said to me, "Would you like me to be your second?" — "I would, indeed, Father Palbrois." — "Be

off, then," said he, "and no more ado!" All four of us started out. We went a little way into the garden of the Luxembourg where there were two old tumble-down buildings, and they took me in between two old walls. There with my coat off I stood ready. "Now, strike first," said I to him. — "I won't," he answered. "All right, look out." Then I rushed upon him, and gave him no time to recover himself. My master ran in between us, sabre in hand. I pushed him aside. "Get away, let me kill him!" — "Come, come, that will do; shake hands, and we will go drink a bottle of wine." — "But that drop of my blood, doesn't he want it any longer?" — "It was all a joke," said my master.

[1] I. e., the other party to the quarrel.

I was now recognized as a good grenadier. I saw what they were after; this was a trick to make me pay my scot, which I did with a good grace, and they set it down to my credit. The grenadier, who wanted to kill me in the morning, was my best friend. He paid me all sorts of attentions and rendered me any number of small services. My two masters pushed me forward; four hours of drilling, two hours in the fencing school, making six hours daily. This life lasted three months, and I paid for many drams for these drunkards. Happily for me, M. and Madame Potier had filled my belt-pouch. I reaped the benefit of their goodness a long time.

We passed the winter in Paris. The First Consul's review took place in the month of February, at the Tuileries; the three half-brigades (24th light, 43d and 96th of the line) formed a division of fifteen thousand men, the command of which was given to General Chambarlhac. The First Consul put us through the evolutions, rode down the ranks and seemed satisfied. He called the colonels, and desired to see the conscripts apart. The company of grenadiers of the battalion of Seine-et-Marne was brought out. He told our captain, Merle, to make us go through the evolutions before him. He was surprised. "But these must be old troops you are drilling?" — "No," answered the captain, "'tis a company of the auxiliary battalion which has been formed at Fontainebleau." — "I am greatly pleased with this company; send it back to the battalion. Hold yourselves in readiness to march."

We received orders to set out for the camp of Dijon, which really had no existence, at least we never saw it. The whole division started for Corbeil, where Chambarlhac made us camp among the vines in the good department of Seine-et-Marne, which had made so many sacrifices for our battalion. We camped thus all along the route. From Auxerre he led us to St. Nitasse. The citizens were willing to lodge us, they brought us wagon-loads of wood and straw; but all in vain, we were forced to burn their trellises and cut down their poplars. We were called "Chambarlhac's brigands." He, however, never bivouacked with his soldiers. This life continued till we reached Dijon, where we were lodged among the citizens and remained there six weeks.

General Lannes formed his advance guard, and set out for Switzerland. We were the last to leave Dijon for Auxonne, where we lodged. The next day we went to Dôle where we only passed the night, and went on to Poligny. Thence we went to Morez. The next day we slept at Rousses, and thence to Nyon, where we brought all our little force together in a beautiful plain. We were reviewed by the First Consul, assisted by his generals, among whom was Lannes. We were put through the evolutions, and made to form a square. The Consul kept us occupied the whole day; the next morning he marched us out, and started us for Lausanne, a very pretty village. The Consul passed the night there, and we were kindly received.

Here one comes upon a wooded height which overlooks a wide extent of country, with Geneva on one hand and the shores of the lake on the other. As far as the eye can reach extends the wooded and rocky shore of that majestic lake, the water of which is always a deep blue. To the left a road winds along this beautiful shore, which is cultivated in the form of an amphitheatre. It is a series of espaliers from bottom to top. This shore is a source of great wealth to the whole country; it is a masterpiece of nature. Guides are needed through all the towns of Switzerland, for the country is woody and mountainous. The people are good to the soldiers; we never started out without a good bit of ham wrapped in a paper. We had guides all along our route, for we were in danger of losing our way.

Leaving Lausanne, we went around the end of the Lake of Geneva, and then went up the valley of the Rhone, and arrived at St. Maurice. Thence we started for Martigny. All these villages were as wretched as can possibly be imagined. We went into another valley, which might well have been called the valley of Hell. After that we left the valley of the Rhone, and went into the valley which leads to the St. Bernard, and came to the town of St. Pierre, situated at the foot of the gorge of the St. Bernard. This village was composed entirely of barracks covered with planks, and immense barns where we slept pell-mell. Here we dismounted our entire park in the presence of the Consul. Each of our pieces was placed in a trough; at the end of the trough there was a large mortise by which to drag our piece, managed by a strong and intelligent gunner with forty grenadiers under his orders. We had to obey in absolute silence every movement made by his piece. If he commanded "Halt," we could not budge; if he cried "Advance," we had to move on. He was our master.

Next morning at daybreak all was ready, and rations of biscuits were distributed to us. I put them on a string and

hung them around my neck (the necklace was very inconvenient), and we had two pairs of shoes given us. That very evening our cannoneer made up his teams, which were composed of forty grenadiers to each piece; twenty to drag the piece (ten on each side, holding on to sticks put through ropes which served for traces), and twenty others who carried the others' muskets and the wheels and caissons of the piece. The Consul had taken the precaution to collect the mountaineers together for the purpose of picking up all the things which should have been left behind, promising them six francs for the journey and two rations a day. In this way every thing was brought together at the place of rendezvous, and nothing was lost.

The next morning at daybreak, our master placed us by twenties at our pieces, ten on each side of a gun. I was put in the first place, to the right, in front; it was the most dangerous side, because it was next to the precipices. Then we started off with our three pieces. Two men carried each axletree, two carried a wheel, four carried the upper part of the caisson, eight carried the chest, eight others the muskets. Every one had his special duty and position. It was a most terrible journey. From time to time there were commands of "Halt," or "Advance," and not a word was spoken. All this was mere pastime, but when we reached the snow, matters became more serious. The road was covered with ice which cut our shoes, and our gunner could not manage his piece; it slipped constantly. He was obliged to mount it anew. This man needed all his courage to be able to hold out; "Halt!" "Advance!" he cried every moment, and all moved on in silence.

We had gone over a league of this terrible road, and it was necessary to give us a moment to rest and to put on some new shoes, for those we had on were in tatters, and also to take a bite of our biscuits. As I was taking my string from around my neck so as to take one off, the string broke, and all my biscuits went rolling down the precipice. How grieved I was to find myself without bread, and how my forty comrades laughed at my misfortune! "Come," said our cannoneer, "we must make up a feed for our lead horse, he always obeys the first word of command." This made my comrades laugh again. "All right," they answered, "let each of us give a biscuit to our lead horse!" Then I recovered my spirits. I thanked them with all my heart and found myself richer than my comrades. We started off again well shod. "Come, my horses," said our gunner, "fall into your places, advance! When we reach the snow fields, we shall move more easily and not have so much trouble."

We did reach those terrible fields of perpetual snow, and found much less difficulty; our gun-trough slid along more rapidly. General Chambarlhac came up with us and wanted to hasten us; he went towards the cannoneer and assumed the tone of command, but was ill received. "You don't command my piece," said the cannoneer. "I alone am responsible for it. Go your own way! these grenadiers do not belong to you for the present; I alone command them." Then he tried to approach the cannoneer, but the latter commanded him to halt. "If you do not move out of my way I will knock you down with one blow of my crowbar. Pass on, or I will throw you over the precipice!"

He was compelled to go away, and after the greatest exertion we reached the foot of the monastery steep. For four hundred feet the ascent is very rapid, and we could see that some troops had gone on ahead of us. The road had been opened and paths cut out leading to the monastery. We planted our three pieces, and four hundred of us grenadiers with a party of our officers entered the house of God, where men devoted to the cause of humanity are stationed to give aid and comfort to travellers. Their dogs are always on hand to guide unfortunate creatures who may have fallen in the avalanches of snow, and conduct them to this house, where every necessary comfort is provided.

While our colonel and other officers were in the halls beside bright fires, we received from these venerable men a bucket of wine for every twelve men, and a quarter of a pound of Gruyère cheese and a loaf of bread for each. We were lodged in the large corridors. These good monks did every thing that they possibly could, and I believe they were well treated.

For our part, we pressed the good fathers' hands when we parted from them, and embraced their dogs which caressed us as if they knew us. I cannot find words to express the veneration I feel for those men.

Our officers decided to take our pieces down the descent, and then our terrible task would be accomplished. Our brave captain, Merle, was appointed to conduct the three companies. As we crossed the lake which is at the foot of the monastery, we saw that in one place the ice had been broken. The good monk who showed us the way told us that it was the first time for forty years that he had seen the water. He pressed our captain's hand and bade us all farewell.

We descended almost perpendicularly, and reached St. Rémy. This village is down in a perfect hell of snow; the houses are very low, and covered with very broad tiles. Here we passed the night. I lay down on the floor of a stable where I found some straw, and passed a comfortable night along with twenty of my comrades; we were not cold. The next morning we had roll-call, and started to go to a place three leagues farther on. We were going to get out of hell and descend to paradise. "Be saving of your biscuits," said our captain, " we are not yet in Piedmont. We must go through many a difficult pass before we reach Italy." We came to the place of general rendezvous for all the regiments; it was a long gorge with a village set against the mountain. To the right, up a steep slope, there was a very high rock. In two days all our forces were gathered together in this plain. Our brave officers had come through without any boots and with no sleeves to their coats; it was pitiful to see them.

This rendezvous seemed to be the end of the world; there was no way leading out of it. The Consul arrived and immediately ordered some heavy timbers to be brought. He superintended in person, with all the engineers, and they made a hole in the rock, which was on the edge of the precipice. This rock was so steep that it seemed as though it had been cut. A piece of timber was placed in the hole; then he made them put another piece across it (this was more difficult to accomplish), and placed a man at the end. When the second piece was in position, with beams on the first two, it was no longer difficult to establish our bridge. Railings were put on the side next the precipice, and this wonderful piece of work was completed in two days. Meanwhile all our pieces had been remounted, and nothing was lost.

On the other side the descent was easy to the valley, which led to the fort of Bard, which is surrounded by rocks. This fort is impregnable, it is impossible to batter it down; it is one great rock, with rocks all around it which tower above it, and which cannot be surmounted. Here the Consul took many pinches of snuff, and had quite enough to do, with all his genius. His engineers set to work to pass by out of range

"He had a path cut in the side of this mountain." — Page 63.

of the guns. They discovered a foot-path among the rocks which was four hundred yards long, and he had it cleared out and made smooth. This foot-path led to the foot of a mountain; he had a path cut in the side of this mountain with iron sledge-hammers, wide enough for a man to ride through on horseback. But this was not his most difficult task. The ordnance was at hand, sheltered in a cave, but it could not follow the foot-path, but must pass near the fort. So this is the way he managed it; he first placed two pieces on the road in front of the fort and fired into it. He was, however, obliged to withdraw them immediately, for a cannon-ball entered one of our pieces. He sent a flag of truce and summoned the commander to surrender, but received an unfavorable reply. He was then obliged to employ strategy. He chose good sharp-shooters, gave them provisions and cartridges, and placed them in the clefts of the rocks or had niches made for them in the rocks which overlooked the fort. Their shot fell on the backs of the soldiers, they could not move about in their court-yard. The same day he discovered a very broad flat rock to the left of the fort. He immediately made an examination of it so as to plant two pieces on it. Men and ropes were called into requisition, and the two pieces were placed upon this flat rock which was at least a hundred feet higher than the fort. Grape shot was poured into it, and the soldiers could not move from their casemates during the day; but still, there were our pieces and our caissons which must be taken past the fort.

As soon as Bonaparte learned that the horses belonging to the artillery trains had passed by, he made preparations to send his artillery under the walls of the fort; he had the wheels and every part which could make any noise, even the soldiers' shoes, padded with straw, so as not to attract attention. At midnight all was ready. The cannoneers of our half-brigade asked for grenadiers to drag the artillery, and the twenty men who had climbed Mont St. Bernard were detailed for that purpose. I was among those who were under the same cannoneer under whom I had made the passage of the St. Bernard; he put me at the head of the first piece, and each of the others at his former post. The signal for departure was given; not a breath was heard. We passed by without being noticed.

On reaching the opposite side, we turned immediately to the left; along the way for forty feet, we were protected by the rock which overlooked the road and concealed us from the fort. We found the horses all ready; we hitched them up at once and started off. We returned by the same road on tip-toe, holding on to each others' coat-tails; but we were heard, and grenades were thrown upon us over the ramparts. As they fell upon the opposite side of the road, no one was struck; we were only frightened and went back to get our guns. This was a mistake; we should have been told to put them on the caissons, and go forward on our way. As it was, we were much exposed; but it is impossible to think of everything.

On our return from this perilous undertaking, the colonel congratulated us upon our success: "I thought you were lost, my brave men." Our captain made us form a circle around him, and said, "My grenadiers, you have just accomplished a great work. It is a great credit to the company." He shook us all by the hand, and said to me, "I am much pleased with your first services. I shall remember you." Then he pressed my hand again, saying, "I am very well pleased." We all answered, "Captain, we all love you."—"Ah, you are very kind; I shall not forget it, and I thank you."

We now went up a steep foot-path; when we reached the top of the mountain, we saw the beautiful plains of Piedmont. The descent being practicable, we soon found ourselves in that paradise, and went on by forced marches as far as Turin, where the inhabitants were surprised to see an army arrive with its artillery.

This is the best-built city in Europe. All the houses are alike, all built after the same model, with streams of pure water in the gutters; all the streets are straight and very magnificent. Next day we set out for Milan. We made no halt, the march was forced. We made our entrance into the beautiful city of Milan, where all the people lined the streets to see us pass. They are very fine-looking. The street which leads to the Roman gateway is as handsome as can well be imagined. Passing through this gate, and turning to the left, we found a camp already established, and barracks completed. We saw that there was an army there ahead of us. We were made to stack arms, and men were detailed to go for provisions, and I was among the number. No one was allowed to enter the city. I stole off, while rations were being distributed, to go and see the cathedral. There is nothing like it, with all its columns of white marble. I went back to carry my bag of bread, and full rations were distributed to us.

We left there the next morning, and went to the right down to the river Po, which is a very deep stream. Here we found a flying bridge, which would hold five hundred men at a time, and by means of a heavy rope, which was thrown across the river, one could cross by pulling on the rope. This consumed a great deal of time, especially in transferring the artillery. It was very late when we reached the heights, which were completely laid waste, and there we passed the night. Our division was sent on to Piacenza, a superb city. General Lannes was defeating the Austrians, and driving them back upon the Po. As for our division, we were sent from one place to another, and made to march in every direction to assist the divisions of the advance guard, and still we did not fire a gun. We only manœuvred.

We again marched down to the Po. The Austrians seized upon the heights before reaching Montebello. Their artillery cut down our troops as they came up. We were obliged to send the 24th and 43d half-brigades forward to take possession of the position. General Lannes finally succeeded in driving them back toward Montebello, and pursued them all night. The next morning he bade them good-by, and our half-brigade occupied the heights, which had cost us so much to take, for they were twice as strong as we were. Next morning we started out to follow in the wake of that immense advance-guard, and we were stationed about half a league back of Montebello, in a broad walk in a beautiful plantation of mulberry-trees. There we were made to stack arms.

We were regaling ourselves upon the ripe fruit with which

the trees were loaded, when suddenly at eleven o'clock we heard cannonading. We thought it was very far off. But we were mistaken, it was coming nearer to us. An aide-de-camp came up with orders for us to advance as rapidly as possible. The general was hard pressed on all sides. "To arms," said our colonel, "forward, my brave regiment! To-day it is our turn to distinguish ourselves." And we shouted, "Hurrah for our colonel and all our brave officers!" Our captain, with his one hundred and seventy-four grenadiers, said,

"I will answer for my company. I will lead them to the front."

We were made to march by platoons, and load our guns as we were marching, and here I put the first cartridge in my gun. I made the sign of the cross with my cartridge, and it brought me good luck. We reached the entrance of the village of Montebello, where we saw a great many wounded soldiers, and then came the charge which won the day.

I was in the first platoon in the third rank, according to my height. As we were going out of the village, a cannon gave us a volley of grape-shot, which did no one any harm. I ducked my head at the sound of the cannon, but my sergeant-major slapped me on the knapsack with his sabre, and said, "You must not duck your head." — "No, I won't," I answered.

After the first discharge, Captain Merle cried, "To right and left into the trenches," so as to prevent our receiving another volley. As I did not hear the captain's command, I was left entirely exposed. I ran past our drummers, towards the cannon, and fell upon the cannoneers. They were loading again, and did not see me. I bayoneted all five of them, then leaped upon the piece, and my captain embraced me as he went by. He told me to guard my cannon, which I did, and our battalions dashed upon the enemy. It was a bloody charge of bayonets, with firing by platoons. The men of our demi-brigade fought like lions.

I did not remain long in that position. General Berthier came galloping up, and said to me, "What are you doing here?" — "General, you see what I am doing. This is my

piece, I took it all by myself." — "Do you want something to eat?" — "Yes, general." (He talked through his nose.) Then he turned to his groom, and said, "Give him some bread." And taking out a little green memorandum-book, he asked me my name. "Jean-Roch Coignet." — "Your half brigade?" — "Ninety-sixth." — "Your battalion?" — "The first." — "Your company?" — "First." — "Your captain?" — "Merle." — "Tell your captain to bring you to see the

Consul at ten o'clock. Go and find him; leave your piece here."

Then he galloped off, and I, delighted, went as fast as my legs would take me to rejoin my company, which had turned into a road to the right. This road was a sunk road, bordered on each side with hedges and filled with Austrian grenadiers. Our grenadiers were fighting them with bayonets. They were in complete disorder. I went up to my captain, and told him that my name had been taken down. "That is good," said he. "Now, come through this opening, so we can get ahead of the company; they are marching too fast, they will be cut off. Follow me." We went together through the opening. About a hundred steps off, on the other side of the road, there was a large wild pear-tree, and behind it a Hungarian grenadier, who was waiting till my captain came in front of him to fire upon him. But as he saw him, he cried to me, "Fire, grenadier." As I was behind the Hungarian, I took aim at a distance of only ten steps, and he fell, stone dead. Then my captain embraced me. "Do not leave me through the whole fight," said he; "you have saved my life." And we hastened on to get ahead of the company which had advanced too rapidly.

There was a sergeant who came from the other side as we did. Three grenadiers surrounded him. I ran to help him. They had hold of him, and called to me to surrender. I pointed my gun at them with my left hand, and with my right I made it play see-saw, plunging my bayonet into the body of first one and then a second of the grenadiers. The third was thrown down by the sergeant, who took him by the head, and threw him at his feet. The captain finished the work. The sergeant recaptured his belt and his watch, and in his turn plundered the three Austrians. We left him to recover himself, and put on his clothes, and hastened forward to get in front of the company, which was filing into an open field, where the captain once more took command, and reunited it to the battalion, which was marching forward at a quick step.

We were encumbered with three hundred prisoners, who had surrendered on the sunk road. We turned them over to some of the *hussars de la mort* who had escaped, for they had been cut to pieces that morning, and only two hundred out of a thousand were left. We took more prisoners; we did not know what to do with them; no one wanted to take charge of them, and they went along unguarded. They were routed completely. They ceased firing upon us, and ran like rabbits, especially the cavalry, which caused a panic throughout the infantry. The Consul came up in time to see the battle won, and General Lannes covered with blood (he looked dreadfully), for he had been constantly in the thick of the fight, and it was he who made the last charge. If we had had two regiments of cavalry, all their infantry might have been taken.

That evening, the captain took me by the arm, presented me to the colonel, and told him what I had done during the day. He answered, "Why, captain, I knew nothing about it all." Then he shook me by the hand, and said, "I must make a note of this." — "General Berthier wishes to present him to the Consul at ten o'clock this evening," said my captain; "I am going to take him." — "Ah! I am glad of it, grenadier."

We went to see General Berthier, and my captain said to him, "Here is my grenadier who captured the cannon, and since then he has saved my life and that of my first sergeant. He killed three Hungarian grenadiers." — "I will present him to the Consul." Then General Berthier and my captain went to see the Consul, and after talking a while with him they called me in. The Consul came up to me, and took me by the ear. I thought he was going to scold me, but, on the contrary, he was very kind; and still holding me by the ear, he said, "How long have you been in the service?" — "This is my first battle." — "Ah, indeed! it is a good beginning. Berthier, put him down for a gun of honor. You are too young to be in my guard; for that, one must have made four campaigns. Berthier, make a note of him at once, and write it in the portfolio of notes. You may go now." said he to me, "but you shall one day be one of my guards."

Then my captain took me away, and we went off with our

arms locked as if I had been his equal. "Do you know how to write?" said he. — "No, captain." — "Oh, that is a pity; if you did, your fortune would be made. But, never mind, you will be specially remembered." — "Thank you, captain."

All the officers shook hands with me, and the brave sergeant, whose life I had saved, embraced me before the whole company, who cheered me. How proud I was!

Thus ended the battle of Montebello.

THIRD NOTE-BOOK.

THE BATTLE OF MARENGO. — EXCURSION INTO SPAIN.

The next night we slept on the field of battle. The morning of the 19th, the drums called to arms. Lannes and Murat set out with their van-guard to bid the Austrians good-morning, but could not find them. They had not slept, and had marched all night. Our half-brigade finished picking up the wounded Austrians and French whom we had not found the night before. We carried them off to the ambulances, and it was very late before we left the battle-field.

We were all night on the march through cross roads. At midnight, M. Lepreux, our colonel, called a halt, and passed down the ranks saying, "Maintain the most perfect silence, — absolute silence." Then he ordered the first battalion to move. We passed through narrow roads where we could not even see each other. The officers, who were on horseback, had dismounted, and the most profound silence reigned through the ranks. We passed out, and found ourselves in ploughed fields. We were still forbidden to make any noise, or to light any fire. We were obliged to lie down among the great clods of dirt, with our heads on our knapsacks, and wait for the day.

The next morning we were ordered to rise, with empty stomachs! We went on only to find villages completely pillaged. We crossed ditches and marshes, a large stream, and came to villages filled with shrubbery. No provisions anywhere. All the houses were deserted. Our officers were overcome with fatigue and hunger. We left these marshy places, and turned to the left, into a village surrounded by orchards and gardens. Here we found some flour, a little bread, and a few animals. It was time, for we were dying of hunger.

On the 12th our two half-brigades came up on our right wing, and our division was reunited. We were told that the name of the village was Marengo. In the morning the breakfast-drum sounded. What joy! Twenty-seven wagons filled with bread had arrived. What happiness for the famished! Every one was willing to do extra duty. But what was our disappointment! The bread was all damp and mouldy. But we were obliged to put up with it.

On the 13th, at break of day, we were made to march forward into an open plain, and at two o'clock we were placed in line of battle and piled arms. Aides-de-camp arrived from our right, who flew around in every direction. A general engagement took place; the 24th half-brigade was detached and sent forward unsupported. It marched a long distance, came up with the Austrians, and had a serious encounter, in which it lost heavily. It was obliged to form a square in order to resist the attack of the enemy. Bonaparte abandoned it in this terrible position. It was said that he desired to leave it to be destroyed. The reason was this. At the time of the battle of Montebello, this half-brigade, having been forced to fire by General Lannes, began by firing upon its officers. The soldiers spared only one lieutenant. I do not really know what could have been the motive for this terrible vengeance. The Consul, informed of what had taken place, concealed his indignation. He could not give way to it when in face of the enemy. The lieutenant who had survived the destruction of his comrades was appointed captain; the staff immediately re-formed. But, nevertheless, it was understood that Bonaparte had not forgotten.

About five or six o'clock in the evening we were sent to extricate the 24th. When we arrived, soldiers and officers heaped insults upon us, declaring that we had wantonly left them to destruction, as if it depended upon us to march to their assistance. They had been overwhelmed. I suppose they had lost half their men; but this did not prevent their fighting still better the next day.[1]

There was no longer any doubt that the Austrians were in front of us, in the city of Alessandria. All night long we were under arms; the outposts were placed as far forward as possible, and small guard-posts advanced. On the 14th, at three o'clock in the morning, they surprised two of our small posts of four men and killed them. This was the signal for the morning reveille. At four o'clock there was firing on our right. Our drums beat the general, and the aides-de-camp came and ordered us to form our lines of battle. We were made to fall back a little behind a beautiful field of wheat, which was on a slightly rising ground and concealed us, and there we waited a little while. Suddenly their sharpshooters came out from behind the willows and from the marshes, and then the artillery opened fire. A shell burst in the first company and killed seven men; a bullet killed the orderly near General Chambarlhac, who galloped off at full speed.[2] We saw him no more all day.

A little general came up, who had fine mustaches: he found our colonel, and asked where was our general. We answered, "He is gone." — "Very well, I will take command of the division." And he immediately took charge of the company of grenadiers of whom I was one, and led us to the attack in one rank. We opened fire. "Do not halt while loading your guns," said he. "I will recall you by the beating of the drums." And he hastened to rejoin his division. He had scarcely returned to his post when the column of Austrians started from

---

[1] This paragraph and the preceding one were added during the printing of the first edition made at Auxerre, under the supervision of the author. They are not found in his manuscript.

[2] Yet in October, 1793, the Moniteur speaks of this Chambarlhac, then chief of battalion, as having contributed by his courage to the occupation of the territory of Mont Blanc. But those shine in the second rank who are eclipsed in the first.

behind the willows, deployed in front of us, fired by battalions, and riddled us with small shot. Our little general answered, and there we were between two fires, sacrificed. . . . I ran behind a big willow tree, and fired into that column, but I could not stand it. The balls came from every direction, and I was obliged to lie down with my head on the ground in order to shield myself from the small shot, which were making the twigs fall all over me; I was covered with them. I believed myself lost.

Fortunately our whole division now advanced by battalion. I got up and found myself in a company of the battalion; I continued in it all the rest of the day, for not more than fourteen of our hundred and seventy grenadiers remained; the rest were killed or wounded. We were obliged to resume our first position, riddled by small shot. Everything fell upon us who held the left wing of the army, opposite the high road to Alessandria, and we had the most difficult position to maintain. They constantly endeavored to flank us, and we were obliged to close up continually, in order to prevent them from surprising us in the rear.

Our colonel was everywhere at once, behind the half-brigade so as to sustain us; our captain, who had lost his company and who was wounded in the arm, performed the duties of aide-de-camp to our intrepid general. We could not see one another in the smoke. The cannons set the wheat-field on fire, and this caused a general commotion in the ranks. The cartridge-boxes exploded; we were obliged to fall back in order to form again as quickly as possible. This caused us much mortification, but was atoned for by the intrepidity of our chiefs, who looked out for everything.

In the centre of the division was a barn surrounded by high walls, where a regiment of Austrian dragoons had concealed themselves; they burst upon a battalion of the 43d brigade and surrounded it; every man of it was captured and taken to Alessandria. Fortunately General Kellermann came up with his dragoons and restored order. His charges silenced the Austrian cavalry.

Nevertheless, their numerous artillery overwhelmed us, and

we could hold out no longer. Our ranks were thinned visibly; all about us there were only wounded men to be seen, and the soldiers who bore them away did not return to their ranks; this weakened us very much. We had to yield ground. Their columns were constantly re-enforced; no one came to our aid. We began to retreat, but in good order. Our cartridges were giving out and we had already lost an ambulance, when the consular guard arrived with eight hundred men having their

linen smock-frocks filled with cartridges; they passed behind our ranks and gave us the cartridges. This saved our lives.

Then the fire redoubled and the Consul appeared; we felt ourselves strong again. He placed his guard in line in the centre of the army and made it march forward. They immediately arrested the enemy, forming a square and marching in line of battle. The splendid horse-grenadiers came up at a gallop, charged the enemy at once and cut their cavalry to pieces. Ah! that gave us a moment to breathe, it gave us confidence for an hour. But not being able to hold out against the consular horse-grenadiers, they turned upon our half-brigade and drove in the first platoons, sabring them. I received such a blow from a sabre on my neck that my queue was almost cut off; fortunately I had the thickest one in the regiment. My epaulet was cut off with a piece of my coat and shirt, and the flesh a little scratched. I fell head over heels into a ditch.

The cavalry charges were terrible. Kellermann made three in succession with his dragoons; he led them forward and led them back. The whole of that body of cavalry leaped over me as I lay stunned in the ditch. I got rid of my knapsack, my cartridge box, and my sabre. I took hold of the tail of a retreating dragoon's horse, leaving all my belongings in the ditch. I made a few strides behind that horse which carried me away, and then fell senseless, not being able to breathe any longer. But, thank God, I was saved! But for my head of hair, which I still have at seventy-two years of age, I should have been killed.

I had time to find a gun, a cartridge box, and a knapsack (the ground was covered with them). I resumed my place in the second company of grenadiers, who received me with cordiality. The captain came and shook my hands. "I thought you were lost, my brave man," said he; "you got a famous sabre stroke, for you have no queue and your shoulder is badly hurt. You must go to the rear."—"I thank you, I have a cartridge box full of cartridges, and I am going to revenge myself upon such troopers as I meet; they have done me too much harm; they shall pay for it."

We retreated in good order, but the battalions were visibly reduced, and quite ready to give up but for the encouragement of their officers. We held out till noon without being disordered. Looking behind, we saw the Consul seated on the bank of the ditch by the highway to Alessandria, holding his horse by the bridle, and flirting up little stones with his riding whip. The cannon-balls which rolled along the road he did not seem to see. When we came near him he mounted his horse and set off at a gallop behind our ranks. "Courage, soldiers," said he, "the reserves are coming. Stand firm!"

Then he was off to the right of the army. The soldiers were shouting, "Vive Bonaparte!" But the plain was filled with the dead and wounded, for we had no time to gather them up; we had to show ourselves everywhere. The discharges by battalion, by échelons formed in the rear, arrested the enemy, but those cursed cartridges would no longer go into our fouled musket barrels. This caused us to lose time.

My brave captain, Merle, passed behind the second battalion, and the captain said to him, "I have one of your grenadiers; he has received a famous sabre-cut." — "Where is he? Make him come out, so I may see him. Ah! it is you, is it, Coignet?" — "Yes, captain." — "I thought you were among the dead, I saw you fall into the ditch." — "They gave me a famous sabre-cut; see, they have cut off my queue." — "See here, feel in my knapsack, take my 'life-preserver,' and drink a cup of rum to restore you. This evening, if we live, I shall come and seek you out." — "Now I am saved for the day, my captain; I shall fight finely." The other captain said, "I wanted him to go tó the rear, but he would not." — "I can readily believe it; he saved my life at Montebello." They took me by the hand. How beautiful is gratitude! I shall feel the value of it all my life.

Meanwhile, do all we could, we were beginning to fail. It was two o'clock. "The battle is lost," said our officers, when suddenly an aide-de-camp arrived at a sweeping gallop. He cried, "Where is the First Consul? Here is the reserve. Courage! you will be re-enforced at once, within half an hour." Then up came the Consul. "Steady," said he, as he passed along, "here is my reserve." Our poor little platoons gazed down the road to Montebello every time we turned around.

Finally came the joyful cry, "Here they are, here they are!" That splendid division came up, carrying arms. It was like a forest swayed by the wind. The troops arrived without running, with a fine park of artillery in the spaces between the half-brigades, and a regiment of heavy cavalry bringing up the rear. Having reached their position, they took possession of it as though they had chosen it expressly for their line of battle. On our left, to the left of the highway, a very tall hedge concealed them; not even the cavalry could be seen.

Meanwhile we continued to sound a retreat. The Consul gave his orders, and the Austrians came along as though they were on their way home, shouldering arms; they paid no attention to us; they believed us to be utterly routed. We had gone three hundred paces past the division of General Desaix, and the Austrians were also about to pass the line, when the thunderbolt descended upon the head of their column. Grape-shot, shells, shot from the battalions, rained upon them. Our drums beat a general charge; the whole line wheeled about and ran forward. We did not shout, we yelled.

The men of the brave 9th demi-brigade ran like rabbits through the hedge; they rushed with their bayonets upon the Hungarian grenadiers, and gave them no time to recover. The 30th and 59th fell in their turn upon the enemy and took four thousand prisoners. The regiment of heavy cavalry fell upon the whole. Every man did his duty, but the 9th excelled them all. Our other cavalry joined this, and rushed in solid column upon the Austrian cavalry, whom they so completely routed that they rode off at full gallop to Alessandria. An Austrian division coming from the right wing charged us with bayonets. We ran up also and crossed bayonets with them. We overcame them, and I received a small cut in the right eyelid, as I was parrying a thrust from a grenadier. I did not miss him, but the blood blinded my eyes (they had a grudge against my head that day). It was a small matter. I continued to march and did not suffer from it. We followed them until nine o'clock in the evening: we threw them into the ditches full of water. Their bodies served as a bridge upon which others could cross over. It was frightful to see these unfortunate creatures drowning, and the bridge all blocked with them. We could hear nothing but their cries; they could no longer return to the city, and we took their carriages and their cannons. At ten o'clock, my captain sent his servant to ask me to take supper with him, and my eye was dressed and my hair put in good condition.

We slept on the battle-field, and the next day at four o'clock

"I received a small cut in the right eyelid." — Page 78.

in the morning, a party with flags of truce came out of the city. They demanded a suspension of arms, and went to the headquarters of the Consul. They were well escorted. The camp became gay once more. I said to my captain, "If you please, I would like to go to headquarters." — "What for?" "I have some acquaintances among the guard. Let me have a companion." — "But it is very far." — "No matter, we will return early, I promise you." — "Very well, go."

We set out, our sabres at our sides. Upon reaching the grating of the château of Marengo, I asked for a cavalry sergeant who had been long in the corps, and a very handsome man appeared. "What do you want with me?" said he. — "I wish to know how long you have been in the guard of the Directory." — "Nine years." — "It was I who trained your horses, and who rode them at the Luxembourg. If you remember, it was M. Potier who sold them to you." — "That is so," said he to me; "come in, I will present you to my captain." He told my comrade to wait, and introduced me as follows: "Here is the young man who trained our horses at Paris." — "And who rode so well," added the captain. — "Yes, captain." — "But you are wounded." — "Ah! it is a bayonet thrust from a Hungarian. I punished him. But they cut my queue half off. If I had been on horseback that would not have happened to me." — "I dare say," said he, "I know your skill in that respect. Sergeant, give him a drink." — "Have you any bread, captain?" — "Go get four loaves for him. I am going to show you your horses and see if you will recognize them." I pointed out twelve of them to him. "That's right," said he, "you recognized them very easily." — "All right, captain. If I had been mounted on one of those horses, they would not have cut off my hair; but they shall answer for it. I shall enter the Consul's guard. I am marked out for a silver gun,[1] and when I shall have made four campaigns, the Consul has promised to put me in his guard." — "Very likely, my brave grenadier. If you ever come to Paris there is my address. What is your captain's name?" — "Merle, first company of grenadiers of the 96th half-brigade of the

[1] The arms of honor had a silver mounting.

line." — "There are five francs to drink my health. I promise to write to your captain. We must give him some brandy in a bottle." — "I thank you for your kindness, now I must go; my comrade is waiting for me at the grating. I must take him some bread at once." — "I did not know it, go along. Take another loaf and be off to join your corps." — "Farewell, captain, you saved the army by your splendid charges. I saw you well." — "That is so," said he.

He, with his sergeant, accompanied me as far as the grating. The wounded of the guard were stretched on some straw in the court-yard, and amputations were being made. It was heart-rending to hear their cries on all sides. I came out with my heart rent with grief, but a more horrible spectacle was to be seen on the plain. We saw the battle-field covered with Austrian and French soldiers who were picking up the dead and placing them in piles, and dragging them along with their gun straps. Men and horses were laid pell-mell in the same heap, and set on fire in order to preserve us from pestilence. The scattered bodies had a little earth thrown over them to cover them.

I was stopped by a lieutenant, who said to me, "Where are you going?" — "I am going to carry some bread to my captain." — "You got it at the Consul's headquarters. Could you give me a bit?" — "Yes." I said to my comrade, "You have a small piece, give it to the lieutenant." — "Thank you, my brave grenadier, you have saved my life. Pass down the road to the left." And he had the kindness to accompany us a good bit of the way, fearing we might be arrested. I thanked him for his goodness, and soon reached my captain, who smiled when he saw my package. "Have you been on a marauding party?" — "Yes. captain, I have brought you some bread and some brandy." — "And where did you find it?" I related to him my adventure. "Ah," said he, "you were born under a lucky star." — "See, here is a loaf and a bottle of good brandy. Put them in your 'life preserver.' If you want to take a loaf for the colonel and the general, you can divide with them; they are, perhaps, very hungry." — "That is a happy thought; I will do so with pleasure, and I thank you on their part." — "Come, first eat and drink some of this good brandy. I am delighted to be able to return the service you rendered me and the good meal you enabled me to enjoy." "You shall tell me all that some other time. I am going to carry this bread to the colonel and the general."

All this, however, the captain set down to my account. On the 16th the army received orders to carry laurels, and the oak trees had a hard time. At noon we filed before the First Consul, and our excellent general marched on foot in front of the remnant of his division. General Chambarlhac appeared on horseback at the head of his division, but he was saluted with a volley from our half-brigade, and he disappeared. We never saw him again, and the sequel of that story is unknown to us. But we shouted, "Hurrah for our little general," for him who had led us so bravely on the day of the battle.

On the morning of the 16th, General Melas sent back our prisoners (there were about twelve hundred of them), and this was a great delight to us. Provisions had been given them, and they were triumphantly received on their arrival. On the 26th, the first Austrian column filed before us, and we watched them go by. What a superb column it was! there were men enough in it to have overwhelmed us at that moment, seeing how few of us there were. It was frightful to see such a body of cavalry and artillery; they were three days in passing. There were only baggage wagons. They left us half of their stores; we got considerable provisions and ammunition. They yielded to us forty leagues of country, and retired behind the Mincio. We brought up the rear of the last column. We travelled along together; our lame ones mounted on their carriages; they marched on the left and we on the right side of the road. No one quarrelled, and we were the best friends in the world.

Marching thus, we came to the flying bridge over the river Po. As only five hundred men could cross at one time over this flying bridge, we lost no time, and continued our march to Cremona, the place which we were to garrison during the three months of truce agreed upon. Cremona is a beautiful city which is proof against surprise. Splendid ramparts and solid gates. The town is considerable; there is a handsome cathedral with an immense dial-plate; an arrow-hand makes the circuit of it once in a hundred years. In the markets they weigh everything; even onions and grass; it is filled with delicious melons called watermelons; there are milk taverns there. But it is the worst garrison in Italy; we slept on the ground, on straw filled with vermin. Breeches, waistcoats, and undervests were in a deplorable condition. Inconceived the idea of killing these vermin which bit me. I made some lye in a copper boiler and put my waistcoat in it. Alas for me! The waistcoat melted away like paper, nothing was left me but the lining. There I was entirely naked, and nothing in my knapsack to put on.

My good comrades came to my assistance. I at once had letters written to my father and my uncle; I informed them of my distress, and begged them to send me a little money. Their answers were long delayed but came at last. I received both letters at the same time (not prepaid); they each cost me a franc and a half, in all three francs for postage. My old sergeant happened to be present. "Do me the kindness to read them." He took my two letters. My father said, "If you were a little nearer I would send you a little money." And my uncle said, "I have just paid for some state lands, I can send you nothing." Such were my two charming letters! I never wrote to them again in my life. After the truce, I was obliged to mount guard at the outposts four times, as a forlorn sentinel on the shore of the Mincio, at fifteen sous a watch, in order to pay this debt.

These two letters have made me lose sight of my subject. I return to Cremona, where we passed three months in utter misery. Our half-brigade was made up and our company was organized; they took a third from each of two companies so as to make them all equal, and they took grenadiers from the battalion so as to finish our quota. Every day we were led out on military parade, on the great road, with our knapsacks on our back, and forbidden to quit our ranks; the discipline was severe. General Brune was the commanding officer of this fine army. We could say that we were commanded by a good general. May France give us many such! One would be willing to follow him anywhere. Then during the three months' truce our army was magnificently re-enforced; troops came in from every direction. How we longed for the 15th of September when we should leave this wretched garrison and go again into the field!

The happy day arrived, and the whole army rejoiced. We set out to join the line at a strong town called Viédane,[1] where we began to breathe freely and found provisions. Our scouts discovered a wine cave under a mountain; we held a council to determine how we should get the wine. It was dangerous to rob the house, seeing that war had not been declared. So we decided that we should have an order. "But who will sign it?"—"The pen," said the quartermaster, as he signed it with his left hand.—"How many rations?"—"Five hundred," said the sergeant-major.—"We must show the order to the lieutenant and see what he will say."—"Take it," said the lieutenant, "and see if it will work."—"Come, let us go, we will see." We started off after having affixed the colonel's seal. His servant said to us, "I understand; I'll seal it with lamp-black." We presented our order, the distribution was immediately made, and "the pen" gave us five hundred rations of good wine. The captain and the lieutenant laughed heartily the next day.

We now departed for Brescia where the army was assembled in a beautiful plain; the commanding general reviewed us.

[1] This is the town of Viadana, on the right of the road from Cremona to Brescia, near Montechiari.

Brescia is a strong city, easily defended; a river flows by it which is deep but not wide. Next day we set out for a march to the Mincio; there the whole army was in line, and it was decided to cross at a very high point which overlooked the other shore. A village concealed it from the Austrian army, which was very numerous. Twenty-five thousand men were sent over. There was a terrible battle; our troops, thoroughly

beaten, were obliged to fall back, with loss, upon the Mincio. Fortunately our army was protected by its very elevated position overlooking the plain, which prevented our being thrown head over heels into the Mincio. General Suchet, with fifty heavy pieces, fired broadsides upon them which passed over our columns, cut down their ranks, and held them in the plain. Every one was working the pieces, and our three battalions of grenadiers were obliged to watch the whole affair without being able to take any part in it.

I saw a brave act done by a little voltigeur. Being left alone in the plain by the retreating army, he fired upon the advancing column, and shouted "Forward!" His boldness caused the division to wheel about; they sounded a charge and went to his aid. The general kept his eye upon him; he sent his aide-de-camp for him. When the aide-de-camp reached the spot and saw the voltigeur, who was still in front of the line, he hastened to him and said, "The general wishes to see you."—"No," said he.—" Come with me; obey your general." —" But I have done nothing wrong."—" He wants to reward you."—"Ah! that is another matter. I am with you." When brought before the general he was triumphantly received by all the officers, and entered on the list for a gun of honor.

That evening we started for a position three miles higher up, near a mill which was on our left with a fine rising ground behind us. The regiment of *hussars de la mort* asked that they might be the first to cross over so as to avenge themselves for Montebello. Their colonel promised fifty louis to the hussar who should give the first sabre cut ahead of him, and they were given eighteen hundred men of the Polish infantry,[1] without knapsacks. They crossed the bridge and went to the right along the Mincio; the Poles followed them on the run. They fell upon the head of the Austrian column, gave them no time to form a line of battle, sabred them and carried off six thousand prisoners and four flags. Our three battalions of grenadiers crossed immediately, commanded by General Lebrun, a good soldier. General Brune ordered him to take the redoubt which was battering the bridge, and we marched on it at once. They surrendered under fire; there were two thousand men and two flags. The whole army passed over, and formed in line of battle. The columns faced each other; we overcame them, took their baggage, caissons, and some pieces of cannon. The carnage was terrible.

The Austrians took the road to Verona so as to pass the Adige. Our divisions pursued them; we blockaded the fort which

---

[1] A Polish legion was, indeed, already fighting for France; but as the law forbade the employment of foreign troops, this legion was set down as marching on behalf of Italy.

overlooked the city at a height of three hundred feet. General Brune sent a flag of truce into the citadel to warn them that he was about to enter Verona, and that if a single gun was fired upon the city, he should immediately blow up the fort. Our three battalions of grenadiers passed through the city, and the Austrians only looked at us. We camped two miles farther on; at midnight we were placed on the right wing of the army as outposts. I was on guard at the advanced post. The adjutant-major came and posted us. I was the first to stand sentinel; they stationed me in a meadow, giving me the countersign. "Fire upon everything which passes on your right, without calling out 'Who goes there?' and listen attentively lest you should be surprised."

There I was for the first time alone as a forlorn sentinel; in utter darkness, and kneeling on the ground to listen. At last the moon rose; I was very glad to be able to look around me, and I was no longer afraid. What should I see a hundred steps off, but a Hungarian grenadier with his bear-skin cap! He did not move. I took my best aim, and the whole line answered the sound of my gun.[1] I thought that the enemy was everywhere. I reloaded my gun, and the corporal came up with three men. I pointed to my Hungarian; they said, "Fire beyond, and we shall see all five of them." I took aim, I fired; nothing stirred. The adjutant-major came up; "Hold on," said I to him, "don't you see him below there?" We walked over. It was a willow-tree with a big head which had frightened me. The major told me that I had done well, that he should have been deceived himself, and that I had done my duty.

We marched upon Vicenza, a beautiful city; but the Austrians were marching on Padua by forced marches. There was joy everywhere on account of our good cantonments; but our half-brigade with a regiment of chasseurs was appointed to go on to the Venetian coast. The general who commanded this expedition had only one arm. He had lanterns made so that we could march at night, and during the day we remained concealed among the reeds. We had to make small bridges

---

[1] In 1870, such panics were known; they may occur at any time.

over the great ditches so as to take our cavalry and artillery across; there were only marshes and fishermen's huts. By dint of exertion, we reached the appointed place; it was a river of strong current, with an embankment separating it from the sea. This river, farther on, joined four others which emptied together into the sea and formed an estuary. We had to take possession of all these rivers in order to secure fresh water.

A corps of the Austrian guard was stationed as advance guard upon the great causeway; redoubts faced the river at the distance of a quarter of a league. A sentinel was stationed upon the embankment. The sentinel spoke German and made acquaintance with the Austrian sentinel. Our sentinel asked him for some tobacco, and the German asked our sentinel for wood. Our sentinel told him that he would come with two of his comrades and bring him some when he was off duty. So our grenadiers set off with the wood; the others brought the tobacco. The next day we promised them a large supply; they were delighted and said, " We will give you some tobacco."

In the morning fifty grenadiers arrived laden with wood and were kindly received; they seized the Austrians' guns and took them prisoners. Immediately the trench was opened and the pieces placed in position. This was a good strategic point. The ships loaded with flour which were coming down the river on their way to the sea, fell into our hands, also two ships loaded with eels and fish. We had a ship all to ourselves, and we ate them cooked in every way.

When the Venetians were thirsty they came and drew water, and the general got as much as he wanted for it. He had promised us three francs a day, but the accounts were soon settled up. He did not give us a sou, and sent everything home. Then General Clausel took the command. We were quiet only a little while; Mantua surrendered; we saw its garrison pass by, and we had orders to set out for Verona to celebrate the peace. In this place, which is magnificent, the order of the day was read to us, and we learned that our half-brigade was appointed to go to Paris. What joy for us!

We crossed the whole of Italy; nothing can be seen more beautiful than Turin, it is magnificent. We crossed Mont Cenis, reached Chambéry, and from Chambéry we went to Lyons.

When our old regiment reached the place Bellecour, all the *incroyables* quizzed us through their eye-glasses and asked if we came from Italy. We answered, " Yes, gentlemen."—" And you have not got the itch ? "—" No, gentlemen." Then rubbing their eye-glasses on their sleeves, they replied, " Incredible !"

They did not wish to have us quartered in the city, but General Leclerc compelled them to give us billets, and immediately he was

granted seven permits for each company, for the oldest soldiers. What a delight this was for those old soldiers ! The Consul never granted so many of them as on this occasion. The next day we were informed that we were not going to Paris as we had expected, but in fact to Portugal. The general counted us among the forty thousand men of his army; we were obliged to resign ourselves to going off in a deplorable condition, with clothing made of all sorts of cloth.

We started for Bayonne ; the distance was great; we suffered from the heat, but at last we reached the bridge of Irun. Our comrades found a stork's nest and took the two young ones. The authorities came to the colonel to reclaim them; the alcalde requested him to restore them, because these birds were necessary in that climate for the destruction of serpents and lizards; he said that the galleys was the penalty for those who killed storks in that country. Consequently they are seen there everywhere; the plains are covered with them, and they walk about in the streets of the towns. Old wheels are put up for them on the top of high posts, and they make their nests in the gable-ends of the buildings.

Having reached our first halting place, some of our soldiers found some Malaga wine at three sous a bottle, and they drank it as though it had been whey; they fell down dead drunk. We had to put them in wagons and carry them along as if they had been calves. At the end of a week it was still necessary to feed our drunkards; they could not hold the soup in their spoons. Not a soldier could eat his ration, the wine had been so strong. We reached Vittoria, a lovely town; from there we went to Burgos, and from Burgos to Valladolid, a fine large city, where we remained a long time among the vermin. The lice make up the soldiers' beds by dint of rustling among the straw, which is only thrown down in a heap. It is the custom among the Spaniards to take these lice up between their fingers and throw them on the ground, saying, "Let him who created thee nourish thee."

I had the good fortune to be made a sapper; I had a very long beard all round my face, and I was selected by Colonel Lepreux. I was dressed anew in full uniform, and we were quartered in the house of a citizen where we could get rid of the vermin; but at night we were obliged to remain indoors for fear of being killed.

As I was walking along the river, I met two French priests, *émigrés*, who were in great want; they stopped me to ask news from France. I told them that I had only passed through, but that I heard that the *émigrés* were to be recalled, and that if they wished to go and see General Leclerc, they would be welcomed, and that the general was the brother-in-law of the First Consul. They went to see him the next day and heard good news; they came again to me and took me by the hand, telling me that I had saved their lives. A fortnight after they received an order to return to France, and these unfortunate refugees embraced me; I advised them to travel in disguise lest they should be insulted on their way to France.

From Valladolid we departed for Salamanca, a large town where we remained a long time going through reviews and making petty warfare; our vanguards reached the frontier of Portugal, and still there was no fighting. They brought away seventeen wagons with a strong escort, and peace was made without a battle.[1]

We returned to France by way of Valladolid. As we were leaving the city, the Spaniards killed our quartermasters with clubs,[2] and had the audacity to come and take our flags from the colonel's guard-house in a village near Burgos. All the men were asleep; the sentinel cried, "To arms," and it was time; they were just going out of the village. They were caught by our grenadiers, who bayoneted them without mercy.

We reached Burgos, and set out for Vittoria. Thence we crossed the frontier on our way to Bayonne, our frontier city. We passed all the halting places until we came to Bordeaux, where we were to stop. I was quartered upon an old lady who was sick. I presented myself with my billet, and she was a little frightened on seeing my long beard. I reassured her as well as I could, but she said, "I am afraid of soldiers." — "Fear nothing, madame, I ask nothing, and my comrade is a very nice fellow." — "Very well, I will keep you at my house; you shall be well fed and have comfortable beds." Ah! how comfortably we were housed! After dinner, she sent her maid for me. "I sent for you to tell you that I am reassured, and that you are very quiet; I have ordered my servant to take good care of you." — "Thank you, madame."

We set out to go to Tours following the appointed halting-places, and on arriving there we were received by General Beauchou, who presented to us an old soldier who had served

---

[1] By the two treaties of June and September, 1801, Portugal engaged to pay 25,000,000 francs to France.

[2] Quartermasters go on ahead of the forces, to prepare lodgings.

eighty-four years as a private in our half-brigade. The Consul had given him, on retiring, the general's table; he was one hundred and two years old, and his son was chief of the battalion. A footstool was brought to him; he wore the uniform of an officer, but without epaulets. There was in the corps a sergeant of his time, who had served thirty-three years.

After leaving this beautiful city of Tours, we went into quarters at Le Mans (in the department of the Sarthe), which is considered the best garrison in France. The splendid national guard marched in front of us, and there was great joy in the town, on seeing a good old regiment quartered there. The walls of the barracks were still stained with the blood of the victims who had been murdered by the Chouans, and we were lodged for two months in private houses where we were received as brothers. The barracks were repaired and we remained there a year. The colonel married a young lady of Alençon who was very rich, and entertainments were given in the town. There were a great many invitations. I was appointed to carry the invitations to the houses in the country. The colonel was generous to the regiment; all the officers were invited.

At the expiration of three months, the barracks made the bread-offering, and there were three litters trimmed with velvet, loaded with bread and borne by six sappers. The colonel's bride took up the collection, and my captain, Merle, who was appointed commandant, escorted our fair collector. The drum-major was the porter. I carried the plate and madame made the acknowledgments. Nine hundred francs were taken up in the collection for the poor; the whole regiment was at the mass. A litter loaded with blessed bread was taken to the colonel's house, and there the parcels were made up, with a laurel branch in each package and a letter of invitation. Two sappers carried the large hamper full of blessed bread, and I was appointed to accompany the two sappers who carried the hamper. They remained at the door; I took a package and a letter; I presented myself; each time from three to six francs were given me. This tour through the city and the country houses was worth a hundred crowns to me. The colonel wished to know whether I had been well paid for the trouble; I showed him my pockets. When he saw all that money, he divided it in two portions and said to me, "There, take half for yourself, and the other half you can divide between the sappers."

My two porters knew nothing of what had taken place. I led them back to the barracks and laid the money down before the sergeant and the corporal. They were overcome with joy, when they saw me place on the table before them several handfuls of silver. "What! have you stolen the regiment cash-box? For whom is all this money?" said the sergeant. — "It is for you, divide it; it is earnings from the blessed bread." We each had fifteen francs; they were pleased with me, they pressed my hand. I had my fifteen francs, and my hundred and fifty francs; this was a fortune for me. They wanted to treat me, I would not consent: "Excuse me. To-morrow I will pay for a bottle of brandy, and that is all that is necessary to be done. I'll do the treating, sergeant, do you understand?" — "There is nothing more to be said; he is wiser than we."

And the next day I got a bottle of brandy, and they were quite satisfied. That fine dinner of the colonel's was worth a louis to me; he gave it to me for staying all night. The ball was kept up until daylight; the guests sat down to the table at three o'clock, and I was well rewarded. A fortnight after, I received a letter from Paris, and I was surprised (but what a surprise!). It was from my dear sister, who had discovered me through the efforts of her master, who had a relative in the office of the minister of war. It was a great joy for me to know that she was in Paris, as cook at the house of a hatter, on the Place du Pont-Neuf.

The council of administration of the regiment had orders to nominate soldiers for the cross of honor, and my name was put on the list of those who deserved it. My commandant, Merle, and the colonel called me up to tell me about it; it had come from the office of the minister of war. I replied, "I thank you, my commandant." — "The colonel and I have claimed the promise of the Consul to you in reference to the guard, and I have signed this application with the colonel, it is your due." A fortnight after, the colonel sent for me. "The good news has come. You are appointed to the guard; you shall be paid off and depart. I will give you a letter of recommendation to General Hulin, who is a great friend of mine. Go, tell your commandant about it, he will be very glad to hear of it." I was glad to set out for Paris, and to be able to go and embrace my good sister whom I had not seen

since she was seven years old. My commandant did me the kindness to say, "If ever I go to Paris, I shall ask to see you. Now lose no time, go back to the barracks."

I told the good news to all my comrades, who said, "We will all see you off." The sergeant and the corporal also said, "We will all go as escort to our brave sapper." When I was paid off, I set out from Le Mans with two hundred francs in my purse (a fortune for a poor soldier), accompanied by my good comrades with the sergeant and corporal at their head. They had to make a halt and leave us after going a mile, and I reached Paris the 2d Germinal, year XI, and went to the barracks of the Feuillants, near the Place Vendôme; it is called the barrack of the Capuchins.

I was appointed to mess with the third company of the first battalion. My captain's name was Renard; he had only one fault, and that was being too small. As a compensation for this, he had the voice of a Stentor; he was big when he gave command; he was a man who had had much experience, and was my captain ever afterward. I was conducted to his house, he received me cordially. My long beard made him laugh, and he asked my permission to touch it. "If you were larger, I would give you a place among our sappers; you are too small." — "But, captain, I have a gun of honor." — "Is it possible?" — "Yes, captain. I have a letter for General Hulin from my colonel, also a letter for his brother, a cloth merchant on the Porte St. Denis." — "Very well, I will keep you in my company. To-morrow, at noon, I will go with you to the office of the minister, and there we will see." — "It was the minister himself who found me on my gun at Montebello." — "Ah! after hearing all this, I wish to-morrow were here, that I might see if he would recognize you." — "I wore no beard at Montebello, but he has my name, for he wrote it down in a little green memorandum book." — "Very well, tomorrow at noon, I will present you."

The next day, at noon, we started out to go to the minister's office; we sent in our names and were taken into the presence of the minister. "Well, captain, you bring me a fine sapper. What does he want with me?" — "He says that you recommended him for a position in the guard." — "What is your name?" — "Jean-Roch Coignet, it was I who was on the gun at Montebello." — "Indeed! it was you?" — "Yes, general." — "Did you receive my letter?" — "My colonel, M. Lepreux, did." — "You are right. Go into the office opposite, ask for the portfolio of the officers of the 96th halfbrigade, tell your name and bring me a paper which I have signed for you."

I went to inquire at the office; they gazed at my beard without granting my request. This beard was thirteen inches long, and they thought it was artificial. "Is it natural?" asked the chief. I took hold of it and pulled it; "See," said I to him, "it sticks to my chin and is well rooted." — "Well, my good sapper, here is a paper worthy of you." — "Thank you."

Then I took the paper to the minister, who said to me, "You see I have not forgotten you. You shall wear a little machine,"[1] said he, as he laid his hand on my coat. "And you, Renard, you will receive a letter for him to-morrow at ten o'clock; he is a soldier worth having, be sure to keep him in your company." I thanked the minister, and we started off at once to go to the house of General Davoust, colonel-general, of the foot grenadiers. He received us pleasantly, and said, "You bring me a sapper who has a fine beard." — "I want to keep him in my company," said my captain to him; "he has a gun of honor. But he is very small."[2]

He made me stand beside him and said, "You are not tall enough for a grenadier." — "But I would like to keep the place, general." — "We must cheat the measure. When he passes under the measure make him put some packs of cards in his stockings. See there," said he, "he lacks six lines. Never mind, you will see that with two packs of cards under each foot, he will have his six inches; you must go with him." — "Certainly, general." — "If he is accepted, he will be the smallest of my grenadiers." — "But he is to be decorated." — "Ah! that makes a difference, do your best to have him accepted."

Then we went off to get the cards and put them in my stockings. My captain managed everything well; he was nimble as a fish and soon got it all over. That very evening, I was standing straight as a line under the measure, and my captain was there also, holding himself very erect, thinking by that means to make me taller. However, I measured my six inches, thanks to my packs of cards. I went off triumphant.

---

[1] An allusion to the decoration which was to ornament his button-hole.

[2] To walk about so much with a simple grenadier would not accord with the habits of military administration in our days; the story shows how much pains was then taken with the recruiting of the guard.

My captain was also delighted; I was admitted into his company. "You must cut off your fine beard," said he. — "Permit me to wear it a fortnight longer; I would like to make a few visits before cutting it off." — "I grant you a month, but you must drill." — "Thank you very much for all your trouble on my account." — "I shall have you entered on the pay-roll from yesterday." — "Permit me to take my letter?" — "Certainly," said he.

He sent for a sergeant-major and said to him, "Here is a little grenadier. Give a permit to Coignet to attend to his business, and have it delivered to him at once so he can go in and out. Put him in the smallest mess. You have the biggest man in it, and now you shall have the smallest." — "Just the thing, he is alone; he is a good comrade; we can say 'the smallest with the biggest.'" The sergeant-major conducted me to my room, and presented me to my comrades. One of the grenadiers, a jolly fellow, six feet four inches tall, burst out laughing on seeing how small I was. "Well," said the sergeant to him, "here is your bedfellow." — "I could hide him under my coat and smuggle him off." I laughed at this, and supper being ready (we did not eat from one dish, each one had his own soup-tureen), I gave ten francs to the corporal. Every one was pleased at this. The corporal said, "You must go with your comrade and buy a soup-tureen to-morrow." The next day we went to buy my soup-tureen, and I treated my comrade to two bottles of beer. On returning to the barracks, I asked permission to go out until the roll-call at noon. "Go," said my corporal.

I flew to see my good sister at the hatter's house on the Place du Pont-Neuf. I presented myself with the letter which the master of the house had had the kindness to write me, and they were surprised to see such a beard as mine. "I am the soldier to whom you were so good as to write at Le Mans. I have come to see my sister Marianne; here is your letter." — "It is actually so," said he; "come, but wait a moment, your long beard might frighten her."

He returned and said to me, "She expects you, I will go with you."

"He received us pleasantly, and said, 'You bring me a sapper who has a fine beard.'" — Page 95.

I went up to that big mother and said, "I am your brother; come, do not be afraid to kiss me." She came to me, crying with joy. I said to her, "I have two letters from my father, dated from Marengo."

Then the master said to me, "That was a hot day."—"Ah, true enough, sir." But she said, "My elder brother is here in Paris."—"Is it possible?"—"Yes, he is coming to see me to-morrow at noon."—"I am so glad. I am in the Consul's guard; I will run back to the roll-call and return to see him. I shall be back in an hour."

I thanked the master and hastened to the roll-call; I returned as quickly as possible, but my brother had already arrived. My sister had told him that I was in the Consul's guard. "Beware," said he to her, "of making the acquaintance of a soldier; do not bring shame upon us, we have had trouble enough already."—"But, my dear," said she, "he is coming back after the roll-call and you will see him."

She saw me as I was returning and made him conceal himself. I said, "Well, sister, has not my brother Pierre come yet?"—"Yes," she replied, "but he says you are not my brother."—"Indeed," said I, "very well, tell him that it was he who carried me away from Druyes to Étais, where he hired me out, when he had a sore arm."

At this he rushed to me, and we were all three locked in one another's arms, weeping for joy so loudly that every one in the house hastened to see the poor creatures who were now restored to one another after seventeen years of separation.

The joy and grief were so intense that my brother and sister could not sustain it; I lost them both. I buried my poor sister at the end of six weeks; she fell sick a week after we met, and we were obliged to take her to a hospital, where she died. I accompanied her remains to their last resting place. My brother could not survive her loss. I sent him back to the country, where he died also. I lost them both within the space of three months. I have never recovered from that trouble.

Having done all I could for them I returned to my military duties, and told my sorrows to my captain, who pitied me sincerely. I was promptly provided with a uniform and drilled. I continued to be skilful as before in the use of arms and in fencing; I was introduced to the drill-masters, who pushed me forward rapidly. At the end of a year, there was a contest, and I was applauded for my strength and my modesty in yielding the point of honor. Afterwards I was presented by the head master in the Rue Richelieu for a contest with some very skilful young men, and there I showed what I could do. The masters embraced me and skilful pupils invited me out. Our own fencing-master overwhelmed me with attentions, and said to them, "Don't let him deceive you, you have seen nothing; he has concealed his skill and behaved like an angel. We could make a master of him, if he wished, but he said, 'No. I will continue to be a pupil.' That's what he said."

Every day I went to the drills so as to learn the movements of the guard, and I was not long in becoming acquainted with them; at the end of a month I was dismissed and put into the battalion. The discipline was not severe; we turned out to the roll-call every morning in our linen shirts and breeches (with no stockings on our legs) and then went back to our beds. But a colonel, named Dorsenne, came to us from Egypt all covered with wounds; he was just the sort of soldier needed to discipline and drill an efficient guard. In a year's time we might have served as a model for the whole army. He was so severe that he made the most unruly soldier tremble; he reformed all abuses. He might have been held up as an example for all our generals, both for courage and bearing. A finer looking soldier was not to be seen on the battle-field. I have seen him one moment covered with dirt by shells, and the next he would be up again saying, "It is nothing, grenadiers, your general is near you."

We were informed that the First Consul was to pass through our barracks, and that we must be on the lookout for him. But he took us by surprise and found us in our beds; he was accompanied by his favorite general, Lannes. A misfortune had just happened to us; some grenadiers had committed suicide, no one knew why. The Consul went through all the rooms and finally came to my bedside. My comrade, who was six feet four inches tall, stretched himself out on seeing the Consul beside our bed; his feet stuck out of the bedstead more than a foot. The Consul thought that there were two grenadiers in a line, and came to the head of our bed to assure himself of the fact, and passed his hand along the body of my comrade, to be sure he was not mistaken. "Why!" said he, "these bedsteads are too short for my grenadiers. Do you see, Lannes? All the beds of my guard must be changed. Make a note of it, and have new bedsteads made for the whole guard; these will do for the garrison." So my bedfellow caused an outlay of more than a million francs, and the whole guard had new beds seven feet long.

The Consul delivered a severe lecture to all our officers, and looked into everything; he had a piece of bread brought to him. "That is not the right kind," said he. "I pay for white bread, I wish to have it every day. Do you understand, Lannes? Send your aide, and order the quartermaster to come to me." To us he said, —

"I will review you on Sunday; I want to see you. There are malcontents among you. I will hear your complaints."

Then they returned to the Tuileries. In the order that he sent for the Sunday review, Colonel Dorsenne recommended that nothing should be neglected in the uniforms of the men. The whole store of clothing was turned upside down; all the old uniforms were renovated, and he inspected us at ten o'clock.

He was so stern that he made the officers tremble. At eleven o'clock we set out for the Tuileries; at noon the Consul came down to review us mounted on a white horse, which, it was said, Louis XVI. had ridden. This horse was of great beauty, with a tremendous mane and tail; he marched through the ranks with the step of a man; he was a magnificent looking horse.

The Consul had us open ranks; he walked slowly and received many petitions; he took them himself and then handed them to General Lannes. He stopped wherever he saw a soldier presenting arms, and spoke to him. He was pleased with our appearance and ordered us to march on. We found some casks of wine at the barracks, and a quart of it was distributed to each man. The petitions were almost all granted, and the content was general.

FOURTH NOTE-BOOK.

MY DECORATION. — I AM POISONED. — RETURN TO MY COUNTRY. — THE CAMP OF BOULOGNE AND THE FIRST AUSTRIAN CAMPAIGN.

The non-commissioned officers and soldiers who had been appointed to receive the cross were summoned, and there were eighteen hundred of us in the guard. The ceremony took place in the dome of the Invalides, June 14, 1804. We were stationed in the following order: to the right on entering, the guard occupied the steps all the way to the top, the soldiers of the army were on the opposite steps, and the disabled soldiers filled the back part of the dome up to the ceiling. The corps of officers were on the floor; the whole chapel was full.

The Consul arrived at noon, mounted on a horse covered with gold; his stirrups were of solid gold.[1] This elegant horse was a present from the Grand Turk; it was necessary to set a guard over him, so as to prevent any one from approaching him (the saddle was covered with diamonds). He entered. The most profound silence reigned in the chapel. He passed before the whole corps of officers, and seated him-

---

[1] This "solid gold" existed only in Coignet's imagination; but I have not been willing to omit any of his naïve statements, which give such originality to his narrative.

self on the throne, which was to the right in the back part of the dome. Josephine was opposite in a loge to the left, Eugene at the foot of the throne holding a pin cushion stuck full of pins, and Murat had a little boat filled with crosses. The ceremony began with the officers of high rank, who were called up according to their degrees. After all the grand crosses had been distributed, one was sent to Josephine, as she sat in her loge, and was presented to her on a salver by Eugene and Murat.

Then they called out, "Jean-Roch Coignet!" I was on the second step. I passed in front of my comrades, through the main body of the dome and on to the foot of the throne. Here I was stopped by Beauharnais, who said to me, "You mustn't go any farther." But Murat answered him, "Prince, the candidates for the cross of the Legion of Honor are equals; he has been called, he can pass up." I mounted the steps to the throne. I presented myself straight as an arrow before the Consul, who said that I was a brave defender of my country, and that I had given proof of it. At the words, "Accept thy Consul's cross," I lowered my right hand, which was at salute against my fur cap, and took my cross by the ribbon. Not knowing what to do with it, I was about to move backwards down the steps of the throne when the Consul called me up to him again, took my cross, passed it through the button-hole of my coat and fastened it there with a pin taken from the cushion which Beauharnais held. I descended the throne, and as I passed by the staff which occupied the floor, I met my colonel, M. Lepreux, and Commandant Merle, who were awaiting their decorations. They both embraced me before the whole corps of officers, and I went out of the dome.

I could scarcely make my way, the crowd pressed so eagerly around me to see my cross. Some beautiful women who could get near enough to me to touch my cross asked permission to embrace me.[1] I served as a paten that day for all the ladies and gentlemen I met as I went out. I reached the bridge of

---

[1] There is much less embracing nowadays. But at that time it was still considered a testimonial of esteem, and was quite customary.

the Revolution, where I found my old regiment, which was in line on the bridge. Compliments were showered upon me from all sides. I finally passed through the crowd and entered the garden of the Tuileries, where I had great difficulty in making my way to my barracks.

When I came to the door the sentinel presented arms. I turned back to see if there was an officer near, and found that I was all alone. "Is it to me that you are presenting arms?" — "Yes," he answered, "we are ordered to present arms before those decorated with the cross of the Legion of Honor." I took his hand and shook it heartily, and asked him his name and his company. Then forcing him to take the five francs I put in his hand, I said, "I invite you to breakfast with me as soon as you are off guard." Lord! how hungry I was! I ordered ten litres of wine for my mess, and said to the cook, "That is for my comrades." The corporal saw the bottles and said, "Who sent up this wine?" — "Coignet ordered it; he was nearly starved. I gave him his supper at once, for the lieutenant had come for him; they went off arm in arm, and he told me to tell you to drink his health."

My lieutenant, who had seen me receive the first decoration, had kept his eye upon me, and had caught up with me. He said very kindly, "You must spend the whole evening with me. We will go and see the illuminations, and afterwards we will go to the Palais Royal and take a cup of coffee. The roll will not be called till midnight, and we need not return till we choose; I will take the responsibility."

We walked about in the garden for an hour. He took me to the café Borel, at the end of the Palais Royal, and made me go down into a large cellar,[1] where there were a great many people. They crowded around us. The master of the café came to my lieutenant and said, "I will order for you anything you want. The members of the Legion of Honor are entertained gratis." The big citizens who heard M. Borel, first stared at us and then took possession of us. Punch flowed freely. My lieutenant told them that I was the first man

---

[1] Afterwards known by the name of the Café des Aveugles, on account of the blind musicians who composed the orchestra.

decorated, and then all of them rushed up to me crying out, "Come, let us drink his health." I was filled with confusion. They said to me, "Drink, brave fellow!"—"I cannot drink, gentlemen, I thank you." Everybody feasted us, we were invited to sit down at every table. At last we thanked the host and bade him farewell, and at midnight we returned to our barracks. My lieutenant was as sober as I was; we took very little to drink. How delightful that evening had been to me! I had never known anything like it before.

Next morning my lieutenant took me to see our captain, and he embraced us both and made us take a drink of brandy with him. "At noon," said he, "you will go with the lieutenant and be presented to M. de Lacépède, as the man who received the first decoration; that is the order."

We took a cab. On reaching the court we mounted the great stairway, then the folding-doors opened and we were announced. The chancellor appeared; he had a long, big nose. My lieutenant told him that I had been the first man decorated. He embraced me and guided my hand while I wrote all the letters of my name in the great register. He accompanied us to the door of the great stairway. All the guard came in carriages to the chancellor's office. I paid a visit to the brother of my colonel at the Porte St. Denis, where I purchased some nankeen to make some short breeches. Long stockings and silver garter-buckles were the rule for a summer uniform.

Nothing could be handsomer than that uniform. When we were on dress parade we wore a blue coat with white lapels, sloped low down on the breast, a vest of white basine, short breeches, gaiters also of white basine, silver buckles on the shoes and breeches, a double cravat, white underneath and black on the outside, with a narrow edge of white showing at the top. In undress, we wore a blue coat, white basine vest, nankeen breeches, and seamless white cotton stockings. In addition to all this we wore pigeon wings powdered and a queue six inches long, cut off at the end like a brush and tied with a black worsted ribbon, with ends exactly two inches long. Add to this the bearskin cap and its long plume, and you have the summer uniform of the imperial guard. But one thing of which I can give no real idea is the extreme neatness which was required of us. When we passed through the grating of the barracks the orderlies inspected us, and if there was a speck of dust on our shoes or a bit of powder on the collar of our coats we were sent back. We were splendid to look at, but abominably uncomfortable.

When I was ready to present myself to General Hulin, he received me and made me a present of a piece of the ribbon of the Legion of Honor. The next day I wanted to go to see M. Champromain, a wood merchant living near the Jardin des Plantes. I went along the Rue St. Honoré; when I reached the Palais Royal I met a superb looking man, who stopped me to look at my cross and asked me to do him the kindness to take a cup of coffee with him. I refused, but he insisted so that I allowed myself to be tempted. He took me to the Café de la Régence, on the square with the Palais Royal, which occupies the right side of the square. When we reached that fine café he ordered two cups of black coffee. As for me I was looking at the woman behind the counter, who was very beautiful. I gazed at her with all the strength of my twenty-seven years. The gentleman said to me, "Your coffee will get cold, drink it." And as soon as I had done so he rose and said to me, "I am in a hurry." Then he paid his bill and went out. As soon as I had finished my cup I got up, but he had disappeared.

As I was going out of the café I fell on the pavement. My whole body was writhing with pain. I was drawn double. I had fearful cramp in my bowels. The people in the café ran to my assistance, had me taken to our hospital at Gros-Caillou, and I was treated at once. They made me drink all sorts of stuff, warmed my bed, and sent for M. Suze, the head physician, an excellent man who was badly scarred by the small-pox and blind in one eye. A nurse with bare arms rubbed my stomach with all his strength, and another was at hand to relieve him, and thus it was day and night for eight days. But still the cramp never left me.

They were obliged to put cupping glasses on my stomach, to draw a blister, and when the fire went out under them they cut the skin with a penknife. Then they put a glass bowl turned upside down on my stomach to pump the blood. In this way I became so exhausted that one could almost see through me. And the nurses continued to rub me night and day, and changed my clothing four times a day on account of the profuse sweats. Every morning I gave twenty-four sous to my two nurses for their kind care. M. Suze came

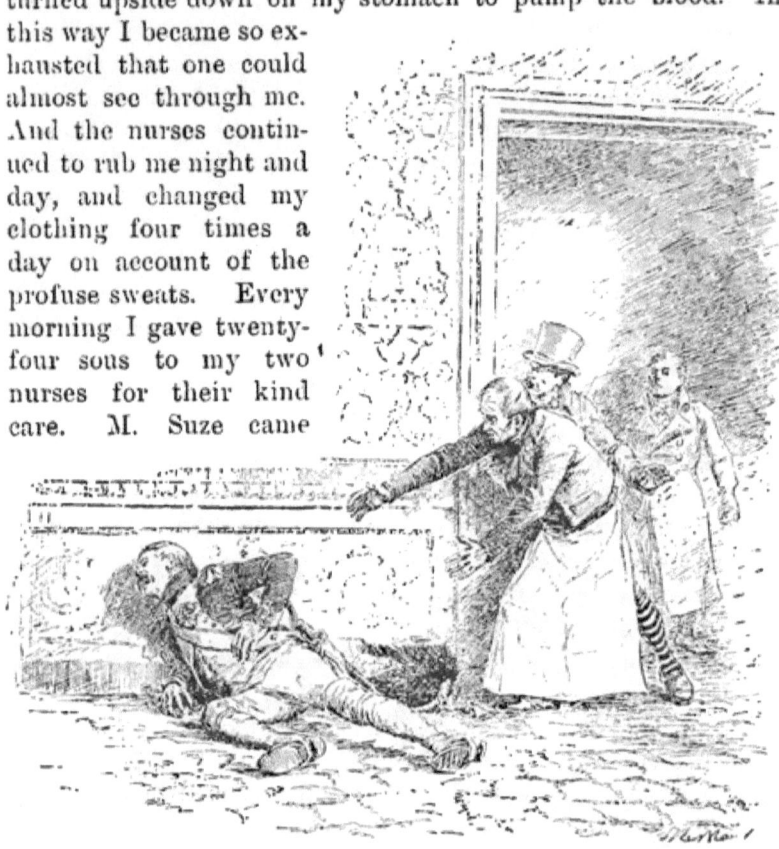

three times a day, and they cupped me constantly and applied all sorts of remedies, but nothing had any effect. Nothing passed through my bowels. My condition was reported to the First Consul, who ordered two physicians to attend me during the night, and nurses night and day. An officer of the regular service came every day to ask after me. Every possible care was lavished on me. An order was given to allow all who wished to see me to enter without permits, and my greatest consolation was gazing upon my cross which was placed near me. I endured all sorts of suffering in the hope of being cured.

I remained in this condition forty days. A consultation of physicians was held and Baron Larrey was called in. They put me on a mattress on a table well covered up, and he said to them, "Gentlemen, this brave soldier is full of pluck; consult and tell me your opinion." They consulted together and I could not hear what they said. M. Larrey said, "Have a bucket of ice and some lemonade brought, and we will make him drink it; if that passes through him we will see what can be done."

A large silver goblet of lemonade well sweetened was brought me; I drank it and did not vomit it up. The doctors watched by me and half an hour after they gave me a second. M. Larrey said to them, "I have saved the upper part, now you save the lower." They concluded to make me take a remedy of their own concoction, and it had a good effect. There came away three lumps, one about the size of a walnut, and the others not quite so large, and the first was full of verdigris. These were carefully put aside, and the doctors remained two hours longer with me. M. Larrey said to me, "You are saved. I will come to see you;" and he did come to see me three times. I owe my life to him and M. Suze. I was well cared for; preserves were given me, and when I was able to eat I had some excellent chocolate and four ounces of Malaga wine which I could not drink. I gave it to the sickest man in the room. After the end of another week fried fish was given me and mutton and a bottle of wine of Nuits. I gave half of it to my comrades. The preserves came from outside, I know not from whose kind hand. I received visits every day. M. Morin, who had a château in my native country, heard that I was at the hospital, and came to see me, and offered to take me to stay at his château till I recuperated. I accepted his offer gratefully. "You will find plenty of good milk there," said he, "and I will give orders that you shall be well taken care of."

The faithful care of the physicians and nurses saved me

from the revenge which had been attempted upon me by one who could not wreak it upon the First Consul himself; for it was one of the spies of Cadoudal who had watched his opportunity to kill me. When I was convalescent I was laid on a sofa near the window to get the fresh air. M. Suze had my hair combed and told the nurse that he did not wish to have it cut off. It required a great deal of time and powder, and the nurse had to put on a mask. There was a double glass to the mask so as to prevent inhaling the poison, my hair was so filled with the verdigris. This operation occupied a whole hour. I gave the nurse three francs for having preserved my hair. In those days pigeon wings were worn, and we had to put our hair in curl papers at night, and in the morning the hairdresser came to the guard-house to arrange our hair. At noon the guard going on duty looked very differently from the guard coming in. We were greatly relieved when the order came to cut off all the queues. It created quite a revolution in the army, particularly among the cavalry.[1]

My convalesence was apparent. I told M. Suze that I felt very well and that I wanted a permit to try the air of my native region, as I was invited to go to a château in that country till I was entirely well again, that the milk there would be very good for me. "I will give you three months' leave if you wish," said he, "but promise me to be prudent." — "I swear I will."

He gave me a pass, and on my return to the barracks I presented it with my sick leave to the captain, who had me paid off. I started off dressed in a new uniform at the expense of the government, and went by coach to Auxerre, where I lodged at Monfort's, at the Paris gate. I remembered a relative of mine there, Father Toussaint Armancier. I sent for him and asked him if he had ever heard what had become of my little brother whom I had not seen since he was six years old. He answered, "I know where he is. He is at Beauvoir,

---

[1] This was not only a question of ornament in certain branches of the cavalry. The hussars, for instance, had a habit of hiding there what gold pieces they possessed.

living with Thibault the miller." — " Send for him. My God, I am so thankful ! "

Next day he came and threw himself into my arms. He could scarcely bear his joy at seeing me so fine, all dressed in uniform and wearing the cross. " My brother," said he, " I am so glad." — " I am going back to our native place," said I, " and if you wish it I will take you with me and put you in business. I have some good friends in Paris." — " All right," said he, " come for me and I will go with you." — " I promise you I will be ready. Have you any money ? " — " Yes," said he, " I have seven hundred francs." — " That is a proof of your good character, my dear fellow." Then we dined together like two children who had just found each other.

The next day, after breakfast, we each started for our respective abodes. On my arrival at Courson, I was stopped by a brigadier of the gendarmes, named Trubert, who asked me if I was under orders. I answered, " Look at my cross and my uniform ; they are my passport." He was completely dumfounded. I went on to Druyes. On Saturday night I reached M. Morin's château of Bouloy, where I found I was expected. As I had come up the valley no one had seen me. The next morning being Sunday, I dressed myself in full uniform to go to mass. I asked where I could get a seat in one of the stalls. One was shown me next the mayor, M. Trémeau, who is still living, and I went into the choir. I sat down in the seat pointed out for me, and the mayor seated himself on my left. I bowed to him. " Ah ! indeed, is it you, Coignet ? " — " Yes, sir." — " I was expecting you. I received a letter from M. Morin announcing your arrival." — " Thank you. I shall have the honor of paying you a visit after mass." — " I shall expect you."

Everybody came over on the side of the choir to see the fine soldier with his decoration. I recognized my stepmother in front of me, and my father who stood with his back towards me. He sang among the choristers. I left the church before the mass was quite over, and went to my father's house. The door was not shut. I remained standing, and my father came and found me waiting for him in the middle of the room. I went up to him to embrace him; he pressed me in his arms, and I returned the embrace. My stepmother came forward also to kiss me. "Do not come near me," said I to her. "I do not like Judas kisses. Go away, I have a horror of you." — "Come, my son," said my father, "be seated. "Why did you not come to your father's house?" — "I did not wish to receive your hospitality in the presence of your wife whom I detest. Strangers offered me a resting-place for friendship's sake, and I have accepted it. I am going now to see the mayor, and I will come to see you

to-morrow at noon, if you will permit me." — "I shall look for you."

I started for the village and found a crowd awaiting me along the way, who called out, "There he is, good M. Coignet; he has not wasted his time, he has earned a beautiful cross! The good God has blessed him on account of all the suffering his stepmother made him endure!" — "Let me pass," said I to them. "I will see you all, my good friends. Allow me to go on to the city to see M. Trémeau."

I was received with open arms by M. Trémeau, who said to me, "I have ordered a seat for you at my table, and my brothers and I will take you out hunting to cheer you up;

you carry your passport on your breast." — "Thank you; I will come to see you." What a comfort all this kindly welcome was to me!

I returned to my hotel, and the next day I went down to my father's. I said to him, "I have at last found my little brother, after being so unfortunate as to lose both the others, one of whom died not far from you without receiving any kind care from you. This is another of your wife's terrible acts, and you, poor weak man, closed your door upon your oldest son. You must now settle your accounts with us; you know that you owe us three thousand francs."

My stepmother, who was seated beside the fire, said to me, "How could we pay you all that money?" — "I cannot permit such a wretch of woman as you are to have anything to say in what concerns me. This matter is altogether between me and my father. If it were not for the respect I owe him, I would knock your head off your shoulders; you will never pull my nose with the tweezers again. Miserable wretch, are you not ashamed of having taken those two innocent creatures into the woods and left them there to the mercy of God? Look at your crime, you serpent! If the fear of God did not restrain me, I should kill you." My father was very pale. I was trembling from the outburst I had permitted myself to make before him, but I felt that I had gained some satisfaction from it.

All through the country they talked of nothing but me. I received visits from every direction, which I returned, and was everywhere received with friendly kindness. I received a letter from M. de la Bergerie, prefect of the Yonne, written by command of Marshal Davoust, who had arrived at Auxerre, requesting me to meet the marshal and take part in a wolf-hunt in the forest of Frétoy, near Courson. I went, accompanied by the Messrs. Trémeau, who very kindly told me that to save my uniform I ought to go in hunting dress. I looked like a real huntsman with my ribbon of the Legion of Honor. The marshal recognized me immediately. "Here is my grenadier," said he to the prefect; "you can follow the hunt all day long." The guards found a place for us, and the huntsmen who beat about the bushes started off at a given signal. Two wolves and some foxes were killed. Shooting deer was forbidden, but we were allowed to hunt other game in the evening and to fire on all. The hunt was over at four o'clock, and the Messrs. Trémeau and I were invited to dinner. The dinner was a splendid affair. I was triumphantly received. The marshal said to the prefect, "This is the smallest of my grenadiers. Now make yourself thoroughly happy in your native place." We left at eleven o'clock in the evening, and the Messrs. Trémeau were charmed with the cordial welcome of the prefect and the marshal; our game-bags were well filled with hares.

I spent my time in hunting. I went to see my father, who invited me to go on a hunting-party with him. I could not refuse. When we reached the rendezvous, he said to me, "Here is the trail of three deer which must have spent the night in this underwood; they cannot be far off. Come, I will station you. Hold on to my dog, and at the end of a quarter of an hour, walk on right ahead of you. As soon as I fire let him loose." I started off, and about half way I heard two reports of a gun. I let the dog loose, and heard my father cry to me, "This way." I ran to him, and to my astonishment saw two deer upon the ground. "I have killed two of them, and would have killed the third if I had not been in such a hurry. Let us go to the farm. They will come to look for us; but first each of us must have a hare. I know where to find them." In an hour's time the hares were in our game-bags. "That is enough," said I, "let us go back."

I went around to all my friends and said good-by before going to Beauvoir to see Father Thibault, and get my young brother to take him with me to Paris. I let no one know when I was to leave except my comrade Allard, and I started off at two o'clock in the morning.

When I reached Paris, I immediately placed my brother with a wine-merchant; I returned to my barracks, where my comrades welcomed me heartily. I drew my whole pay and three months of my pension, as member of the Legion; this gave me two hundred francs, and quite set me up. Being exempt from service for a month by order of the captain, I was completely restored to health, and ready for the next campaign.

It was said that preparations were being made for a descent upon England. Hammocks were made for the whole guard, with bedclothes for each. The camp of Boulogne was in great commotion, and we were pretty lively at Paris. But our turn came to take part in movements by land and sea, after grand reviews and drills in the plain of St. Denis, where we were obliged to be out in the rain all day long. The barrels of our guns became filled with water when we carried arms. The "great man" never budged; the water ran down his sides; he did not let us off even for half an hour. His hat drooped upon his shoulders, his generals looked discomforted; but he took no notice of any of it. At last he made us march past, and when we reached Courbevoie we were paddling about like ducks in the yard; but we found wine there, and so we thought no more about it. The next day, the order was read that we should hold ourselves in readiness to march. "Make up your knapsacks," said our officers, "and say good-by to every one, for only the veterans will be left."

The order came; we were obliged to put all the bedding into the storehouse, and sleep on the straw, so as to be ready to leave for Boulogne. We camped at the port of Ambleteuse, where a splendid camp was formed; General Oudinot was above us with twelve thousand grenadiers, who formed a part of the reserve force. And every day we drilled and drilled. We were divided into brigades for service by turns on sea. We were put very far out, in a line, with two hundred pinnaces. The whole of this little fleet, divided into sections, was commanded by a good admiral, who was on a fine frigate in the middle.

Thus for twenty days we worked the pieces, and were both gunners and sailors. The sailors, gunners, and soldiers all moved as one man; there was perfect harmony on board the fleet. At night there was the cry of "All's well!" and the last man answered, "All's well, ay, ay!" In the morning, the speaking trumpets asked the news of the night. "What is the news on board your ship?"—"Two grenadiers threw themselves into the water."—"Were they drowned?"—"Yes," was the answer, "yes, my commander."—"All right." He said "all right" merely to indicate that he had understood.

Once I was put on a sloop of war with ten heavy pieces of cannon, a hundred grenadiers, and a captain covered with wounds. I was right-hand man to one of the guns, for it was necessary to do something of everything; and one half of us remained on deck all night. When my turn came to go down to rest in my hammock, I said, "Come on, old man, here you go to your hammock; now you can rest." The head steward's mate heard me. "Where is this old soldier?"—"It is I," said I.—"Where is your hammock? I want to put you in a good place." Then he hung my hammock near the biscuit chests, and raised a plank. "Eat some biscuits, and to-morrow I will give you a gill." This was a small measure for brandy. We ate out of wooden bowls, with wooden spoons, beans which dated from the creation of the world. All the rations for each mess were put up in bundles; we had fresh meat and sole.

While I was at the camp at Ambleteuse, I received a visit from my old bedfellow, from the company to which I had first been admitted as a member of the guard. I have already said that he was the tallest of all the grenadiers; he was, moreover, a jolly fellow, good-natured and full of fun, and somewhat of a joker. I cannot remember his name, I only remember that he was the son of an innkeeper in the neighborhood of Meudon. He had left the guard in consequence of a singular adventure. One day we were on duty at the Tuileries; he was stationed at the door opening into the Consul's own chamber. When the Consul came at night to go to bed, he stopped, dumfounded. There was more than sufficient cause for his astonishment. Imagine a man six feet four inches tall, wearing a bear-skin cap eighteen inches high and a plume at least a foot higher than the cap. He called me his dwarf, and when he held out his arm horizontally, I could walk under without touching it. The First Consul was still shorter than I, and I think he was obliged to raise his head higher than usual to see my comrade's face. After examining him a moment, he saw that, moreover, he was perfectly formed. "Would you like to be a drum-major?" said he to the man. — "Yes, Consul." — "Very well, go send your officer to me."

At these words the grenadier put down his gun and rushed off, then he stopped and came back to get it again, saying that a good soldier should never leave his gun. "Never mind," said the First Consul, "I will watch it, and wait for you." A minute after, my comrade arrived at our post. The officer, surprised at seeing him, asked roughly what had happened. "Well, by my soul," replied he with his bantering air, "I had stood guard long enough. I have left some one on duty in my place." — "Whom, then?" cried the officer. — "The little corporal, to be sure." — "Come, none of this ill-timed joking." — "I am not joking; he ought to take his turn mounting guard; besides, he is asking for you; come to him, he sent me for you."

The officer's astonishment gave place to terror, for Bonaparte rarely sent for the officers to come to him except to give them a scolding. This one of ours went out discomforted, following his new guide. They found the First Consul walking up and down the vestibule, beside the gun. "Sir," said he to the officer, "does this soldier bear a good character?" — "Yes, general." — "Then I appoint him drum-major in my cousin's regiment. I will pay him three francs a day from my private purse, and the regiment will give him as much more. Give orders to have him relieved from duty, and let him start off to-morrow."

No sooner said than done. My comrade immediately entered upon his new duties, and when he came to see us at

Ambleteuse, he had on a prodigiously fine uniform, all covered with gold lace, as handsome as that of the drum-major of the guard. He got permission for me to leave the camp, took me to Boulogne and treated me to a dinner.

That evening I left him to return to Ambleteuse. I was alone; as I was going along I met two grenadiers of the line, who wanted to arrest me. At that time the soldiers of the guard were exposed to frequent attacks. There was in the camp of Boulogne what was called the "company of the moon," which was composed of brigands and jealous fellows who took advantage of the night hours to plunder those of us whom they found alone, steal their watches and silver buckles, and throw them into the sea. It was found necessary to forbid our returning to the camp at night unless there were several in a party. I got out of my difficulty by dint of audacity. I had my sabre and my seven years in the fencing-school. I drew sabre, and defied my assailants. They thought it prudent to allow me to pass on; but if I had shown any signs of weakness I should have been lost, and my drum-major's dinner would have cost me very dear.

One day Messrs. the Englishmen came in a large squadron to make us a visit. A vessel of seventy-four was insolent enough to come near the shore. She brought her broadside to bear, and sent a volley of balls into our camp. We had some big mortars on the height; a sergeant of grenadiers asked permission to fire on this ship, saying that he would guarantee to send her a-leak the first or second fire. "Go to work then. What is your name?" said the Consul.— "Despienne."— "Give me your address."

The first bomb passed over it. "You have missed your aim," said our little corporal.— "All right," said the sergeant. "Watch this one." He took aim, and sent a bomb into the middle of the ship. Then there was a cry of joy. "I will make you lieutenant in my artillery," said he to Despienne. Then the English fired blank cartridges calling for aid, for their ship was on fire. They leaped into our boats as well as into their own. Our little flotilla pursued their big ships. It was a sight to see our little pugs after their big house-dogs. The

English tried to return to the charge, but they were roughly received. We were in good condition. Our little boats made havoc of them. Every one of our shots struck, and their broadsides passed over our pinnaces. We were ordered to return to port so as to make a general movement all along the line. Never had there been seen such a sight as a hundred and fifty thousand men firing by battalions; the whole shore shook.

All the preparations were made for the descent, and one Thursday evening we set sail for the coasts of England, expecting to reach there on Friday. But at ten o'clock in the evening we were made to land with our knapsacks on our backs, and start for the bridge of Briques where we were to leave our blankets. There were shouts of joy. In an hour the whole of the artillery was on the march for the town of Arras. Never was there such a terrible march. We had not a moment for sleep, marching by platoon all day and all night, and at last holding on to each other to prevent falling. Those who fell could not be wakened. Some fell into the ditches. Blows with the flat of the sabre had no effect upon them. The music played, drums beat a charge; nothing got the better of sleep. The nights were terrible. I was on the right of a section. About midnight I fell down on the right on the declivity of the road. I turned over on my side, and went rolling down, never stopping till I reached an open field. I did not let go my gun, but I rolled into the other world. My brave captain sent some one down to look after me. I was all broken up. They took my knapsack and my gun. I was now thoroughly awake.

When we reached the heights of Saverne, the sleepers had to be put into carriages. At last we arrived at Strassburg, where we found the Emperor, who reviewed us the next day and distributed crosses. Two nights' rest put us in good condition. We crossed the Rhine and marched by long stages upon Augsburg, and thence on to Ulm, where we found a considerable army which we had to drive beyond a rapid river, before taking possession of a convent on an impregnable height.

Marshal Ney, standing in the water up to his horse's belly, had the bridge repaired in spite of the grape-shot. The sappers were cut down, and still this intrepid Ney did not budge. As soon as the first truss was placed, the grenadiers and light-horsemen crossed over to support the sappers, and the marshal came galloping up to Prince Murat, took him by the hand and said, " Prince, the bridge is finished. I need your support." — " I will start at once," said he, " with my division of dragoons."

Off they went at a gallop. The weather was so terrible that the bridge was flooded; we never saw it again. We  were stationed near this river in a meadow; the water rose rapidly, it was soon up to our knees. The guard had to paddle about like ducks. Every one began to laugh and walk gayly through the water. I had my pot in my knapsack; it was not upside down, so it got full of water, and I poured it over my comrades' legs. The barrels of our guns were full also. We could not change our position; the whole of the marshal's corps were waiting for the water to fall so they could cross; the soldiers were in the mud; we were in the best place. At last the waters subsided. We could see the planks of the bridge. The troops pulled themselves out of the mud and washed their legs as they were crossing the bridge. Our ducks in their turn came up out of the meadow, and the columns arrived at the foot of that tremendous mountain, defended by very considerable forces. But nothing could resist Marshal Ney. On reaching the village of Elchingen, he attacked it, one house after another, and there were gardens surrounded by walls, over which we had to climb. This extraordinary village was taken with the bayonet, and our columns reached the convent which overlooked the town.

The Emperor then marched us off at quickstep to complete the overthrow of General Mack. The Austrians fought with determination. Behind this village were some scantily wooded fields, where we could manœuvre, and the chain of mountains extended from the convent to the front of Ulm. We did not leave the enemy at peace for a moment. Murat covered himself with glory by his splendid charges, and Ney did not stop till he was in front of Ulm. The Emperor surrounded the town on all sides, and gave us at last time to dry ourselves. As ill-luck would have it, a beautiful house belonging to one of the citizens took fire. It was impossible to save it. "You shall pay for it," said the Emperor angrily. "I will give six hundred francs and you shall give a day's pay. Let that sum be immediately paid over to the owner of the house." Our officers made wry faces at this, but were obliged to submit, and the guard owns a house in that town. The proprietor did a good day's work, for he received a considerable sum.

The Emperor summoned General Mack to surrender, which he did on the 19th of October. Orders were given to march next morning at five o'clock; the whole guard went to the foot of the Michelberg, in front of Ulm. The Emperor stationed himself on the top of this height and had a good fire made; it was there that he burned his gray cloak. He was surrounded by the whole of his guard, and fifty pieces of cannon were turned upon the town. I was standing guard on the top of the eminence near the Emperor who was talking to Count Hulin, general of the foot grenadiers. Suddenly we saw an endless column file out of the town of Ulm, and march up in front of the Emperor in a plain at the foot of the mountain. All the soldiers had hung their cartridge-boxes on their knapsacks ready to take them off when they reached the place appointed to disarm; they threw their arms and cartridge-boxes in a pile as they passed. General Mack came at their head to surrender his sword to the Emperor. This the

Emperor refused to accept (all the officers and generals retained their swords and knapsacks), and he talked a long time with the superior officers.

This evacuation lasted four or five hours (there were twenty-seven thousand of them), and the city was full of sick and wounded. We made our entrance into Ulm amid the shouts of the whole populace; the officers were sent off to their own country on parole not to take up arms against France, and the Emperor made a proclamation to us. The next day after the surrender of Ulm, Napoleon set out for Augsburg with the whole of his guard; they made forced marches so as to reach Vienna. The soldiers were required to march eighteen or twenty leagues a day. They used to say: "Our Emperor makes war not with our arms but with our legs."

When the Emperor learned that Prince Ferdinand had escaped from Ulm with his cavalry, he sent Prince Murat with Oudinot's grenadiers in pursuit of them. We came up with them ten leagues down the road; they had only wagons, cannons, caissons, and cavalry; they had carried off half of their arms with four thousand horses; the roads were filled with prisoners.

We started at midnight to join the advance-guard, and were obliged to pass by the troops who were already marching along the sides of the road. We had to take the middle, in the mud, and so pass columns two leagues long. Our grenadiers took strides a fathom long, and passed two soldiers at each step; as for me, with my short legs, I trotted along, to keep up with my comrades. The Emperor slept in his carriage, and when he stopped we had to mount guard, and the army corps passed on.

When the troops had gone on fifteen leagues, the Emperor would start again; we had to put our knapsacks on our backs, and swallow as we went along, all in the darkness. We could see neither town nor village. Fortunately the Russians expected us. Oudinot's grenadiers, with Marshal Lannes and Murat, made their acquaintance; this gave us time to reach Lintz, a town a little to the left of the road to Vienna. This city has, at its back, some high mountains, at the foot of which flows the Danube, among the rocks; it is so shut in that it has cut its way through the rocks. The torrent makes one tremble. We stayed there two days; certain princes sent from Vienna arrived, and then an aide-de-camp of Marshal Lannes, announcing that the Russians were defeated. The next day, the Emperor started off at a gallop; he was sullen. "All does not go well," said our chiefs; "he is angry."

He gave orders to start at once for St. Polten. Just before reaching there, to the left, there are mountains which are covered with trees to a considerable height; here an army corps was camped. Thence we marched to Schoenbrunn, the residence of the Emperor of Austria. This palace is magnificent, having forests surrounded by walls and filled with game. We remained here a few days to rest; carriages came out from Vienna. Overtures were made to Napoleon, to induce him to spare the town. The army corps came in from all directions; that of Marshal Mortier had suffered a great deal, and was held in reserve for refreshment. The Emperor lost no time; he gave orders that the guard should appear in dress uniform, and rode at its head through that great city, amid the acclamations of a populace full of joy at the sight of such a splendid corps. We passed through without stopping, and came to the bridges, a little distance from the faubourgs, in a woody place, where we were somewhat concealed. The great wooden bridge was superb; we said to each other, "How is it that these Austrians have allowed us to pass over on this bridge and have not blown it up?" Our officers told us that this was managed by a stratagem of Prince Murat, Marshal Lannes, and the officers of the engineers.

We slept in villages completely devastated by a terrible season of snow. The Emperor went in front; he visited the outposts, and overlooked the army corps, and then went on to Brunn, in Moravia, where he established his headquarters. We could not catch up with him; this was one of our most terrible marches, we had to go forty leagues to rejoin him. We arrived there on the third day, utterly broken down with fatigue. This city was beautiful, and here we had time to rest. We were near Austerlitz. The Emperor went out every day to make reconnoissances along the line, and returned satisfied. He seemed joyous; his pinches of snuff took effect (this was always a proof of his contentment), and with his hands behind his back he went about talking to every one.

We received orders to go forward, near the Pratzen mountains. In front of us there was a river to cross, but it was so frozen that it presented no obstacle. We camped to the left of the road, over the Pratzen mountains, with Oudinot's grenadiers on the right and the cavalry behind us.

On the first of December, at two o'clock, Napoleon came with his marshals to visit our line. We were eating some quince marmalade, of which we had found salt-boxes full in the village, and had made tarts. The Emperor laughed. "Ah!" said he, "I see you are eating preserves, don't get up. You must put new flints in your guns; to-morrow morning you will need them. Be ready."

The horse grenadiers were carrying off a dozen big pigs; they passed along in front of us. We charged them with our sabres and took all their pigs. The Emperor laughed. He divided them; six for us and six for the horse-grenadiers. The generals took a pint of good blood, and we had some good broiled ham.

That evening the Emperor came out of his tent, and mounting his horse, started off with his escort to visit the outposts. It was twilight, and the horse-grenadiers carried four lighted torches. This was the signal for a charming sight; the whole guard took up handfuls of straw from their barracks and set it on fire. Holding a bunch of it in each hand, the men lighted it one from other, and all cried out, "*Vive l'Empereur!*" as they leaped into the air. The whole army corps took it up, and I am sure that two hundred thousand torches were lighted. The music played and the drums beat to arms. The Russians, from their heights, more than a hundred feet above us, could see seven army corps, and seven lines of fire in front of them.

The next morning early, all the musicians were ordered to be at their posts, on pain of severe punishment. It was then the 2d of December. The Emperor started out very early in

"There were twenty-five thousand of us jolly fellows with our bear-skin caps." — Page 123.

the morning to visit the outposts and see the position of the Russian army: he returned and took a position on a plateau, above where he had passed the night. He placed us, with Oudinot's grenadiers, in line of battle behind him. All his marshals were with him; he sent them to their several posts. The army ascended this eminence, in order to descend to the country below, cross a river and come to the Pratzen mountain, where the Russians were waiting for us as quietly as possible. When the columns had passed by, the Emperor ordered us to follow them up. There were twenty-five thousand of us jolly fellows with our bear-skin caps.

Our battalions mounted the hill carrying arms, and when within reach, saluted the first line with fire by battalions, and then crossed bayonets with the first line of the Russians, beating a charge. Contrary to custom, the Emperor had ordered that the musicians should remain at their post in the centre of each battalion. Our corps of musicians was full, with its chief, an old trooper of at least sixty years, at its head. They played a song we all knew well.

> On va leur percer le flanc,
> Ran, ran, ran, rantanplan, tirelire,
> Rantanplan tirelire en plan,
> On va leur percer le flanc,
> Que nous allons rire!
> Ran, tan, plan, tirelire,
> Que nous allons rire!

While this air was played, the drums, under the direction of M. Sénot, their major, an accomplished man, beat a charge loud enough to break their drumheads in. The drums and music mingled together. It was enough to make a paralytic move forward!

When we reached the summit of the plateau we were only separated from the enemy by the remnant of the corps, who had been fighting in front of us since morning. Our right wing suffered very much. We saw that they could not ascend that steep mountain. The whole of the guard of the Russian Emperor was massed on this height. But we were strongly supported on the right. Their cavalry charged upon a battalion of the 4th, and strewed the field with their dead bodies. The Emperor perceived this, and ordered General Rapp to charge. Rapp dashed forward with his horsemen and the Mamelukes, delivered the battalion, but was driven back by the Russian guard. The Emperor ordered us to halt, and sent forward first the Mamelukes and light-horsemen. These Mamelukes were marvellous riders; they could do anything they chose on horseback. With their curved sabres, they would take a man's head off with one blow, and with their sharp stirrups they could cut the loins of a soldier. One of them came three different times up to the Emperor bringing a Russian standard. The third time, the Emperor wished to stop him, but he dashed in again, and returned no more. He rested on the field of battle.

The light-horsemen were no less effective than the Mamelukes, but they had to contend with a force too strong for them. The Russian imperial guard was composed of gigantic men who fought with desperation. Our cavalry was at last driven back. Then the Emperor let loose his "black horses," that is, his horse grenadiers, commanded by General Bessières. They passed by us like a streak of lightning, and fell upon the enemy. For a quarter of an hour there was a desperate struggle, and that quarter of an hour seemed to us an age. We could see nothing through the smoke and dust. We feared we should see our comrades sabred in their turn. We were advancing slowly behind them, and if they had been defeated it would have been our turn.

There was a confusion for several minutes; everything went pell-mell, and no one knew which had the upper hand; but our grenadiers came off conquerors, and returned to their position behind the Emperor. General Rapp came back covered with blood, bringing a prince with him.

We had been sent forward at a quick step to assist in this struggle; the Russian infantry was behind this mass, and we thought that our turn had come, but they beat a retreat into the valley of the ponds. Not being able to pass on the causeway, which was blocked up, they were obliged to cross over the pond to the left, in front of us; and the Emperor, perceiving their embarrassment, sent down his artillery and the 2d regiment of grenadiers. Our gunners manned the batteries, and balls and shells rained on the ice, which yielded beneath this mass of Russians. All the troops clapped their hands, and our Napoleon wreaked vengeance on his snuff-box; it was a total rout.

In the midst of these solemn circumstances we found a chance to laugh like children. A hare, frightened almost to death, was trying to escape, and came right up to us. My captain, Renard (*Fox*), seeing it, rushed forward to sabre it, but the hare made a turn. My captain pursued it, and the poor animal had barely time to run, as a rabbit should, into his hole. We who were watching this chase, cried out as loudly as we could, "The fox will not catch the hare, the fox will not catch the hare." And sure enough he could not catch it; so we all laughed at him, and we laughed so much the louder, because the captain was the best man in the world, esteemed and loved by all his soldiers. The day ended in following up and capturing cannons, wagons, and prisoners. That night we slept on the fine position which the Russian guard had occupied in the morning, and the Emperor occupied himself in seeing that the wounded were taken up. There were two leagues of battlefield to be gone over in search of them, and each corps furnished men for this sad service.

That evening we went into the village on the opposite side of the mountain, facing the ponds, to get wood and straw. We were obliged to descend rapidly and could not see where we were going. But our marauders found some beehives, and in order to take some honey, they set fire to an immense shed. The flames gave sufficient light to enable us to carry off all that we needed most to spend a bitterly cold night, and to show us the way back up the winding pathway. Finding no provisions, I seized upon a big pine cask. I took a feather bed, punched it into the cask and got one of my comrades to put it on my back. Then I mounted the hill; the miserable cask rolled about on my back, but I had the courage to reach my bivouac. I put down my burden, and my captain, Renard, came up at once to beg me to give him a place in my cask. I immediately went back to the village and brought a load of straw, which I put into my cask and put my feather bed in on top of it. We got in head foremost, and stuck our feet out before the fire. No one ever passed a more comfortable night. My captain said, "I shall remember you all my life."

The next day we set out for Austerlitz, a poor little thatched village, with an old castle; but we found six hundred sheep in the stalls of the manor, and rations of them were distributed to the guard. The Emperor of Austria came to see Napoleon. After the two emperors had come to an understanding, we

started for Vienna, marching by moderate stages, and went to Schoenbrunn, where we were lodged in that beautiful palace until the settlement of affairs. The guard received orders to return to France by short stages and by way of the halting places. How glad we were! And to think we should be well fed! But the army did not return; it was necessary that the peace should be signed and that our troops should have time to be re-enforced. The halting places were twenty leagues apart; it was so comfortable to find our food ready for us when we arrived. We were kindly received in Bavaria, and we recrossed the Rhine transported with joy at seeing our country once more.

We were triumphantly received by the good people of Strassburg. I went straight to my lodgings, where I had left all my belongings as I passed through. I found everything as I had left it. Those good people felt me and said, "So you are not wounded?" Their young daughter said, "We have prayed for you; all your linen is clean and white, and your silver buckles are shining bright. I made the goldsmith polish them." — "Thanks, my dear young lady. I bring you a beautiful shawl from Vienna, which I beg you to accept." She blushed at this in presence of her mother, and the father and mother were both delighted. I said to them, "If I had died, my things would have gone to your daughter." The father took me by the hand. "Come, let us go to the café," said he; "the guard is here for the day; you will have time to rest."

I had gotten this beautiful shawl from an imperial castle, where I had been stationed as safe-guard. The lady of the castle[1] asked me if I was a married man. I answered, "Yes, madame." — "Then I will make you a present for your wife, in return for your treatment of my husband."

We now went on to the beautiful city of Nancy, and from Nancy to Épernay. The first battalion was detached at the town of Ay, about a league from Épernay; it is here that they make the sparkling wine. This city has grown very rich upon its trade in these wines; for fifteen years no troops had been quartered there. We could not possibly have been more kindly received than we were; they would not allow the guard to pay for anything, they defrayed every expense. "You shall not drink the champagne now," said they, "but this evening we will try it. Rest assured, you shall have plenty of it." That evening, after dinner, the champagne was brought out, and the hosts were obliged to take their soldiers up in their arms and carry them to bed; they had no use of their legs.

The next day all the heads of households escorted us out, taking with them servants carrying baskets of wine, and our

---

[1] Probably the wife of some official. Coignet's reply shows that he scented the possibility of a present.

officers were obliged to beg these kind men to go away. Our drunkards fell about in the ditches; the soldiers were demoralized. We had to rest three hours in the plain, two leagues from Épernay, so as to give time for the men to get together. Our hosts of Ay were obliged to pick up the stragglers and take them back. We were not all reunited till the next day; but no one was punished.

We reached Meaux, in Brie, where we were kindly received. I was alone; I went to present my billet in Rue Basse, which leads to Paris. I got some one to read my billet for me, as I could not read myself. A big man said to me, "This lady is rich, but she will send you to an inn. Here, go to this locksmith's shop." I went to the locksmith and showed him my billet. "My good man," said he, "my landlady is going to send you to an inn." — "Very well, I hope to stay with this lady. Come to see me in an hour." — "But you will not be there." — "You will see that I shall, without any fuss." I went up to the first floor. "Good-morning, madame, here is your billet." — "But, sir, I do not take lodgers." — "I know it, madame; but I am very tired, I must rest a little while. If madame will have the goodness to go and get me a bottle of wine, there are fifteen sous. After that I will go away."

She took my fifteen sous and went for the bottle of wine. As soon as she went out, I took off my clothes and bound my handkerchief around my head; I rolled myself up in her bed and began to tremble as hard as I could. Presently madame came back; she saw me in her bed and began to scream. Then she went for her tenants and consulted with them; they told her she must make me some warm wine with plenty of sugar in it, put on the pot to make me a good broth, and cover me up well, for I had a terrible chill. These wicked creatures enjoyed themselves at the expense of the miserly woman. That night they came up to see me, and the lady spent the night on her lounge. The next day madame returned my fifteen sous, and I was escorted to other quarters. The neighbors were delighted with the joke I had played.

We went to Claye, and from Claye to the Porte St. Denis, where the people of Paris were waiting for us; they had made us a triumphal arch. We found, in the Champs-Élysées, tents prepared, with tables served with cold meats and sealed wines. But as ill-luck would have it, the rain fell in such torrents that the plates were filled with water. We could not eat, but we drew the corks from the bottles and drank standing. It was a pitiful sight to see us; we were as wet as ducks.

Three battalions of us set out for Courbevoie; one remained on duty. The Emperor gave us some rest, and we received new uniforms. We had splendid reviews; the good city of Paris gave us a magnificent dinner under the galleries of the Place Royale; nothing was wanting; and that night we went free to a comedy at the Porte St. Martin. There was a representation of the Passage of Mount St. Bernard, and we could see the good monks descending the mountain with their big dogs following them. As I looked at those good Capuchins and their dogs, I could almost believe that I was dragging my cannon along. I clapped my hands and stamped my feet. My comrades said to me, "Are you crazy?" I answered, "You see, I saw them on Mount St. Bernard, those splendid dogs; and those are the very same monks."

The roll was not called till two o'clock in the morning; no one was punished, and all our little shortcomings were pardoned.

FIFTH NOTE-BOOK.

PRUSSIAN AND POLISH CAMPAIGNS. — CONFERENCE AT TILSIT. — I AM MADE CORPORAL. — SPANISH AND AUSTRIAN CAMPAIGNS. — I AM APPOINTED SERGEANT.

The allied princes came to pay their court to Napoleon, and he entertained them with splendid reviews. We mounted guard at the princes' hotels, who all gave us something, more or less. Among the great officials M. Cambacérès was the least generous; he never gave more than a half-bottle to the sentinel who was stationed at his door. Consequently we made a wry face when it was our turn to go to his house.

We were overwhelmed with duty; eight hours of guard and two hours of patrol duty, that made ten hours each night, and picket duty at the barracks for twenty-four hours, without taking off our clothes. We were obliged to be out at the first sound of the roll-call to answer, "Here." Each day the guard going on duty had twenty-four hours' picket duty. Then there were grand drills which kept us all day long in the plain of the Sablons and at the Tuileries.

The Emperor ordered up a great deal of artillery, wagons

and caissons; he had them opened, so as to assure himself that nothing was wanting. He got up on the wheels to see that nothing had been forgotten, especially the medicine-chest, the shovels, and pickaxes. He had a strict inspection. M. Larrey was responsible for the medicine-chest, and the engineering officers for the shovels and pickaxes. He dealt severely with them if all was not as it should be. He was at the same time the kindest and the severest man; we all feared him and we all loved him.

An order was given to examine the condition of our linen and shoes, and to inspect our arms for another campaign. The Emperor reviewed us, and we were ordered to hold ourselves in readiness to march. Our officers told us that we were to start for a conference, at which the Emperor of Russia and the King of Prussia were to be present. But when we reached the frontiers of Prussia, an order was read to us informing us that war had been declared against Prussia and Russia.

Very early in the year 1806 we set out for Würzburg, where the Emperor was awaiting us. This is a beautiful city, and there is a magnificent castle; the princes gave Napoleon a grand reception. From there the army corps were sent on to Jena, by forced marches; we reached that city the 13th of October, at ten o'clock in the evening. We passed through the town without being able to see anything of it; there was not a light anywhere; the inhabitants had all deserted it. Absolute silence reigned. On the other side of the city we found ourselves at the foot of a mountain as steep as the roof of a house; this we had to climb, and immediately form battalions on the table-land. We were obliged to grope our way along the edge of the precipice; not one of us could see the other. It was necessary to keep perfect silence, for the enemy was near us. We immediately formed a square, with the Emperor in the middle of the guard. Our artillery came to the foot of this terrible mountain, and not being able to pass over it, the road had to be enlarged and the rocks cut away. The Emperor was there, directing the engineers; he did not leave till the road was finished, and the first piece of cannon, drawn by twelve horses, had passed on in front of him, in absolute silence.

Four pieces at a time were carried up and immediately placed in battery in front of our line. Then the same horses went back to the foot of the mountain to be hitched to others. A good part of the night was employed in this terrible task, and the enemy did not perceive us. The Emperor placed himself in the middle of his square, and allowed them to kindle two or three fires for each company. There were a hundred and twenty of us in each company. Twenty from each company were sent off in search of provisions. We did not have far to go, for from the eminence we could throw a stone into the village. All the houses were deserted, the wretched inhabitants had abandoned their homes. We found everything we needed, especially wine and sugar. We had our officers along to keep order, and in three-quarters of an hour we were on our way back up the mountain, loaded with wine, sugar, copper boilers, and all sorts of provisions. We carried torches to give us light in the cellars, and we found a great deal of sealed wine in the large hotels.

Wood was brought and fires lighted, and wine and sugar put into the boilers. We drank to the health of the King of Prussia all night long, and all the sealed wine was divided among us. There was the greatest quantity of it; each grenadier had three bottles, two in his bear-skin cap, and one in his pocket. All night long we had warm wine; we carried some to our brave gunners, who were half dead with fatigue, and they were very thankful for it. Their officers were invited to come and drink the warm wine with ours; our mustaches were thoroughly wetted, but we were forbidden to make any noise. Imagine what a punishment it was not to be able to speak or sing! Every one of us had something witty ready to say.

Seeing us all so happy, put the Emperor in good spirits. He mounted his horse before day and went on his rounds. The darkness was so profound that he was obliged to have a light in order to see his way, and the Prussians, seeing this light moving along their lines, fired on Napoleon. But he went on his way, and returned to his headquarters to order the men to arms.

Day had scarcely broken when the Prussians greeted us (October the 14th) with cannon shots, which passed over our heads. An old Egyptian soldier said, "The Prussians have bad colds, hear them cough. We must take them some sweetened wine." The whole army now moved forward without being able to see one step ahead of them. We were obliged to feel our way like blind men, constantly falling up against each other. At the sound of the movement which was going on in front of us, it was considered necessary to call a halt and commence the attack. Our brave Lannes opened on our left; this was the signal for the whole line, and we could only see each other by the light of our firing. The Emperor ordered us to advance rapidly on their centre. He was obliged to order us first to moderate our pace and finally to halt. Their line had been pierced, as was that of the Russians at Austerlitz. The accursed fog was a great drawback to us, but our columns continued to advance, and we had room to look around. About ten o'clock the sun came out and lighted up the beautiful plateau. Then we could see in front of us. On our right we saw a handsome carriage drawn by white horses; we were told that in it was the Queen of Prussia, who was trying to escape. Napoleon ordered us to halt for an hour, and we heard a terrible firing on our left. The Emperor immediately sent an officer to learn what was going on; he seemed angry, and took snuff frequently as he stamped up and down in front of us. The officer returned and said, "Sire, it is Marshal Ney who is fighting desperately, with his grenadiers and his light-horsemen, against a body of cavalry." He immediately sent forward his cavalry, and the whole army advanced. Lannes and Ney were victorious on the left; the Emperor joined them and recovered his good humor.

Prince Murat came up with his dragoons and his cuirassiers; his horses' tongues were hanging out of their mouths. They brought with them a whole division of Saxons, and it was pitiful to see them, for more than half of these unfortunate fellows were streaming with blood. The Emperor reviewed them, and we gave them all our wine, particularly to the wounded, and also to our brave cuirassiers and dragoons.

We had at least a thousand bottles of sealed wine still left, and we saved their lives. The Emperor gave them their choice, either to remain with us or to be prisoners, telling them that he was not at war with their sovereign.

After winning this battle, the Emperor left us at Jena; he went on to see the corps of Davout and Bernadotte. On our right we could hear distant cannonading, and the Emperor sent an order for us to hold ourselves in readiness to march. We spent the night in that poor deserted town. The Emperor returned; we gathered up our wounded and carried them on to Weimar, which is a lovely town.

We had a hard fight with a large body of cavalry, at the assault of Hassenhausen; but Prince Murat gained the victory over them. We marched upon Erfurt, without being able to catch up with the army corps of Davout and Bernadotte, who carried off all the baggage wagons and cannons of the Prussians. We lost heavily.

On the 25th we reached Potsdam; we spent the 26th and 27th at Charlottenburg, the splendid palace of the King of Prussia, which is opposite Berlin. The country here is covered with woods up to the very entrance-gate to this beautiful city; nothing can be more beautiful than it is. The gateway is surmounted by a triumphal arch, and the streets are straight as a line. From the Charlottenburg gate to the palace, there is a broad walk, with benches on each side for those who wish to look on. The Emperor made his entrance on the 28th, at the head of twenty thousand grenadiers and cuirassiers, and all our splendid foot and horse-guards. The uniform was as magnificent as at the Tuileries; the Emperor moved proudly along in his plain dress, with his small hat and his one-sou cockade. His staff was in full uniform, and it was a curious sight to see the worst-dressed man the master of such a splendid army.

The people were gazing out of the windows as the Parisians did on the day we came back from Austerlitz. It was grand to see this great populace crowding the streets to see us, and following us wherever we went.

We drew up in line of battle in front of the palace, which

is isolated by beautiful squares in front and at the back of it, and a handsome square filled with trees, where the great Frederick stands on a pedestal with his little gaiters on.

We were lodged in private houses and fed at the expense of the inhabitants, with orders to give us a bottle of wine every day. This was hard upon the citizens, for the wine costs three francs a bottle. Not being able to procure wine, they begged us to take instead, beer, in little jugs. At roll-call, all the grenadiers spoke about it to their officers, who told us not to force them to give us wine, as the beer was excellent. This was a great comfort to all the people in the town, and the beer in jugs was unsparingly bestowed. It would be impossible to find better beer. Peace and good-will were universal; we could not have been more comfortable; all the citizens came with their servants to bring us our well-served meals. The discipline was strict; Count Hulin was governor of Berlin, and the service was severe.

The Emperor reviewed his guard in front of the palace; he stood near some fine linden-trees, near the statue of Frederick the Great. Behind the statue are three rows of stones, five feet high, joined together by bars of iron. We were in line of battle in front of the palace; the Emperor came up, ordered us to carry arms, and cross bayonets; our colonel repeated the command. He ordered, "Wheel about." The colonel repeated it. Then, "Forward, double quick, march." We halted in front of the five-foot stones. The Emperor seeing us stop, said, "Why do you not march on?" The colonel answered, "We cannot pass." — "What is your name?" — "Frédéric." The Emperor said, in a severe tone, "Poor Frédéric! Order them to 'Forward.'" And there we went, leaping over the stones and the bars of iron. It was a sight to see us go over.

The corps of Marshal Davout was the first to enter Berlin; and then marched on to the frontier of Poland. We learned, before leaving, that Magdeburg had surrendered. The Emperor settled matters with the authorities at Berlin, and we set out to rejoin the corps, which was marching on Poland. When we reached Posen, we rested there some time. Our corps marched without intermission to Warsaw. The Russians were good enough to give those two beautiful cities up to us; but they were not so generous about provisions; they ravaged the whole country, and carried off everything to the other side, leaving only what they could not take away. They even blew up all the bridges, and carried off all the boats. The Emperor showed some ill-temper. Once before, at Posen, I saw him, when he was angry, jump on his horse so violently that he flew over to the other side, and give his equerry a cut with his whip.

We were ordered into position before reaching Warsaw. We saw the Russians on the opposite side of the river, on a

height overlooking the road. Five hundred swimmers were detailed, and made to swim across with their cartridge-boxes and guns on their heads; they fell upon the Russians at midnight, as they were sleeping beside their fires. We seized upon their position, and made ourselves master of the right shore of the river; but we were still without boats. Marshal Ney, who had accomplished wonderful things at Thorn, sent us some boats to make bridges. The Emperor was in the highest spirits, and said, "That man is a lion."

The Emperor entered Warsaw during the night. Oudinot's grenadiers and ourselves arrived next day. The kind people of this city came out to look at our splendid column of grenadiers. They made an effort to receive us kindly. The Russians had carried off everything. We had to buy grain and beeves to feed the army, and the Jews made good contracts with Napoleon. Provisions came in to us from all sides, and biscuits were made for us. It must be said that the Jews saved the army as well as made their own fortunes.

When the Emperor was in condition to recommence the campaign, and his troops had been supplied with provisions, he had splendid reviews. The last of them took place in the midst of the most intense cold. During one of these reviews, a handsome carriage drove up, and a small man got out, and presented himself to the Emperor, in front of the guard. He was a hundred and seventeen years old, and walked as if he were sixty. The Emperor offered him his arm: "Thank you, sire," said he. He was said to be the oldest man in Poland.[1]

The ice being considered in proper condition, a distribution of rations of biscuits for fourteen days was made to us. I bought a ham for twenty francs, and did not eat a pound of it; nothing could be had for love or money. It was December, the beginning of a most terrible winter, in a deserted country, covered with woods, and with roads heavy with sand. We found no inhabitants in the wretched villages; the Russians fell back before us, and we found their camps deserted. We had to march all night, and at midnight we came to a castle. Not knowing where we were, we put down our knapsacks under some walnut-trees, in a camping-ground deserted by the Russians. As I put my knapsack on the ground, I felt a small pile of something. I felt about in the straw. My God, what joy! there were two loaves of bread of about three pounds each. I knelt down, and opened my knapsack, took one of my loaves, and put it in. The other, I broke into pieces. It was so dark that no one saw me. "What are you doing?" said Captain Renard. Taking hold of his hand, I put into it a piece of bread, saying, "Keep silence, watch my knapsack, and eat; I am going for some wood."

I started off with four of my messmates, and we found a piece of cannon mounted in front of the castle. We dis-

---

[1] We have found confirmation of this singular fact. The good man was named Naroçki, and he pretended to have been born in 1690. But his great age was only a pretence in order to obtain a pension.

mounted the piece, and carried off the wheels and the carriage. When we got back to our captain with these tremendous pieces of wood, we made a fire big enough to last all night. What a good night we had! My captain and I hid ourselves so we could eat our bread. I said to him. " I have another loaf in my knapsack; you shall have your share to-morrow evening."

The next day we started off again to the right, through the woods and the sands. The weather was terrible: snow, rain, and thaw. The sand gave way under our feet, and the water splashed up over the sinking sand. We sunk down up to our knees. We were obliged to take ropes. and tie our shoes around our ankles, and when we pulled our legs out of this soft sand, the ropes would break, and our shoes would stick in the wet mud. Sometimes we would have to take hold of one leg, and pull it out as you would a carrot, carrying it forward, and then go back for the other, take hold of it with both hands, and make it take a step forward also; our guns, meantime, hanging in our shoulder-belts, so as to leave our hands free. And so we had to go on for two whole days.

Discontent began to spring up among the old soldiers; some of them committed suicide in their moments of great suffering. We lost about sixty of them in the two days previous to our arrival at Pultusk, a miserable thatched village. The hut in which the Emperor had his quarters was not worth a thousand francs. Here we came to the end of our misery, for it was impossible to go any further.

We camped in front of this poor little village, called Pultusk. In order to prepare for our bivouac. we went in search of some straw to put under our feet. Not finding any, we took some sheaves of wheat, and used that to keep us off the ground; so the barns were pillaged. I made several trips. I brought back a trough which the horse-grenadiers had not been able to carry off; they put it on my back, and I reached the camp, thus shaming my comrades, who were colossal creatures compared to me. But God had given me legs as fine as those of an Arab horse. I returned again to the village, and brought a small pot, two eggs, and some wood; but I was half dead with fatigue.

No man could give any idea of our wretched suffering. All our artillery was sunk in the mire; the pieces dragged along the ground. The Emperor's carriage, with him inside, could not be drawn out. We were obliged to lead a horse up to the door of the carriage, so he could get over this terrible place, and go on to Pultusk. And here he saw the desolation among the ranks of his old soldiers, some of whom had blown their brains out. It was here that he gave us the name of "grumblers," a name which clung to us, and which honors us to this day.

But to return to my two eggs. I put them into my little pot, in front of the fire. Colonel Frédéric, who commanded us, came towards my fire, for I, who had been bravest in the cold, had been the first to make a good fire. Seeing such a nice fire, he came to my bivouac, and looking at the little pot in front of it, he said, "Is your little stew boiling nicely?" — " Yes, colonel." — " All right, I will stay by your fire."

I went for some sheaves of wheat, and gave him two to sit on. Then I took out my two eggs, and gave him one of them. As he took it, he gave me a napoleon, saying, "If you do not take these twenty francs, I will not eat your egg; it is worth that to-day." I was obliged to take twenty francs for an egg.

The horse-grenadiers occupied the village of Pultusk; they found an enormous hog, and chased it into our camp. As it was passing by our bivouac, I rushed upon this good game, sabre in hand. Colonel Frédéric, who had a loud voice, shouted to me, "Cut his hams." I rushed forward, caught up with him, and cut his hams, and then passed my sabre across his throat. The colonel and his grenadiers came up, and it was decided that as I had captured him, a quarter and the two kidneys belonged to me. I at once went up to the Emperor's house to get some salt. I found my lieutenant on duty, and asked him for some salt and a pot for the colonel, adding that I had captured a big hog, which the horse-grenadiers were chasing. "It is the house hog," said he. "The Emperor was furious; they have deprived him of his stew. Fortunately, however, his canteens have just arrived, so he is in a good humor again; but his stomach was empty as well as ours." — "Lieutenant, I will bring you a broiled ham in an hour." — "All right, my good fellow, go cook it quickly."

When I got back, I found the colonel waiting for me. "Here is some salt and a big saucepan." — "We are saved," said he. — "But, colonel, it was the hog from the Emperor's quarters; we have deprived him of his stew." — "Is it possible?" — "It is, indeed."

The grenadiers and chasseurs went off on a marauding party

to look for provisions for the next day. They came back in the evening with some potatoes, which were distributed to us. When divided out to each mess, there were twenty potatoes for every eighteen men. It was pitiful. Only one potato for each man. The colonel and Captain Renard were well warmed, and each ate a kidney. We divided everything with one another. The colonel took me aside, and asked me if I could read and write. I answered that I could not. "What a pity! I would have made you a corporal." — "Thank you."

The Emperor sent for Count Dorsenne, and said to him, "You are to set out with my foot-guard, and enter Warsaw.

Here is the chart. Do not follow the same road: you will lose my old grumblers. Make me a report of the missing. Here is your route to Warsaw."

Next day we started, going through by-ways, from one forest to another. When we halted, about three miles from Warsaw, we were in a perfect state of starvation; hollow-eyed, sunken-cheeked, and unshaved. We looked like dead men risen from the tomb. General Dorsenne formed a circle round him, and reproached us severely, saying that the Emperor was displeased not to see more courage under hardships which he was sharing with us. "He will treat you," he says, "as grumblers ought to be treated." We shouted, "Hurrah for the general!"

The inhabitants of Warsaw received us with open arms, January 1, 1807: the people could not do too much for us, and the Emperor allowed us to rest in this beautiful city. But this short campaign of fourteen days had aged us ten years.

After having stayed some time at Warsaw, we were sent forward among some miserable villages. The inhabitants had carried off all their provisions, and led their animals into the forests, a great way off from the villages. Like hungry wolves, driven from the forests by famine, twelve of our men, well armed, started out to scour the forests, a league from the village, through snow a foot deep. When we reached the forest, we spied the footsteps of a man; we followed them, and came to a camp of peasants, on the other side of the mountain. All their animals were tied there, and pots were on the fire; they were frightened, and dared not fire on us. They had horses, cows, and sheep. We untied them all, and took some flour and a very small quantity of bread. We returned to our village with two hundred and eight beasts, and a division of them was made: half for us and half for the peasants. We left them all their horses, except four, which we kept to ride from one village to the other; and four peasants, whom we wished to serve us as guides. These were the conditions upon which we divided our spoils, and the unfortunate peasants went off with their portion. We made some bread immediately; it had been so long since we had eaten any, that as soon as it was out of the oven, my comrades ate enough to kill them. Two died; we could not save them. We found some potatoes, six feet down in the ground, under the brick paving of one of the rooms in our house; this saved our lives.

We had but little to thank the Poles for; they had all run away. All their villages were deserted; they would have allowed a soldier to die at their doors without giving him any aid. The Germans never left their houses; they are the personification of humanity. I have seen a postmaster killed in his house by a Frenchman, and yet his house turned into a hospital. The master was lying dead on his bed, and yet his wife and daughter were looking for linen to dress the wounds of our men. They said, "It is the will of God." This trait of character is sublime.

In the early days of January, we received orders to hold ourselves in readiness to march. The Russians had made a movement upon Warsaw. What glad news for the starving soldiers! Now we should cease to be hungry. General Dorsenne received orders to break up the encampment, and start on the 30th of January. The Emperor also started the same day, so as to keep ahead of us. We did not catch up with him till the 2d of February, when he immediately went on. We started again on the 3d, following him. We were told that we were marching upon Eylau, and that the Russians had gone to the city of Koenigsberg for the purpose of embarking; but they were waiting for us in a position in front of Eylau, which cost us very dear. We carried the woods and the heights, and pursued them closely; they took the road which led to Eylau, to the right over the hill-top, and there fought with desperation. They, however, finally lost their position. Prince Murat and Marshal Ney pursued them into Eylau, where they rushed pell-mell through the streets. The town was occupied by our troops, in spite of the efforts made to recapture it.

On the 7th of February the Emperor ordered us to camp on an eminence in front of Eylau. This mountain was in the form of a sugar-loaf, and very steep; it had been occupied a day or two before by our troops, for we found a number of the dead bodies of the Russians scattered here and there over the snow; and some dying ones, who made signs to us that they wished to be finished. We were obliged to clear away the snow so as to set up our tents. We dragged the dead bodies to the other side of the mountain, and carried the wounded to a house quite at the foot of it. Unfortunately night came on, and some of the soldiers were so cold that they took it into their heads to pull down the house to get wood to warm themselves. The poor wounded fellows were vic-

tims of this deed of desperation. They perished under the rubbish.

The Emperor ordered us to light his fire in the midst of our battalions, and asked that each mess should give him a log of wood and a potato. We brought him a score of potatoes, some wood, and some bundles of straw. We used for wood the rails which had formed the summer pens for the cattle. He seated himself in the midst of his "old grumblers," on a bundle of straw, his stick in his hand. We saw him turn over his potatoes, and divide them with his aides-de-camp.

From our bivouac I could see the Emperor distinctly, and he saw all our movements. By the light of the pine logs I shaved those of my comrades who needed it most. They each sat down on the rump of a dead horse, which had been there long enough for the intense cold to freeze it as hard as a stone. I had in my knapsack a towel, which I passed around their necks, and I had also some soap, which I mixed with snow melted over the fire. I daubed it over them with my hand, and then performed the operation. Perched on the top of his bundles of straw, the Emperor watched this strange spectacle, and burst into peals of laughter. I shaved at least a score of them that night.

Early in the morning, on the 8th of February, the Russians greeted us with volleys from their cannon. We sprang to our feet. The Emperor mounted, and marched us forward on the lake with our artillery and all the cavalry of his guard. The thunderbolt caught us on the frozen lake. There were twenty-two siege pieces brought from Koenigsberg firing upon us. The shells passed over the houses, and made great havoc in our ranks. There is no possible suffering greater than to expect to be killed without being allowed to defend one's self. Our quartermaster did a brave thing: a cannon-ball took off his leg; he cut off a small part of flesh which remained, and, saying, "I have three pairs of boots at Courbevoie. I shall have enough to last me a long time," he took two guns for crutches, and went off unassisted to the field-hospital.

Having lost heavily, the Emperor now brought us forward on the height, our left wing resting on the church. He was there himself near the church, watching the enemy. He was rash enough to go close up to the cemetery, where a fearful slaughter was kept up. This cemetery was the burial-place of a great number of French and Russians. We gained the victory here. But to the right, in front of us, the 14th of the line was cut to pieces; the Russians penetrated their square, and the carnage was terrible. The 43d of the line lost half its men.

M. Sénot, our drum-major, was behind us at the head of his drummers. Some one came to tell him that his son had been killed. He was a youth of about sixteen, and belonged really to another regiment; but, as a favor, and out of respect for his father's position, he had been permitted to serve as a volunteer in the grenadiers of the guard. "So much the worse for him," cried M. Sénot; "I told him he was too young yet to follow me." And he went on with his duty with unshaken firmness. Fortunately, the report proved false; the young man had disappeared in a file of soldiers, who were cut down by a cannon-ball, but he received no injury. I have seen him since, captain, adjutant-major in the guard.

A bullet cut off the staff of our eagle while our sergeant-major was holding it, and made a hole through and through his coat. Fortunately, he was not wounded. We shouted, "Forward! Hurrah for the Emperor!" As the peril was great, he decided to send forward the 2d regiment of grenadiers and the chasseurs, commanded by General Dorsenne. The cuirassiers had broken through the squares, and made terrible slaughter. Our grenadiers fell upon the Russian guard with their bayonets without firing a single gun, and at the same moment the Emperor charged them with two squadrons of horse grenadiers and two of chasseurs. They dashed forward with such rapidity that the grenadiers broke through all the Russian lines, and made the circuit of their whole army. They returned covered with blood, having lost some men who had been dismounted and taken prisoners. They were confined in the prison at Koenigsberg, and the next day the Emperor sent them fifty napoleons.

The ardor of the Russians was abated after these repulses, and they were not anxious to recommence the fighting. It was well, for our troops were completely exhausted, and our ranks visibly thinned. But for our guard our infantry would have been overcome. We did not lose the battle, but neither did we win it.

That evening the Emperor led us back to the position we had occupied the day before; he was delighted with his guard, and said to the general, "Dorsenne, you were not joking with my grumblers; I am very much pleased with you." What with cold and hunger, we passed a wretched night. The battlefield was covered with the dead and wounded; their cries were blended into one great shriek. One can convey no idea of that terrible day. The next day was employed in digging ditches to bury the dead, and in carrying the wounded to the field-hospitals. About noon some casks of brandy, which the Jews brought from Warsaw, arrived, escorted by a company of grenadiers. The order was given that each man should have his turn : a cask was turned up on end, and the head knocked in. Two grenadiers held the money bag; four at a time came up, and each dropped in six francs; then dipped a certain sized glass into the cask, and were forbidden to dip in a second time. Then four others came up, and so on. The four casks saved the army, and the Jews made their fortune. They were escorted to Warsaw by a company of grenadiers, who were paid three francs a day.

A truce was agreed upon. It was found impossible to continue fighting; the army had suffered too much. The Emperor ordered us to move our camps; but before departing, we carried off the sick and wounded on sleds, and also the pieces of cannon taken from the enemy and the prisoners.

On the 17th of February we set out for Thorn and Marienburg, where we found better camping grounds. It was time we should, for we had not changed our clothes for a month.

We came to a large deserted village, called Osterode. It was a poverty-stricken place; but we did find a few potatoes. The Emperor took up his quarters in a barn, but finally found more comfortable lodgings; he was always in our midst, and often lived on food that was given him by his soldiers. But for the soldiers the poor officers would have died of hunger. The inhabitants had buried everything underground in the forests and in their houses. After much searching, we discovered their hiding-places. By sounding with the butt ends of our guns we found provisions of all sorts : rice, bacon, wheat, flour, and hams. Our officers were immediately informed of this, and they had the different articles dug up, and placed in the storehouse. Our dear Emperor did everything he could to procure provisions for us; but they did not come, and we were often without rations. So we had to go out, in all that terrible weather, in search of food. "Come, let us start out to-morrow," said I one day. "Let a score of us, well armed,

scour the great pine forests, where they say we shall find fallow-deer and stags. The snow will be an assistance to us in finding the game. We must start at daybreak, and say nothing about it to any one; our sergeant will set it all right."
— "We are agreed," said they; "our little brave fellow wants to eat some venison. Come, let us be off."

With our guns well loaded, we plunged into the forest. A herd of deer passed us about two hundred feet away, and then a great many hares; but we missed them every time we fired. I saw a hare go leaping by, not very far off, and as he went into some small pine-trees about five feet high, which grew thick, near by, I bent some of them over to see if I could find his burrow. To my astonishment one of the pines came up out of the ground. I took hold of another; it came up also. I tried another with the same result, and then I shouted to my comrades, "This way! this way! I have some good news for you. These pines are not growing here." — "What do you mean?" they answered. "Come here and see."

Feeling sure that it was a large hiding-place, we began to sound; but the ramrods were not long enough and the place was a hundred feet square. We were so glad! I said, "My hare was the cause of our wind-fall; we must mark the place. There is no road to it; how could they have accomplished it? The wretches must have brought the things on their backs. Let us now get our bearings, and mark the pine-trees, so that we can find our way back to-morrow."

We went to work and cut off pieces of the bark from the pine-trees on the right and left. Being always on the lookout, I saw a plank nailed upon a large pine, and then another twenty-five feet higher. Of course we had to find out what this meant, so we cut down some pine-trees, and cut notches in the branches to make a ladder. When we reached the box, we took out the peg which held up the plank, which was five or six feet high, and found salt meats, stuffed tongues, geese, hams, bacon, and honey; and afterwards, we found two hundred boxes filled with all sorts of things, among them a great many shirts. We carried off the shirts, some of the stuffed tongues, and geese. After marking our road, my comrades said, "Our ferret has a good nose." It was late when we returned to the camp, loaded down, but glad at heart. The sergeant-major immediately informed the officers of our good fortune. The captain came to see us. "Here is our ferret," said my comrades; "it was he who found it all." — "Yes, captain, a hiding-place a hundred feet long, and so deep underground that we could not sound it with our ramrods. Here is some ham, bacon, and goose; take some. To-morrow we will set out with wagons, shovels, and pickaxes, and a good many men and ammunition, for we must sleep all night in the woods." — "Two lieutenants shall go with fifty men," said our captain. "You will also need some knapsacks and some axes. The lieutenant shall take my horse and a bundle of hay; if you are obliged to stay all night, he can return to give us news of you."

We started off with our officers and all the knapsacks belonging to our mess. We reached the place, and, after a great deal of hard labor, dug down into the hiding-place. What treasures we found there! It took us twenty-four hours to empty the cave. It was good to see our happy faces. There was a large quantity of wheat, flour, rice, and bacon; chests full of linen shirts, and salt meats of every kind. They had replanted the pines, and replaced the moss. One had to go on a hare hunt to discover the treasure.

The lieutenant returned to make his report and send us wagons, and some men from other companies. This hole held twenty-five four-horse wagon loads. We had to make a road to get to it. How rejoiced all our grumblers were when they saw the wagons coming! their faces sparkled. "This is not all," said I; "we have yet to take the hives we found up in the trees, and look around up in the big pines for boxes." Our search was well rewarded: we found more than a hundred boxes filled with salt meats, linen, and honey. We all climbed up, and filled our knapsacks.

On our return with all these provisions, we made a big fire to cook hams, and regale ourselves, at the expense of the Poles, who wanted to starve us, for in our winter quarters we had passed fifty days without tasting bread. They had all left their houses. If any remained, it was to watch over their hiding-places. When we asked them for food, they always refused. They are a people destitute of human feeling; they are willing that men should starve at their doors. Hurrah for the Germans, who are always resigned to fate, and never desert their homes!

On our return to the camp, I was triumphantly received by the whole regiment. Rice was distributed to the grenadiers, and the wheat was ground up to make bread. This discovery led to further searching; taking soundings became our sport. All the barns were ransacked, and the pavements of the houses and barns taken up. There were hiding-places everywhere, and provisions in every place. The Russians were starving, too, and they came to beg some potatoes from our soldiers. They no longer thought of fighting, and left us undisturbed in our quarters. This terrible winter was the cause of great suffering to us.

Seeing a peasant go every morning and look over his garden, I watched him, and went there and sounded. I came to something which seemed soft, and I went to inform my comrades of it. We set to work at once, and discovered the bodies of two cows, which were entirely decayed. The smell was terrible. But under this carrion there were big casks filled with rice, bacon, ham, and all the utensils of the village: saws, axes, shovels, and pick-axes; in short, everything we needed; and also some preserves made of grapes and pears, for our dessert. I jumped for joy at having persisted in removing the carrion (it was a sickening task). We did not tell our officers about this hiding-place, and we got out of it fifteen hundred pounds of rice and quantities of bacon.

Finding that the snows were beginning to melt, the Emperor sent for his engineers to come and lay out a camp, in a fine position in front of Finkenstein. The lines were marked off in the form of a square. In the middle there was a place for a palace, which was to be built of brick. When the plan was made out, we went to look for planks to make our barracks. In this country the gardens are enclosed with big posts and pine planks twenty feet long and a foot wide. We set to work to pull these planks off the posts. We sent off twenty wagons loaded with it, and they returned for more. For three leagues around all the enclosures were torn down. In a fortnight our barracks were completed, and the Emperor's palace was almost done. A finer encampment could not possibly have been found. The streets were named after the battles won since the beginning of the war. Our officers were comfortably lodged, and the whole army was camped in fine positions. The Emperor went

around, and was present at the drills. He sent to Dantzig for brandy and provisions, and for wine for his staff. All the soldiers looked happy. He came often to see us eat our soup, and would say, "Do not let me disturb you; I am much pleased with my grumblers; they have furnished me with excellent lodgings, and my officers have rooms with plank floors. The Poles can make a town of it." As we found some pieces of cloth in the hiding-places, we made some pantaloons, and great bags, six feet long, to sleep in. The Poles came with some beautiful ladies, in carriages, to see our plank city.

We passed the month of May trotting around, all fresh and be-powdered, as when at Paris. But on the 5th of June, our brave Marshal Ney was attacked and pursued by a strong force of the Russians. A courier arrived, bringing the news of it to the Emperor. The camp was at once broken up, and we got ready to start. At six o'clock on the morning of the 6th we set out to join the army. We arrived at our destination the next day, and were immediately placed in line of battle with our artillery. We were near Eylau; we were sent to the right and forward to meet the Russians in the lonely plain of Friedland, at the ford of a river. They were awaiting us in a fine position: they had many redoubts on the heights and bridges behind them.

The brave Marshal Lannes came up from Warsaw, greatly disgusted with the Poles. In a discussion with the Emperor, in front of the grenadiers, we heard him say to him. "The blood of one Frenchman is worth all Poland." The Emperor answered, "If you are not satisfied, go away." — "No," replied Lannes, "you (*tu*) need me."

This great warrior was the only one who dared say "thou" (*tu*) to the Emperor. Pressing his hand, the latter said, "Set off at once with Oudinot's grenadiers, your own corps and the cavalry. March upon Friedland. I will send Marshal Ney to you."

These two great soldiers found themselves opposed by forces more than double as strong as their own. They held out till noon. The grenadiers, light-horsemen, and cavalry held the enemy in check till we came up; but it was all they could do. The Emperor went galloping by all the troops who were marching up. As he went through a wood where Oudinot's wounded men were passing, they called out to him, "Hurry to the aid of our comrades. The Russians have the upper hand just now." The Emperor, finding the Russians near a river, wanted to cut their bridges. He gave this task to the intrepid Ney, who went off at a gallop. All the troops came up. The Emperor ordered an hour for rest, visited the lines, came galloping back to his guard, changed his horse, and gave the signal to attack the Russians from all points. The Russians fought like lions; they preferred to be drowned rather than to surrender.

After this memorable day's fight, which was kept up late by the light of the burning of Friedland and some of the neighboring villages, the fighting ceased, and they took advantage of the night to beat a retreat upon Tilsit. Our Emperor slept on the battle-field, as usual, so as to see that the wounded were cared for, and the next day he pursued the Russians to the Niemen. Our soldiers could only catch up with the rearguard, the stragglers; they captured some savages named Kalmucks, fellows with big noses, flat faces, large ears, and quivers full of arrows. There were eighteen hundred cavalrymen of them; but our *gilets de fer* fell upon them, and hunted them down like sheep. They were commanded by Russian commissioned and non-commissioned officers. We got permission to go to their camp to see these savages. Rations of meat were distributed to them, and they devoured it instantly. On the 19th of June, our troops found themselves in front of the Russians, who had crossed the Niemen, and destroyed all the bridges. The river is not wide at this place; it runs across the foot of a beautiful broad street, which passes through Tilsit, and is closed at one end by a sort of barrack, where the Russian guard is lodged when in the service of the sovereign. His own camp was at the end of a lake, to the right of the city. The Emperor reached the Niemen with his cavalry. The Russians were on the opposite shore, without bread. We were obliged to send them provisions at a distance of six or seven leagues. At last an envoy of the Emperor of Russia came across the river to hold a parley. He was presented to Prince Murat, and then to Napoleon, who gave him an immediate answer, for he sent us an order to hold ourselves in readiness for the next day. Next day a Russian prince came over, and orders were issued that we should be under arms to receive the Emperor of Russia in front of the whole army in full uniform. We were told that a raft was to be built upon the river, and that the two Emperors were to hold a conference, and make peace. God only knows how glad we were to hear this! We acted like crazy people.

The officers inspected us carefully, to be sure that nothing was wanting in our dress; our queues were well tied up and powdered, our shoulder-belts clean and white. No absences were permitted. When all was ready, we were ordered to be under arms at eleven o'clock, so as to go down to the river. There was awaiting us there the most splendid sight that will ever be seen on the Niemen. In the middle of the river there was a magnificent raft, covered with large pieces of handsome tapestry, and on one side of it, to the left, there was a tent. On each shore there was a beautiful barge, richly decorated, and manned by a crew from the guard. The Emperor arrived at one o'clock, and entered his barge with his staff. The Emperors left either shore at the same signal; they had each the same distance to go, the same course to take; but our Emperor was the first to reach the raft. The two great men embraced each other as if they had been brothers returning from exile; and from every side rose shouts of "Vive l'Empereur!"

The interview was prolonged, and then each withdrew to his own shore. The next day we went through the same display. This time it was to receive the King of Prussia. Fortunately, Alexander the Great was there to defend him; he looked like a victim. My God, how thin he was! He was a miserable sovereign, but he had a very beautiful queen. This interview between the three sovereigns was short, and it was agreed that our Emperor should give them board and lodging in the city. This was magnanimous, after having thrashed them well; but he bore them no malice.

The city was then divided in half, and the next day the whole guard was under arms in the beautiful street of Tilsit, three ranks deep on each side. Our Emperor went down to the bank of the river to meet the Emperor of Russia, and took with him horses to mount the Emperor and the princes. The King of Prussia was not there that day. What a fine sight it was! all those sovereigns and princes and marshals, among them the proud Murat, who rivalled the Emperor of Russia in beauty of person; and all in splendid uniform! The Emperor of Russia came in front of us, and said to Colonel Frédéric,

"You have a fine guard, colonel."—"And a good one, sire," said he to the Emperor, who answered, "I know it."

The next day he entertained them with a grand review of his guard, and the third corps, commanded by Marshal Davoust, in a plain about a league from Tilsit. The day was fine; the guard as dazzling as when at Paris, and there was no fault to be found with the marshal's corps. They all had on white pantaloons. After being reviewed by the three sovereigns, we were made to march past by division, commencing with the third corps, and after them the "grumblers." It was like a marching rampart. The Emperor of Russia, the King of Prussia, and all their generals saluted each division of the guard as it passed them.

Orders were issued that we should prepare to give an entertainment to the Russian guard. Very long and wide tents were to be put up, with the openings all on a line, and with beautiful pine-trees planted in front of them. One-half of us went with our officers to get the pine-trees, and the other half put up the tents. Eight days were given us to make our preparations, and a circuit of eight miles of country in which to procure provisions. We started off in good order, and that day the provisions were contracted for. The next day more than fifty wagons, loaded and driven by peasants, came to the camp. The peasants had conformed to this requisition with good grace, and they were sent off entirely satisfied. They thought that the carts, which were drawn by oxen, would be detained at the camp; but they were discharged immediately, and the peasants jumped for joy. At noon, on the 30th of June, our feast was spread. More beautiful tables were never seen, all decorated with *épergnes* made of turf, and filled with flowers. In the back part of each tent there were two stars with the names of the two great emperors formed of flowers, and draped with the French and Russian flags.

We marched out in corps to meet this fine guard, which was to arrive by company. We each offered an arm to one of the giants, and, as there were more of us than of them, two of us offered. They were so tall they might have used us as walking-canes. As for me, the smallest of all, I had one of

"I was obliged to look up to see his face. I looked like a little boy beside him." — Page 155.

them all to myself. I was obliged to look up to see his face. I looked like a little boy beside him. They were astonished to see us so splendidly dressed: even our cooks were all powdered, and wore white aprons to wait in. In fact, everything was in the best style.

We seated our guests at table between us, and the dinner was well served. Everybody was in the highest spirits. These famished men could not control themselves; they did not know how to show the reserve which is proper at table. Brandy was served; it was the liquor used at the entertainment. Before presenting it to them, we had to taste it, and then offer it in a tin goblet, which held a quarter of a litre. The contents of the goblet would instantly disappear. They would swallow pieces of meat as large as an egg at each mouthful. They seemed to become very uncomfortable. We made signs to them to unbutton their coats, doing the same thing ourselves. This rendered them comfortable. They had rags stuffed inside their uniforms to make them full-chested, and it was disgusting to see these rags hanging out.

Two aides-de-camp, one from our Emperor and one from the Emperor of Russia, came to tell us not to move from the tables, as the Emperors were coming to make us a visit. They soon arrived. Our Emperor motioned to us to remain seated. They walked round the table, and the Emperor of Russia said to us, "Grenadiers, your entertainment is worthy of you."

After the Emperors were gone, the Russians, who were now at their ease, began to eat again, as hard as they could. We stuffed them with meat and drink, and when they found they could not eat all that was on the table, what do you suppose they did? They poked their fingers down their throats, threw up their dinner in a pile between their legs, and began eating again with all their might. It was disgusting to see such conduct. They thus made three meals at one dinner. That evening we accompanied those who could be taken away, to their quarters, and left the rest of them in their vomit, under the table.

One of our fellows took a notion to disguise himself as a Russian, and offered to change uniforms with one of them.

The exchange was made, and they started off, arm in arm. On reaching the beautiful street of Tilsit, our fellow let go the Russian's arm. He met a Russian sergeant to whom he made no salute, and who gave him three blows over his shoulder with his cane. At this he forgot his disguise, leaped upon the sergeant, and threw him down. He would have killed him, if he had been allowed to do so, and that under the very balcony from which the two Emperors were watching the merry soldiery. This scene caused them to laugh heartily. The sergeant was left on the ground, and everybody was glad of it, especially the Russian soldiers.

When the Emperor had arranged his affairs, he made his adieux to the Emperor of Russia, and, on the 10th of July, left Tilsit for Koenigsberg, where he arrived the same day. We set out at once to join him by way of Eylau. Here we saw the graves of our brave comrades who had died for their country. Our officers ordered us to carry arms, and pass through the battle-field in solemn silence. We went on to Koenigsberg, a beautiful maritime city, and there we were lodged and fed by the inhabitants. The English, not knowing that peace had been signed, came into port with ships loaded with provisions for the Russian army. One of these ships was loaded with herrings, and the other with snuff. We concealed our troops in the houses along the harbor. As soon as the ships entered the harbor we fired on them, and they surrendered. Good Lord, what a quantity of snuff and herrings! Six packages and a dozen herrings were given to each man in the troop. The Russians who were on board the captured vessels were glad to be taken prisoners, and our Emperor sent them back to their sovereign.

At this time we received orders to plant trees along the principal street, and to sand it, to receive the Queen of Prussia, who was coming to visit our Emperor. She arrived at ten o'clock at night. Lord, how beautiful she looked with her turban on her head! It was said that she was the beautiful queen of an ugly king, but I think that she was both king and queen. The Emperor came to the bottom of the great stairway to receive her, and offered her his hand; but she could not make him yield. I had the good fortune to stand guard at the foot of the stairway that evening, so I could see her near at hand; and the next day, at noon, I was put at the same post. I had a good chance to look at her. How beautiful she was, and what a queenly bearing! At thirty-three, I would have given one of my ears to stay beside her as long as the Emperor did. This was the last time I ever went on guard as a common soldier.

General Dorsenne received orders to distribute to us the shoes and shirts which were in the Russian and Prussian storehouses, and have us inspected. The Emperor was to review his guard before leaving. All was in commotion. We found everything as it should be in that beautiful city. Its cleanliness was unrivalled. French ladies should go there, if they want to see dazzling apartments: shovels, tongs, doorways, balconies, everything was shining. There were spittoons in all the corners of the rooms, and the linen was as white as snow. It was a perfect model of neatness. After the shoes and linen had been distributed, the general ordered his captains to inspect their companies. The review was to take place on the square at eleven o'clock.

Captain Renard went to see the adjutant-major, M. Belcourt, to talk with him about me. They sent for me to tell me that I was to be made corporal in my company, as they wished to reward me. "But," said I, "I do not know how to read or write."—"You shall learn."—"Ah! I thank you; but that is impossible."—"You shall be corporal to-day, and if the general asks you if you can read and write, you must answer, 'Yes, general,' and I will undertake to have you taught. I have some well-educated young soldiers, who will be very glad to teach you." I was very much ashamed to have to learn to read and write at the age of thirty-three, and I cursed my father for having abandoned me.

Finally, at noon, M. Belcourt and my captain went up to the general, and had a talk with him. "Order him out of the ranks." He eyed me from head to foot, and, seeing my cross, he asked me. "When were you decorated?"—"Among the first. I was at the Invalides."—"The first one, were you?"

said he. "Yes, general." — "Have him made corporal at once." I felt relieved, for I was trembling in presence of this man, so strict and so just. The whole company was surprised at seeing me appointed corporal in my own company; no one had suspected it. All the corporals came around me, and said kindly, "Never mind; we will show you how to write." As soon as I reached my lodging, I went immediately to see my sergeant-major, who took me by the hand, saying, "Let us go at once to see the captain."

He received me cordially, and said that he should give me a mess of nineteen men, and put into it seven of the most negligent but best educated recruits. "He will train them," said he to the sergeant-major, "and they will show him how to read and write. I give you charge of this good work. He deserves it, for he saved our lives; we always found something to eat at his bivouac." I went to see M. Belcourt, who remembered the eagerness with which I had returned to him his lost watch. Seeing him one day galloping about in the rear, I said to him, "Where are you going so fast, major? You have lost your watch; there it is." — "That was one of the kindnesses one does not easily forget," said M. Belcourt. "Go on; do your duty; you will not be left behind." Lord, how pleased I was with that reception!

I now found myself the head of a mess of twelve "grumblers" and seven well-educated recruits. The sergeant-major had told them what to do, for they started out at once for the bookseller to buy paper, pens, ruler, pencil, and an old Testament. I was surprised to find that I was to have seven teachers. "See here," said they; "these are what we are going to work with." — "I," said the one whose name was Galot, "am going to set your copies." — "And I," said he whose name was Gobin, "will teach you to read." — "We will all teach him to read by turns," said they all. "All right, I thank you all," said I; "I will repay you by taking care of your uniforms, which need putting in order."

But this was not all. The seven corporals of the company came and brought me two pairs of straps, and the tailor to sew them on. "Come," said they, "take off your coat.

These straps belonged to two of our comrades, who died on the field of honor." — "Indeed," said I to them, "you take too much trouble on my account; we must christen them." — "No," they replied; "there are too many of us." — "No matter; we will take a cup of coffee and a little glass of something. But I beg you will allow me to invite my teachers and the tailor who sewed on my chevrons to join us." — "All right," said they, "we will go." So I started off with my fifteen men for the café. I seated them at a table, and went

to find the host, and said to him, "I shall pay the bill for all, you understand." — "All right," said he. "Be sure to let us have some French brandy." — "You shall have some." I was twelve francs out of pocket, and we left the café well pleased.

I said my lessons regularly, like a child, beginning by making crooked marks, and learning verses in the Testament, and reciting them to my teacher. But we had to pass the final review, and the next day, July 13, we started for Berlin in high spirits. The people of Berlin came out to meet us; they knew that peace had been made. We could not have been more kindly received: we were comfortably lodged, and many of them took us to cafés. They said to us, "So the Russians found their masters, did they? But they say that our soldiers do not fight well." — "Your soldiers are as brave as the Russians, and the Emperor had your wounded men well cared for; we carried them to the field-hospitals, as we did our own. You have also a great general, who took good care of our prisoners; our Emperor knows him well." Then they grasped us by the hand, saying, "That is like Frenchmen!" But I said to them, "Your prisoners are better off than your soldiers; they have good bread, work well paid, and not beaten."[1] — "How kind you are, corporal! you make us very happy. You have behaved yourselves in Berlin as though you were our own countrymen." — "I thank you in the name of my comrades."[2]

We marched by way of the regular halting-places. The large towns of Potsdam, Magdeburg, Brunswick, Frankfort, and Mayence received us with triumphant demonstrations. Joy was painted on every countenance. The country people came out on the roads to see us go by. All along the way refreshments were prepared for us in the villages. The villages vied with the cities in their attentions to us. Well fed and triumphant, we returned to the gates of our own capital, which surpasses all others that I have ever seen. There triumphal arches awaited us, magnificent receptions, the theatres, and the beautiful ladies of Paris, who were there looking down upon us.

The Emperor received us at the Tuileries in our clean, but threadbare, uniforms. Then we marched through the garden of the Tuileries, and sat down to dinner at a table in the Avenue de l'Étoile, and thence on to Courbevoie to rest awhile. But the Emperor did not allow us to remain quiet long. He immediately established regimental schools, and sent to Paris for two professors to instruct us: one in the morning and the other in the evening.

---

[1] Corporal punishment formed and, indeed, still forms a part of Prussian military discipline.

[2] One cannot help thinking here of the contrast presented by our relations as belligerents sixty-four years later. And yet we are told that civilization softens the manners.

This was a great help to me. I immediately purchased a grammar and a <u>theory</u>. Twice a day I had recitations, and, with the assistance of my recruits, I made rapid progress. I never left my studies, except to go on guard. As soon as my recitations were over, I went off, and concealed myself in a very secluded part of the Bois de Boulogne, and there studied my theory. At the end of two months, I could write a large hand, and I can say I did it well.[1] The professors said to me, "If we have you for a year, you will know how to write very well; you have a good hand." How proud I felt!

The Emperor also established a swimming-school, where we could learn to swim. He had some barges placed near the bridge of Neuilly, and there a broad girth was passed under the stomach of each grenadier who did not know how to swim; then two men in each barge would hold on to it, and the soldiers thus became so daring, that in two months there were eight hundred grenadiers who could swim across the Seine. I was told that I must learn to swim. I answered that I was too much afraid of the water. "Very well," said the adjutant-major, "let him alone; do not force him." — "Thank you."

The Emperor ordered that the strongest swimmers should be held in readiness, at noon, in undress with linen pantaloons. The next day he came into the court-yard of our barracks, and the swimmers were ordered out. He was accompanied by his favorite Marshal Lannes. He asked for a hundred of the boldest swimmers. The best of them were pointed out to him. "I want them to swim across with their guns and cartridge-boxes on their heads." Then he said to M. Belcourt, "Can you lead them?" — "Yes, sire." — "Go, then, and get them ready; I will wait for you." He walked up and down the court-yard, and seeing me such a little one among the others, he said to the adjutant-major, "Send that little decorated grenadier to me." I came, feeling very much like a fool. "Do you know how to swim?" said he. "No, sire." — "Why not?" — "I am not afraid of fire, but I am afraid of

---

[1] The sight of Coignet's autograph manuscript compels us to say that he is boasting a little.

water." — "Oh! you are not afraid of fire! Very well," said he to M. Belcourt, "I exempt him from swimming."

I retired quite happy. The hundred swimmers being ready, they went down to the shore of the Seine; there were two boats, manned by sailors from the guard, to follow them, and the Emperor dismounted on the bank. All the swimmers passed under the bridge in front of the castle of Neuilly without any accident. M. Belcourt, alone, was drawn under by the long grass which was dragged along by the current, and wound around his legs; but the boatmen immediately went to his assistance, and he passed on with the others. When they reached the opposite shore, they made a fire. The Emperor galloped off, rode round and went where they were. He ordered that some good wine should be given to the "grumblers" at once, and that they should be sent back in boats. Wine was distributed to all of us, and twenty-five sous to each swimmer. The Emperor also took a fancy to send a squadron of chasseurs, with arms and baggage, across the Seine in front of the Invalides, at the place now occupied by the bridge. They crossed without accident, and reached the Champs Élysées. The Emperor was delighted, but the chasseurs and their baggage were wet.

My duties as corporal increased: two lessons a day, and one from my two recruits, to say nothing of my theory, which I was obliged to recite every day. I used to know it perfectly when I started from the place where I went to study it, but when I came up to M. Belcourt, I could not repeat a single word. "Well," he said, "how is this? Go sit down." — "I knew it," I answered. "Come then, try again." — "I will." And I then recited every word of it. "Very well," said he one day. "That will do. To-morrow no more theory. We will now learn the tone of command." Next day he gathered us around him. "Now," said he, "I am going to begin." We each had to repeat his command in turn. I used my voice so well that he was surprised, and said to me, "Begin again, and do not be in a hurry. I shall give the command, and you have only to repeat after me. Do not be timid; you come here to learn." Then I shouted. "That's right," said he. "See, gentlemen, little Corporal Coignet will make a good tutor. In a month he will surpass us." — "Ah, major, you make me feel abashed." — " You will see," said he, " when you have more self-possession."

As for my theory, I did not get along very well with that; I was always at work on it, but I did not do nearly so well as my comrades, who recited like parrots. I retaliated on them, however, by surpassing them all in practice. I became very skilful in the use of arms, but was always suffering from my ignorance. I purchased two hundred little wooden soldiers, and used to drill them.

When there was a grand drill, I tried to remember every command. The brave general, Harlay, who commanded, was a perfect drill-master; one could learn under him. The flank movement by battalion is the most difficult. It is necessary to start off simultaneously, and to halt in the same manner, turn to the front with a "Left face!" all keeping at the same distance from one another, and in a perfect line with the line guides. Also we had to give the commands, "March" and "Halt" on the left foot. I remembered every word of these difficult tactics. I scarcely ever left my barracks.

About the end of August. the Emperor had grand drills and frequent reviews in the plain of St. Denis. We perceived that he was preparing for another campaign. There were troubles brewing in the direction of Madrid.

We had a good time in Paris until the month of October, 1808, going through reviews, and making cartridges. I especially devoted myself to improving my writing and theory. General Dorsenne held inspections every Sunday. This strict general would come into our rooms, and pass his hand along the bread-shelf overhead, and, if he found one speck of dust on it, four days in the guard-room for the corporal! He raised up our vests to see if our shirts were clean. He even examined our feet, our finger-nails, and our ears to see if they had been attended to. He looked into our trunks to see that we had no soiled clothes in them. He even looked under the mattresses. We were all afraid of him. Once a fortnight, he came with the surgeon-major to visit us while we were in bed. We had to turn out in our shirts, and were forbidden to absent ourselves on these occasions under pain of imprisonment.

Finally, early in October, the Emperor issued orders for us to hold ourselves in readiness to march in a few days. Our officers had our trunks packed so they could be taken to the storehouse. And it was well they did: the order came for us to start for Bayonne. I said to my comrades, "We are going to Spain: beware of the fleas and the lice! They root up the straw in the barracks, and run around over the pavement like mice. Have an eye to our drunkards, too, the wine of that country sets them crazy; it is impossible to drink it." All turned out as I had predicted. At the end of a week's sojourn in Valladolid, we had to feed the soup to our drunkards: they trembled so they could not hold their spoons.

From Bayonne we went to Irun; thence to Vittoria, a pretty town, and thence to Burgos, where we remained a few days. There is a fine church there: the interior of the building is exceedingly beautiful. There is an immense clock inside, and at noon its two doors open, and different curious objects come out. The principal spire of this handsome edifice is flanked by small towers which form four fronts, and contain beautiful rooms, which all communicate. A small stairway, leading from a wide vestibule, runs along the left side of the building; at the end of it there is a beautiful garden. Our horse-grenadiers put up their horses under the fine old arches, which were filled on the left side with bales of cotton. They were about to start out on a foraging party, when, at the foot of the small stairway, appeared a little boy of eleven or twelve years, who seemed to wish to attract the attention of our grenadiers. As soon as one of them saw him, he ran back up the stairway; but the grenadier followed him, and caught up with him at the top of the steps. As soon as he reached the landing-place, the little boy opened a door, and the grenadier entered with him. The door closed, and the monks cut off his head. The little boy came down again, showed himself as before, and another grenadier followed him, and fell a victim to the same fate. The little boy returned a third time, but a grenadier who had seen his comrades go up the stairway, said to those who had just returned from the foraging party, "Two of our men have already gone up to the belfry, and have not returned. They are, perhaps, shut up in the belfry; we must see about it at once."

So they started off in pursuit of the child. They took their carbines along, mounted the narrow stairway, and, to prevent being surprised, fired them off when they reached the top, burst open the door, and found their comrades lying there with their heads cut off and bathed in their own blood. Our old soldiers became perfectly enraged. They slaughtered the wicked monks; there were eight of them, and they had all sorts of ammunition, provisions, and wine. It was quite a fortress. We threw the Capuchins and the little boy out of the dormer-windows down into the garden.

After having rendered a last duty to our comrades, we left Burgos, and marched forward. After going two leagues, we came up with the King of Spain, who had come to meet his brother, our Emperor, and they set off to rejoin the army which was moving on Madrid. They caught up with the advance guard, which was being closely pursued. On the 30th of November, 1808, the battle of the Sierra took place. It was a most difficult position, but the Emperor did not hesitate; he assembled all his sharp-shooters, and stationed them along the mountains. When he saw them coming near the flank of the enemy's artillery, he sent the Polish lancers out upon the highway with the horse chasseurs of the guard, and ordered them to clear the mountain without stopping. It was bristling with pieces of cannon. They started off at a gallop, cutting down everything before them. The ground was strewn with horses and men. The sappers cleared the road by throwing them down into the ravines.

The Spaniards made every effort to defend their capital, but the Emperor turned Madrid, which was blockaded. The garrison was very weak; even the inhabitants and the monks had taken up arms. They had all joined in the revolt, had taken up the pavements of the city, and carried the stones up into their houses. We were ordered to camp near a château a short distance from Madrid, where we remained two days. There was not enough water in the castle well to supply us, and we were obliged to go off in search of some. We returned to camp with two hundred asses laden with wine in leather bottles made of goat-skin, and we had to shave ourselves with wine. We tied our quadrupeds to some posts for the night, but the next morning they made such a fearful noise that the Emperor could not stand it, and sent an aide-de-camp to put a stop to the racket. We let the poor beasts loose, and, finding themselves at liberty, they escaped into the open fields where, having nothing else to eat, they devoured each other.

The cannonading was unceasing; balls were sent into the city from every direction; but they would not surrender. However, their losses were finally so great that they were compelled to do so. The Emperor declared that if a single stone should fall on his soldiers, he would put all the inhabitants to death with the sword. They gained nothing but the trouble of repaving their principal streets.

The city is large and not handsome: great squares filled with ugly barracks. But there is one in the centre of the town which it is impossible not to admire, on account of its beautiful façade, fine walks, and lovely fountain; this is the handsomest square in the city. As for the palaces, the entrances are not set off to any advantage. One enters into a very shabby reception-room, with a guard-room on the left. The palace, on the right, is much below the city; it is built on a ravine or precipice of immense depth. The front of it is superb, and one descends to it by a magnificent stairway. The part of it which fronts the city is only a one-storied building with handsome steps leading up to it. The halls are magnificent, and there is a very costly steel clock.

Marshal Lannes was commanded to take Saragossa, which cost great loss to our army. All the houses were furnished with battlements, and we had to carry them one at a time. The Emperor left Madrid with all his guard, and we came to the foot of a steep mountain, covered with snow like St. Bernard. We encountered untold difficulties in crossing it. Just before reaching this terrible pass, we were overtaken by a snow-storm which almost blew us over. We were obliged to hold on to one another, as we could not see a step before us. It was necessary to have an Emperor like ours to follow, in order to be able to resist it. We slept at the foot of this mountain, which cost our artillery much labor to cross, and then descended on the other side into a plain where there were some miserable villages which had been devastated by the English. We came to the shore of a river, which we found was extremely rapid, and from which all the bridges had been cut away. We had to ford it, holding on to one another, scarcely daring to raise our feet lest we should be carried away by the rapidity of the current. Our caps were covered with sleet. Imagine the delights of such a bath in the month of January! When we stepped into this river it came up to our waists. We were ordered to take off our breeches before crossing the two branches of the river, and, when we came out of the water, our legs and thighs were as red as lobsters.

On the other side, there was a field where our cavalry successfully charged the English. We had to pursue them in order to support the charge, and we marched at a quickstep, without stopping, as far as Benevento, which we found had also been ravaged by the English; they had carried off everything. Our cavalry pursued them as far as possible. They killed all their horses, and abandoned all their baggage-wagons and artillery. The Emperor ordered us to recross the terrible river. Think of two such baths in one day! This was something to grumble at; but he had provided for our comfort, and had had fires lighted a short distance off, so we could warm ourselves.

The whole guard now started for Valladolid, a large city. Here even the monks had taken up arms: all the convents were deserted, and we were at no loss for lodgings. We were ordered to return to France by forced marches, and the

Emperor set out for Paris. He had a little surprise prepared for us on our arrival at Limoges, for he wanted to take care of our legs and our shoes. We were received in this city, and passed the night there. The next day our officers said, "Take the hammers off your guns, and wrap them up well with the screws and the bayonets lest they should be lost. The whole guard will go to Paris in wagons. The wagons are ready outside the city."

As I was taking my gun to pieces, I said to my captain, "They surely take us for calves, putting us in on straw in this fashion." He laughed, and replied, "That is so; but time presses. There is mischief brewing. We are not yet ready to sleep in our beds, and one cannot tell what may happen between here and Paris."

After taking our guns to pieces, we started off. Crowds of people were on the streets. Outside of the city we found the wagons with the bottoms covered with straw waiting for us. The gendarmes were stationed in lines on each side of the road to guard them. We mounted by companies, in perfect order; the number in each wagon was according to the capacity of the vehicle; for instance, if there were three horses, twelve men were put in. When we reached the relay five francs were paid for each draft horse, and, if the horse died, three hundred francs were paid at once. Paymasters were on hand when the troops arrived, ready to pay for everything, and other wagons were ready for a fresh start. Tickets for refreshment had been issued to each company. The inhabitants came out to meet the train of wagons, each having an order for a certain number of men whom they were to feed, and took them off at once to seat them at table. Everything was in readiness everywhere. We had only three-quarters of an hour for eating, and started off immediately after. The drum-major had his food brought to him at his place, so that he could be ready to sound the roll-call at the precise moment. There was no delay. When we were ready to start, the battalion was spread out in a line along the road, so that each company faced the wagons into which they were to mount by messes. There was not a moment lost: each man felt the need of doing his duty. We travelled twenty-five leagues a day. It was as though a streak of lightning passed from the south to the north.

The long journey from Limoges to Versailles was soon made. On arriving at the gates of that beautiful city, we were ordered to get out of the wagons and enter. We had to remount our guns, and march through the city in a state of utter weariness and starvation (we were neither shaved nor combed). We counted on finding wagons on the other side of Versailles, but we were mistaken. We were obliged to go on foot as far as Courbevoie, where we were to pass the night, and where, half dead with fatigue and hunger, we found provisions and wine.

The next day was occupied in making ourselves clean. We drew upon the stores of linen and shoes, and the day after that the Emperor reviewed us. Then we started off at once, but the favor was granted us of being sent in cabs: a requisition had been made for all in the city. Four grenadiers in a cab, with bags and guns, was the arrangement. When we arrived at Claye, we gave some hay to our miserable nags, fed our coachmen, and started off again in the same carriages. At each halting-place we found our dinners waiting on the table.

We went to Ferté-sous-Jouarre, where the big wagons of Brie with big horses and good fresh straw awaited us (twelve men to each wagon). Those cursed roads were full of deep

ruts and large stones. The jolting knocked us together, and threw us down upon one another. Lord, what suffering it was! We travelled twenty-five or six leagues every day. On reaching Lorraine, we found small light horses and small low carriages, which carried us along like the wind; they were hitched one horse before the other. We were able to make thirty leagues with such horses; but it was frightful to descend the steep mountains with them, particularly those where the road turns off towards Metz. When we arrived at the gates of this city, we had to salute it, consequently we were obliged to remount our guns, and put on our full uniforms, unpack our knapsacks, and change our linen. More than ten thousand people had come out to see us, among them a great many ladies who had never seen the Emperor's guard. As soon as our guns were mounted, we opened our knapsacks to change our clothes. It was a high wind, in which to change our shirts; they all flew up in the air, and, consequently, the field was soon cleared. But we could not do otherwise.

Our entrance into the city was magnificent: we were lodged with the citizens, and kindly treated. The Emperor said that the Lorraine horses, by their fleetness, had caused the guard to gain fifty leagues. We then set out from Metz, with orders not to halt night or day. We were guided by a fairy wand. It was night when we reached Ulm. Our billets for lodging were given us, but, after we had eaten something, the drums beat the *grenadière*, and we had to fly to arms immediately. On the road to Augsburg we had a roll-call at nine o'clock at night. No more carriages after that; we were in the enemy's country. We had to rub up our legs, and march all night. We came to a town about nine o'clock in the morning. We were only allowed three-quarters of an hour to eat, and started off again immediately. We were obliged to march twenty-one leagues the first day with our heavy loads on our backs.

Then only a halt of half an hour. The next day no time for rest, except just long enough to eat and be off again. We had still twenty miles to make before reaching Schoenbrunn. After going fifteen or sixteen leagues, we were ordered into line of battle in front of a large village, and there the requisition was sent for twenty-five brave men to volunteer to join the Emperor at the gates of Vienna, and mount guard at the castle of Schoenbrunn. I remembered that I had stood guard there many a time. I was the first to step out of the ranks. "I will go," said I to my captain. "That's right," said General Dorsenne, "the smallest of you sets a good example."

The number was soon made up, and we started off. A bottle of wine was promised to each of us when we should be within three leagues of Vienna. We reached that point at nine o'clock at night, utterly worn out and very thirsty, and counting on the promise of the bottle of wine. But no wine was forthcoming. We had to go right on without stopping. I turned out of the way to look for some water to quench the thirst which was consuming me. I ran along the street, and met a peasant who was coming my way. He was carrying a bucket full of something, and, seeing me, he went into a fine-looking house where a sentinel was standing guard. I passed on, but at the corner of the street I crouched along the wall. The peasant came out again with his pail. I spoke to him in his own language. To my surprise his pail was full of wine. I made him stop in front of me, and hold up his pail with both hands, while I, putting my gun down on the ground, began to drink as hard as I could. I never before was so thankful for something to drink. This set me on my legs for the next three leagues, and I rejoined my comrades with a heart full of contentment.

We reached the village of Schoenbrunn at midnight. Our officers had the imprudence to allow us to rest about a quarter of an hour's march from the castle, awaiting orders from the Emperor, who, when he heard of our arrival, was furious. "What," said he, "have you marched my veterans more than forty leagues in two days? Who ordered you to do this? Where are they?"— "Near by."— "Tell them to come here, that I may see them."

We were ordered to rise, but our limbs were as stiff as the barrel of a gun. We could not go any farther. We had to use our guns as crutches to help ourselves along. When the Emperor saw us coming, all bent over on the butt-ends of our guns, not one erect, all with heads bowed down, he became like a raging lion. "Can it be that these are my veterans in this condition? Suppose I needed them at this moment! You are . . ." He said everything he could to them. He said to the horse-grenadiers, "Have large fires made immediately in the middle of the courtyard, and go for straw for them to lie down on; have some pots of sweetened wine heated."

Large pots were quickly put on the fire to make soup for us; and it was a sight to see the cavalry-men running around, and the Emperor having things brought for us. During the bombardment of Vienna, the inhabitants of the city had concealed some grocery wagons which were in front of the gates of the city; they contained sugar and nuts and raisins. The

"The Emperor never left us; he stayed with us more than an hour." — Page 173.

sugar was now brought out, some of it was put in the basins of warm wine, and all sorts of cups were collected. The Emperor never left us: he stayed with us more than an hour. When the wine was ready, the grenadiers came around the fires to give us some to drink. Not being able to raise ourselves up, they were obliged to raise our heads so we could drink. The wicked grenadiers jeered at us, saying, "Your shoes and the straps of your knapsacks have overcome you. Come, drink to the health of the Emperor and your good comrades. We will stay by you all night, and take care of you. In a little while we will give you something more to drink, and then you can go to sleep; the soup is ready; to-morrow you will be all right again."

The Emperor returned to his palace. At five o'clock we sat up on our straw to eat our soup, meat, bread, and wine. At nine o'clock the Emperor came out again to see us, and ordered our officers to make us rise; but we each had to have two men to assist us to walk, our limbs were so stiff. The Emperor stamped his feet angrily; the grenadiers mocked us, and our officers did not dare show themselves for fear of a scolding. That night lodgings were found for us in that beautiful and wealthy village, and the whole guard arrived, and was comfortably quartered.

The bombardment of Vienna had ceased: our troops had aken possession of the capital. The Austrian armies had blown up the bridges, after crossing over to the other side of the Danube. Great preparations were made for recommencing hostilities; in order to follow them up, we had to cross this terrible river, which was swollen and rushing on like a torrent. The water was very high, and even large boats were anchored with difficulty. Very strong boats were needed to make a bridge of such immense length over such a rapid current. All these preparations required time. The Emperor, we were told, had his large boats brought down about three leagues below Vienna, in front of the island of Lobau and the field of Essling. When the two bridges were completed, the Emperor sent Marshal Lannes' corps down to await orders to cross; he placed a hundred thousand men in Vienna to hold that capital, and keep a strict watch upon all the buildings, so that no one could hold any communication with Prince Charles from the other side. The streets were strictly patrolled, and all the people were shut up in their houses. Then a pretence of crossing was made in front of Vienna so as to keep Prince Charles's army in front of his capital, and prevent them from moving down towards Essling.

When all was in readiness, the Emperor promoted some of his guard. I was appointed sergeant the 18th of May, 1809, at Schoenbrunn. It was an inexpressible joy to me to find myself a non-commissioned officer, with the rank of lieutenant of the line, and the right when in Paris, to carry a sword and a cane. I was to remain with my company; but I did not have any sergeant's chevrons. I had to give up my corporal's stripes to my successor, and be only a private soldier; "But courage," said I to myself, "your time will come."

The Emperor ordered Marshal Lannes to conduct his army corps over the great bridge over the Danube, and march them forward beyond Essling. The fusileers of the guard, Marshal Bessières, and a park of artillery were in position from early morning. The Austrians did not perceive them until Lannes greeted them with a round of cannon-shot, causing them to turn their backs on their capital, and face our army which had crossed without their permission. The whole army of Prince Charles fell into line in front of us, and firing began from one end to the other. More than a hundred thousand men fell upon the corps of Marshal Lannes. The guns sent a thunderbolt upon our troops, but they held out to the utmost. The Emperor ordered us to leave Schoenbrunn for the Danube early in the morning; the whole infantry of the guard with himself at their head. At eleven o'clock he ordered us to cross over, and to throw aside our bear-skin caps. As we were in great haste, and were going over the bridge, three ranks at a time, we unpacked one another's caps as we marched along.[1] This operation taking place as we were going over the bridge, we threw all our caps into the Danube, and have never worn them since. That was the end of caps for the guard.

[1] They were packed in boxes outside of the knapsacks.

We crossed the point of the island, and came to another bridge which we went over at a gallop. The foot chasseurs crossed first, dashed into the field, and made a "column left wheel," instead of a right wheel. This mistaken movement could not be rectified, and we had to fall into line of battle at once, with our right wing near a branch of the Danube. As soon as the fight began a cannon-ball struck the Emperor's horse on the hip. At once all shouted, "We will lay down our arms, if the Emperor does not go to the rear instantly." He was compelled to recross the smaller bridge, and had a rope-ladder made up to the top of a high pine-tree, from which height he could watch all the movements of his own army and that of the enemy.

A second cannon-ball struck the drum-sergeant. One of my comrades went immediately and took off his chevrons and epaulets and brought them to me. I thanked him, and pressed his hand. This was only a prelude. To the left of Essling the enemy planted fifty pieces of cannon in front of us. The fifty pieces thundered upon us without our being able to advance a step, or fire a gun. Imagine the agony we endured in such a position, for I can never describe it. We had only four pieces of cannon in front of us, and two in front of the chasseurs, with which to answer fifty. The balls fell among our ranks, and cut down our men three at a time; the shells knocked the bear-skin caps twenty feet in the air. As soon as one file was cut down, I called out, "Right dress, close up the ranks!" And the brave grenadiers closed up without a frown, saying to one another as they saw the enemy making ready to fire, "That one is for me." — "All right, I will get behind you; that is a good place; keep quiet."

A ball struck a whole file, and knocked them all three head over heels on top of me. I fell to the ground. "Never mind," I called out; "close up at once." — "But, sergeant, the hilt of your sabre is gone, your cartridge-box is half cut off." — "That is no matter; the battle is not yet over."

There were no gunners left to work our two pieces. General Dorsenne had them replaced by twelve grenadiers, and bestowed the cross on them. But all those brave fellows perished beside their guns. No more horses, no more artillery-men, no more shells. The carriages were broken to pieces, and the timbers scattered over the ground like logs of wood. It was impossible to make any more use of them. A shell fell and burst near our good general, covering him with dirt, but he rose up like the brave soldier that he was, saying, "Your general is not hurt. You may depend upon him, he will know how to die at his post." He had no horse any

longer; two had been killed under him. How grateful the country ought to be for such men! The awful thunder continued. A cannon-ball cut down a file of soldiers next to me. Something struck me on the arm, and I dropped my gun. I thought my arm was cut off. I had no feeling in it. I looked, and saw a bit of flesh sticking to my wrist. I thought I had broken my arm, but I had not; it was a piece of the flesh of one of my brave comrades, which had been dashed against me with such violence that it had adhered to my arm. The lieutenant came up to me, took hold of my arm, shook it, and the piece of flesh fell off. I saw the cloth of my coat. He shook my arm, and said to me, "It is only stunned." Imagine my joy when I found I could move my fingers! The commander said to me, "Leave your gun, take your sabre." — "I have none; the cannon-ball cut off the hilt of it." I took my gun in my left hand.

The losses became very heavy. We had to place the guard all in one rank so as to keep up the line in front of the enemy. As soon as this movement had been made, a litter was brought up on our left, borne by grenadiers, who deposited their precious burden in our centre. The Emperor, from the top of his pine-tree, recognized his favorite, left his post of observation, and hastened to receive the last words of Marshal Lannes, who had been mortally wounded at the head of his corps. The Emperor knelt upon one knee, took him in his arms, and had him carried over to the island; but he did not survive the amputation. Thus ended the career of that great general. We were all filled with dismay at our great loss.

Marshal Bessières was still left to us, and was dismounted with all the rest. He came out in front of us. The cannonading continued. One of our officers was struck by a cannonball which cut off his leg, and the general granted permission to two of the grenadiers to carry him to the island. They laid him upon two guns, and were bearing him off, but had not taken more than four hundred paces, when a cannon-ball killed all three of them. A great misfortune befell us. The corps of Marshal Lannes beat a retreat; one part fell back upon us panic-stricken, and covered our line of battle. As there was only a single file of us, our grenadiers took them by the collar, and put them behind us, saying, "Now you need not be afraid."

Fortunately they all had their arms and cartridges. The village of Essling was in our possession, though it had been taken and retaken and burnt. The brave fusileers remained masters of it the whole day. The soldiers behind our file being somewhat restored to presence of mind, Marshal Bessières came up to them, and reassured them by saying, "I am going to station you as sharp-shooters, and I shall be on foot just as you will be."

Then they all started off with this brave general. He then placed them in single file within range of the fifty pieces whose fire we had stood since eleven o'clock in the morning; and there they stood, a single line of sharp-shooters protecting the file-firing which had been opened on the Austrian army. The brave marshal, with his hands behind his back, walked up and down the line, silencing for the moment their fury against us. This gave us a little breathing-space; but time passes slowly when one is awaiting death without the power to defend one's self. The hours seem ages. After having lost a fourth of our veterans without having burnt a priming, I was no longer at a loss for sergeant's chevrons and epaulets; my grenadiers brought me my pockets full. This terrible battle cost us dear. The brave marshal remained behind his sharp-shooters more than four hours. The battle was neither lost nor won. We did not know that the bridges over the broad river had been carried away, and that our army was crossing the Danube at Vienna. At nine o'clock the firing ceased. The Emperor ordered that each of us should light his fire, so as to make the enemy think that our whole army had crossed over.

Prince Charles did not know that our bridge had been carried away, else he would have captured us with little trouble, and would not have asked for a truce of three months, which was immediately granted, for, to tell the truth, we were in a cage: they could have bombarded us on all sides. When we had gotten our fires to burning brightly, we were ordered to recross to the island on our small bridge, and leave our fires burning. We spent the night in getting settled in position without any fire, and waited for the daylight. The next morning some heavy pieces were brought over in front of us, and stationed at the head of our little bridge. To our great surprise we saw nothing of our large bridge upon which we had crossed the day before. There was no more trace of it than of our hats which we had thrown into the Danube.

On the river in front of Vienna, the mills, which were on boats, had been loosened from their moorings, and the wheels taken off; they were filled with stones, and these heavy masses drifted down the current, and carried off our bridge. This sacrifice of their mills blockaded us three days in the island without bread. We ate up all the horses which had not died; not one was left. To the prisoners taken that morning we gave the heads and entrails. Our officers had nothing left but bridles and saddles. It is impossible to describe such destitution; and, in addition, the heart-rending shrieks which we could hear not far off. These came from the field-hospital, where M. Larrey was making amputations; it was frightful to listen to.

The Emperor notified the city of Vienna to col-

lect all its boats, and bring them down to make his bridge again. On the fourth day we were set free from our imprisonment on the island. We recrossed the awful river with joyful hearts, but very pale faces. Provisions awaited us at Schoenbrunn, where we arrived that night. Everything was in readiness to receive us, and our billets for lodgings all made out. We had plenty of time to recuperate during the three months' truce. Then intrenchments were begun in the island of Lobau: a hundred thousand men set to work on redoubts and covered roads. It would be impossible to give any idea of the quantity of earth thrown up during those three months. The Austrians threw up as much more in front of us. The Emperor would leave his palace on horseback, accompanied by his escort, go to the island of Lobau, and mount to the top of his pine-tree; thence he could see all their works, and watch the execution of his own. He would return satisfied and happy. He would come out to see us as soon as he got back, speak to all his veterans, and walk about the courtyard with his hands behind his back. He filled up the vacancies in his guard, and, as he had brought with him some actors from Paris, he gave a play in the castle. The fair ladies of Vienna were invited, and also fifty non-commissioned officers. It was a magnificent sight; but the ball-room was too small for so many people.

My arm having recovered its strength, I worked hard during those three months at my writing; I made great progress. My masters expressed themselves quite satisfied with me. Not one of the guard put his foot into Vienna, not even the Emperor, but he made frequent visits to the island of Lobau to watch his great preparations. He had his whole army drilled so as to keep in readiness to recommence the campaign. When all was ready, he showed a sample of his army to the amateurs of Vienna, in a review of a hundred thousand men, on the heights to the left of the city. There he sent for our Colonel Frédéric, and promoted him as general, saying, "I will make you win your epaulets." All the corps received orders to start for the island of Lobau on the 5th of July. Fortunately Prince Eugene, with the army of Italy, arrived in time to cross the Danube on the 6th of July, at ten o'clock in the morning. The whole army was assembled in the plain.

The Emperor had ordered rafts to be made, large enough to carry two hundred men each, who were to take possession of an island occupied by the Austrians, which interfered with his movements: he could not pass without being seen by the Austrian army. Everything was ready; the light-horsemen and the grenadiers on the rafts with General Frédéric. They were sent out precisely as the hour of midnight sounded, so as to keep to the agreement, for the truce ended on the 6th of July. The rain was falling in torrents. The Austrian soldiers went into their quarters for shelter. Our rafts landed crosswise on the sand. The water being only up to our calves, we took the island without firing a gun; all the Austrians were taken prisoners, and then the enemy could not see our movements. Two thousand sappers were sent with the engineers to make a road for the pontoon-bridges and artillery. The trees which happened to be in the way fell under axes and saws. By daylight we were three leagues beyond the enemy's intrenchments and our own without the enemy's even suspecting it. Within a quarter of an hour three bridges were built, and at ten o'clock in the morning a hundred thousand men had crossed over into the plain of Wagram. At noon our whole army was in line of battle with seven hundred pieces of cannon in battery. The Austrians had quite as many. We could not hear ourselves speak.

It was amusing to see us facing Vienna, and the Austrians with their backs turned on their capital. It must be said for their credit that they fought with determination. The Emperor was informed that the great battery of his guard would have to be replaced, as the gunners were all killed. "What!" said he, "if I relieve the artillery of my guard, the enemy will perceive it, and redouble their efforts to break through my centre. Go at once; let the grenadiers volunteer to serve the pieces." Twenty men from each company started off immediately. It was necessary to make a selection, for all wanted to go. No non-commissioned officers were accepted, only grenadiers and corporals. Off they started to man a battery of fifty pieces. As soon as they reached their position, the firing began. The Emperor took snuff, and walked up and down in front of us. Meanwhile Marshal Davout was seizing the heights, and driving the enemy back upon us as he marched across the great table-land so as to cut off their road to Olmütz. The Emperor, seeing the marshal in front of him, lost no time in ordering all the cuirassiers in a body to go forward, and break through their centre. The whole body started together, and passed in front of us. The earth shook under our feet. They brought back with them fifty pieces of cannon, all harnessed up, and some prisoners. Prince de Beauharnais came galloping up to the Emperor to tell him that the victory was assured. He embraced his son.

That night four grenadiers brought in the colonel who had commanded the fifty pieces, to which the Emperor had sent his "grumblers." This brave officer had been wounded about eleven o'clock. They were carrying him to the rear of his battery. "No," said he, "take me back to my post; that is my place;" and he commanded sitting down.

The guard formed a square, and the Emperor slept in the middle of it. He had all the wounded got together, and carried on to Vienna. The next day we found thirty cannon-balls which had fallen in one spot. It is impossible to give any idea of such a battle. On the 23d all the columns started out early in the morning. The Austrians had left, after suffering great loss; they were compelled to come and ask for peace on the height of Olmütz where the Emperor had erected his magnificent tent. The firing ceased on all sides. We started for Schoenbrunn, and there negotiations for peace were entered upon. The armies remained in sight of each other while the Emperor arranged matters.

SIXTH NOTE-BOOK.

RE-ENTRANCE INTO FRANCE. — THE FESTIVITIES OF THE IMPERIAL MARRIAGE. — I DO THE DUTIES OF SERGEANT-INSTRUCTOR, MESS-CHIEF, AND BAGGAGE-MASTER.

We left Schoenbrunn for the second time. When we came to the Confederation of the Rhine, we were received as though it had been our own country. In the large towns of France the people came out to meet us. We were received most cordially at our lodgings. At the gates of Paris we found a vast multitude assembled, and we could scarcely pass along, the crowd pressed so closely upon us. We were immediately conducted to the Champs-Élysées to partake of a cold collation prepared for us by the city of Paris. The time was pressing. We had to eat and drink standing, and leave at once for Courbevoie. The good city of Paris gave us another collation under the galleries of the Place Royale, and a comedy at the Porte St. Martin. Triumphal arches were erected. The people of Paris were wild with joy at seeing us again. Unhappily there were many missing at the roll-call. A fourth of us had been left on the battle-fields of Essling and Wagram. But no one was better pleased than I to come back to Paris with my sergeant's chevrons, and entitled to carry a sword and cane, and wear silk stockings in summer.

I was, however, much grieved over one thing: I had no calves to my legs. I had to resort to false calves, and this worried me extremely.

After a fortnight's rest in the fine barracks of Courbevoie, all in new clothes, we were reviewed by the Emperor at the Tuileries. Preparations were being made for the burial of Marshal Lannes. A hundred thousand men formed the funeral cortége of this celebrated warrior, which started from the Gros Caillou to go to the Pantheon. I was one of the non-commissioned officers who bore the bier. Sixteen of us carried it down eight or ten steps on the left side of the wing of the Pantheon, and there placed it on some trestles. The whole army marched in front of the remains of this brave soldier. The procession was passing till midnight.

I resumed my duties as non-commissioned officer. I applied myself earnestly to my writing, and one day, being on guard at St. Cloud, I made out a report of my fifty grenadiers, with all the names well written, and carried it myself to M. Belcourt, who was pleased with the neatness of my report, and said to me, "Go on; you are all right." I took the greatest pains to study my theory. I surpassed my comrades in the tone of command, and was considered to have the strongest voice. I was very proud of my rank of sergeant and my forty-three sous a day. Having some visits which I was obliged to make, I proceeded to get myself up. I had to have silk stockings, if I wore my sword. I have already said that I had passed at St. Malo.[1] I had no calves to my legs, so I had to get up some false ones. I went to the Palais-Royal to buy some. I found a pair to suit me, for which I paid eighteen francs, and I got up a good-looking pair of legs, with some fine stockings over the false calves and the silk ones on top of them. I made my visits, and was overwhelmed with compliments upon my appearance. I returned to the barracks at nine o'clock in the evening, delighted with my day, and found a letter from my captain, Renard, inviting me to dine with him on Sunday, without fail, at five o'clock sharp, and saying that his wife and daughter wished to thank me

---

[1] An allusion to the well-known song, *Bon royage, monsieur Dumollet*, etc.

for having put my captain to bed in a cask on the evening before the battle of Austerlitz.

I accepted this invitation. I met some distinguished military men and citizens and ladies of high degree.[1] I felt rather uncomfortable among my superiors in rank, all decorated, and in company of such fine ladies, all dressed up in plumes. I felt very small indeed in that splendid hall, as I waited for the dinner to be announced. My captain came to my relief, presented me to his wife, some other ladies, and some of his friends. I no longer felt alone; but I was very bashful, and would have preferred my mess-table to this grand dinner. We went into the dining-hall, where I was seated between two beautiful ladies, and they paid me much attention, and soon put me at my ease. By the time the second course was served, every face at the table was beaming with pleasure, and the introduction of the champagne put a finishing stroke to the gayety. My officers were obliged to begin to tell stories of their campaigns.

The ladies who sat beside me insisted that I should relate my history. "I beg that you will excuse me; my officers know it all." — "Well," said the captain, "I will tell it for him. You see that he is a good soldier. He was the first one who received the decoration at the Invalides. He saved us from dying of hunger in Poland, by finding out all the hiding-places of the Poles. In fact, ladies, I should have been dead but for him." I was greatly confused at this testimonial from my captain, and overwhelmed by so much attention from everybody. The blood mounted to my face. I had a white handkerchief, which I continually pulled out of my pocket to wipe off the perspiration. My napkin was very fine, and, by mistake, I wiped my face with it, and put it also into my pocket. At the hour when I was obliged to return to my barracks, I got up to go. The captain said to me, "Must you go?" — "Yes, captain; I have to stand guard to-morrow." — "But you will come back to-morrow?" — "Oh, no, I cannot; I shall be on guard." — "But you are carrying off your napkin."

[1] We must not forget that it is a sergeant who is speaking.

Putting my hand in my pocket, I found my napkin and my handkerchief. As I handed the napkin to my captain, I said, "I thought I was still in the enemy's country, you see. There, if you don't steal something, it is thought that you have shown neglect." — "All right," said he, "stay here; I will send my servant to the barracks, and you shall spend the evening with us." Then, pointing to his daughter, "There is your accuser. She said to me, 'Papa, he is carrying off his napkin; but let him do it.'" — "Ah, how happy I am that your daughter should have noticed me."

I went back to my studies in writing and tactics, working unceasingly for the next six months, and only leaving my barracks to go to stand my guard (and always with my *École de Bataillon* in my pocket, so as to learn the manœuvres belonging to my rank). I overcame all difficulties in the use of arms. The Emperor issued an order that the non-commissioned officers and corporals should be drilled alone with the aid of poles to represent the sections. To form a platoon, the platoon-leader took hold of both ends of the pole; to break, the corporal again took hold of the end of the pole. This was called the "pole-drill;" it was a means of resting the "grumblers." M. Belcourt commanded us, and we made rapid progress as we walked rapidly up and down the fine courtyard of the barracks of Courbevoie. With a hundred men we went through all the principal manœuvres of a whole regiment.

"I went back to my studies in writing and tactics, working unceasingly for the next six months." — Page 186.

The Emperor ordered us to form a square; after our going through this manœuvre for an hour he was quite satisfied, and ordered that we should, in the future, only go through it once a week. All the sergeants and corporals had to take command. When my turn came, I was delighted to be able to show my superiors the progress I had made. They watched me closely to see if I would make any mistake. While we were resting, all my comrades congratulated me, and my superiors showed that they were very well pleased with me. But though the Emperor was pleased with us, we were not pleased with him. A report was circulated among the guard that he was about to divorce his wife, and marry an Austrian princess to make up for the second war with the Emperor of Austria, and that he was anxious to have an heir to the throne. In order to do this, he would be obliged to send away this accomplished woman, and take a foreigner, who would be able to bring about a general peace. The Emperor held grand reviews to distract him from his troubles. We were told that Prince Berthier was going to Vienna to carry the portrait of our Emperor to the princess, and ask for her hand.

Great preparations were made for the reception of this new Empress. On the 15th her whole family accompanied her a long way out of Vienna. She showed signs of regret at leaving her dog and her parrot, and orders were issued at once to have them sent to St. Cloud, where, on her arrival, she was surprised to find her bird-cage and birds, her dog, who greeted his mistress, and her parrot, who called her by name.

Our first battalion was ordered to await the arrival of the Emperor at St. Cloud. The couriers arrived, and we were put under arms. We saw that splendid carriage drawn by eight horses, and the Emperor seated beside his betrothed. How happy he looked! They went slowly on to St. Cloud, and we had time to see all the fine equipages pass. The civil marriage took place at St. Cloud, and the next day they left there to make their entrance into the capital. We were ordered to be present at the grand ceremony of the religious marriage, which was celebrated on the 5th of April, in the chapel of the Louvre. It is impossible to give any idea of all the grand prep-

arations. In the great gallery of the Louvre, leading from the
old Louvre to the chapel which is at the end of the pavilion
of the Tuileries on the side next the Pont-Royal (the space is
immense), there were three rows of benches to seat ladies and
gentlemen. In the fourth row were fifty non-commissioned,
decorated officers placed at certain distances from each other
in iron gratings, so as not to be pushed aside by any one.
General Dorsenne commanded us. When he had stationed us

all, he told the ladies that we were to
serve as their knights, and have refreshments brought to them. We had
to be introduced. We each had to
take charge of twenty-four on each
side of us (forty-eight to each noncommissioned officer), and attend to all their wants. Large
niches had been made in the thick wall to hold ninety-six
canteens of all sorts of pleasant refreshments. These little
itinerant *cafés* did a good business.

The dresses of the ladies were as follows: Low in the
neck; behind, almost down to the middle of their backs, and
in front showing half of their breasts; their shoulders and
arms bare. And such necklaces and bracelets and ear-rings!

They were covered with rubies and pearls and diamonds. Here could be seen all sorts of skins: oily skins, skins like mulattoes, yellow skins, and skins like satin. The old women carried salt-boxes [1] containing a supply of perfumes. I must say that I had never before seen the ladies of Paris, half naked, so near. I did not like it.

The men were dressed in French fashion, all wearing the same costume: black coat, short breeches, steel buttons cut in the shape of a diamond. The trimming of their coats cost eighteen hundred francs. They could not present themselves at court without this costume. Cabs being forbidden that day, it is impossible to imagine the number of splendid equipages in front of the Tuileries. The magnificent procession started from the château, and moved on to the Louvre, then mounted the grand stairway of the Louvre, and entered the chapel of the Tuileries. The ceremony was very imposing. The whole assembly remained standing, and the most solemn silence prevailed. The procession moved slowly. As soon as it had passed by, General Dorsenne called us together, marched us into the chapel, and formed us into a circle. We saw the Emperor on the right, kneeling upon a cushion decorated with bees, and his wife kneeling beside him to receive the benediction. After having placed the crown on his own head and on that of his wife, he rose, and sat down with her on a lounge. Then the celebration of mass was begun, chanted by the Pope.

The general made a sign to us to go out and return to our posts, and there we saw the procession return. The new Empress looked beautiful with her splendid diadem. The wives of our marshals carried the train of her robe, which dragged about eight or ten feet upon the ground. She ought to have been proud to have such maids of honor in her suite. But it must be said that she was a beautiful sultana, that the Emperor looked very well pleased, and that her figure was graceful. That was a high day for her, but not so at Malmaison.

All the old guard was under arms to protect the cortége, and we were all excessively hungry. We each received

---

[1] Coignet means the flask of salts, which it was then the fashion to smell.

twenty-five sous and a litre of wine. After the festivities were over, the Emperor went away with Maria Louisa. On the 1st of June they re-entered Paris. The city gave them a reception and a splendid banquet at the Hôtel de Ville. I was put on duty in command of a squad of twenty men inside the building, in front of the beautiful horseshoe-shaped table, and my twenty grenadiers, with arms grounded, in sight of this banquet of cold meats, served in dishes of solid gold. Around the horseshoe table were placed arm-chairs; the largest one in the middle was for the Emperor. The royal party was announced. The general came to station me and give me his orders.

Then the master of ceremonies announced, "The Emperor!" and he entered followed by his wife and five other crowned heads. I ordered carry and present arms; then I was ordered to make them ground arms. I stood in front of my squad, facing the Emperor. He seated himself at the table, and made a sign to the others to take their places on each side of him. When the crowned heads were seated, the table was cleared; every dish was taken up, and carried off. The carvers did their work in a side room. Behind each king and queen there were three footmen about a step from one another. There were others who held communication with the carvers, and passed the plates, without turning more than half-way round to get them. When a plate came within reach of a sovereign, the head footman presented it to him, and, if the sovereign shook his head, the plate disappeared; another plate was brought immediately. If the head did not move, the footman placed the plate in front of his master. How well those meats were carved!

Each one took his piece of bread, broke it, and bit it in the same manner, making no use whatever of his knife, and, after each mouthful, wiped his mouth with a napkin; the napkin then disappeared, and the footman slipped in another. Consequently, in this way, there was a pile of napkins behind each chair which had only been used once.

Not a word was spoken. Each person had a flagon of wine and water, and no one poured out wine for his neighbor.

They ate their bread, and poured out something to drink to suit themselves. They either accepted or refused by a shake of the head. No one was permitted to speak except when addressed by the sovereign master. That may be imposing, but it is not at all jolly.

The Emperor rose. I made my grenadiers carry and present arms, and then they all passed into the great hall. I remained standing near the splendid table. The general came up to me, and took me by the arm: "Sergeant, come with us, I want you to drink some of the Emperor's wine, and, as we go by, I will have some wine given to your twenty men. Stay here. I will go and tell your squad to have patience, and they shall be refreshed in their turn." Those two glasses of wine did me good, and my grenadiers each had a half-litre of it. How proud we were at having drunk the Emperor's wine!

After a few days of repose, the old guard gave a brilliant reception to the Emperor in the Champ de Mars. The whole court was present. We went through the manœuvres for their benefit, and, in the evening, by torchlight, we shot off blank cartridges of all colors. After firing into the air by platoon and battalion, we formed a square in front of the balcony of the École Militaire, where the court was assembled to look at us. At the given signal, this immense square began to fire by file into the air. Never were such baskets of flowers seen before. The guard was crowned with stars. Everybody clapped their hands. I must say, it was a magnificent sight.

The Emperor gave a splendid ball; he opened it himself with Maria Louisa. There never was seen a better formed man. He really was a perfect model: his hands and feet were unequalled for beauty. Maria Louisa was a first-rate billiard-player. She beat all the men; but she was not afraid to stretch herself out across the billiard-table, as the men did, when she wanted to make a stroke. I was always on the watch to get a chance to see her. She was frequently applauded. Duty at St. Cloud was irksome to us. We had to go back and forth from Courbevoie to St. Cloud, and the chasseurs came from Rueil to relieve us. We were well fed, however, and the sergeant had a table to himself. We had soup, bouillon, good chicken-salad, and a bottle of wine. The officer ate with the officers of the household.

In the month of September, 1810, great preparations were made to go to Fontainebleau. The hunting season had come, and the first battalion, to which I belonged, was ordered to set out for duty there. M. Belcourt, the adjutant-major, followed the battalion. We were put into barracks, and the whole court came out in splendid hunting carriages. There were four open carriages with horses all alike, and a relay of horses of another color. It was a magnificent sight. M. Belcourt was ordered to take out for the hunt twelve non-commissioned officers and corporals, who should be under the direction of a game-keeper, and stationed by fours in certain appointed places. On arriving at the rendezvous, we were stationed at our posts in a beautiful circle, well gravelled, and into which several walks led. There was here a beautiful tent with a table ready served, and footmen standing around it. The whole court sat down to the table before going on the hunt.

That day hoops were brought out (with a man inside of each hoop) with falcons perched all around on them. Maria Louisa took one of these birds, and sent it out on the first game that came in sight. The bird swooped down upon it like lightning, and brought it to Maria Louisa. This hunt, a very entertaining one, lasted a whole hour; then the open carriages started off at a gallop for a place where the peasants were to whip the bushes with poles, in a large garden filled with rabbits which could not get out. The Emperor had a great many guns ready loaded; he gave the signal, and the peasants beat the bushes, and crowds of them jumped out. Then the Emperor began to shoot. He fired rapid shots, one after the other. Then he said to his aides-de-camp, "Come, gentlemen, it is your turn now! Take some guns, and amuse yourselves." And soon the ground was covered with victims. He had the guards called up, and said to our adjutant-major, "Have this game picked up, and give a rabbit to each peasant, and four to each of the guard. Put the rest in the wagon, and have them distributed to my old 'grumblers' (there was a wagon full of them). To-morrow you shall lead them on a wild-boar hunt; you shall have provisions to take with you, and spend the whole day in the forest." The adjutant-major gave his orders, and we all started off. This was the first day's hunt, and the whole battalion had rabbit to eat.

The next day four wagons arrived: one for the provisions, two for the great Russian dogs, and one in which to put the boars alive. With the huntsmen, the grooms for the dogs

and the game-keepers, there were fifty of us who started out, besides our adjutant-major. When we came near to the place where this herd of wild boars had their lair, we dismissed the carriages, and coupled up the dogs. There was a physician along, too, to attend to the dogs which should be wounded in the terrible fight in which they were about to engage. "First," said the huntsmen, "we must eat; we shall not have time for it later." And a footman was there, with his napkin on his arm, to wait upon the adjutant-major and the physician.

We all made a hearty dinner, and, as soon as we had finished, we set out for the field of battle. And the footmen each led two of those great long dogs.

They roused up some boars, and six dogs started off after each furious animal. Three boars were soon down, and unable to move. Two dogs took each boar by the ears, and locked themselves together around his body, holding him so tightly that he could not move. Then the guards came up with a gag, and put a strong bit into his mouth before he could defend himself. His four feet were tied together with a slip-knot, and the dogs were unmuzzled, and started off again upon the herd, followed by the grooms who had charge of them. The prisoners were taken to the wagons; the door at the back of the wagons was opened; the boars' trammels were taken off, and they fell down into the deep wagons.

We captured the whole herd of fourteen that day, and the wagon was full. Two of our dogs were wounded by blows of their tusks. We were very hungry after these hunts in the depths of the forest. The Emperor was delighted with such a hunt. He had an enclosure prepared on the road to Paris, where these animals were kept alive. It was round, and the walls high and solid. The wagon was backed up to a door cut in the wall, and the furious animals were thus dropped into the enclosure. This was our second hunt, and it lasted a fortnight. We captured fifty boars and two wolves alive.

Inside of this enclosure, an amphitheatre had been constructed upon piling, and arm-chairs were placed all round it, sufficient in number to seat the whole court. A slight descent brought one to the middle of the enclosure, under a beautiful tent. Sentinels were stationed to prevent any one's approaching. The court arrived at two o'clock. They had to climb up in the top of the pine-trees to see the angry creatures leap upon the palisades. The Emperor fired first. He did not fire at any of the wolves; they were left for the last, and leaped up quite to the top of the palisades. The Emperor allowed the chief officers of his court to finish up the game, and all the boars were divided among his guard. We had a fine feast, and he reserved three of the largest for himself.

Afterwards he gave orders to his guards to go and find out the number of the stags, and the age of each, and report them to him. At the end of two days the number had been ascertained. The ages were told by their feet. The day before this great hunt, he sent out some of the guard and the dog grooms, who had in charge two big bloodhounds in leashes, which were to scent stag number one. The haunt of this animal was discovered by the tracks he had made during the night. The guard then took hold of the bloodhound, and made it smell the footprints of the stag which was to be hunted the next day. This animal, held in a leash, was led slowly forward by the guardsman, and, at a short distance from the haunt, he raised his forepaw in the air as if to spring upon his prey; but the guardsman held him back. All this was done without any noise. The situation of the haunt was marked, and a report of it made to the Emperor, as the rendezvous for the court. Orders were issued for open carriages and relays of horses. There were fifty-two dogs in four relays, thirteen to each relay, and the bloodhound, which was the leader of the whole pack. One dog in each pack of thirteen led the other twelve. As soon as the bloodhound started a stag, this leader followed his footprints, and never turned aside from them; and the twelve other dogs marched in line of battle on each side of him.

The Emperor ordered M. Belcourt to take out twenty-four men (sergeants and corporals), and station them at the three points designated for the relays of carriages. Before beginning the hunt, the whole court sat down to a table served in a nicely gravelled piece of ground, and, after the banquet was over, the open carriages came up. Every one mounted on horseback, and the stag started. The Emperor galloped off to the place where the stag would pass, followed by musket-bearers carrying guns. There he waited for the stag to pass, and, if he missed it, he started off again, like lightning, for another crossing-point.

After the second relay departed, in a little while, the hunt was carried on at a great distance from us. We stood silently at our posts. The major said to me, "You had better go through the drill, and let out your voice. Order them to form a square by division as you march, and do so with the fewest manœuvres." I began, "Form a square on the second division as you are marching: first division, by the left flank and by right file; third division, by the right flank and by left file; fourth division, by the left flank by left file! Quick time! Second division, slow time!" I had made a mistake which I could not repair, and the major said to me, "You are in too much of a hurry; you are too much excited. Order your square to deploy. Now, do not hurry!" But the Emperor had heard me from the spot where he was waiting for the deer; he did not forget one of my blunders. He shot the stag, and the hunting horns sounded a rally. All the open carriages came up to the rendezvous. The Emperor, well pleased, had dismounted, and was standing beside the splendid stag. When the whole court had gathered together, he had us called up, and said to our major, "Who was that commanding the drill in the forest? Send him here; I want to see him."

The major ordered me to leave the ranks, and presented me. "Was it you, then," said he, "who were making the forest resound? You command very well, but you made a mistake."—"Yes, sire, I forgot 'quick time.'"—"That is right. Pay attention next time." The major said to him, "He beat his head with his fist." The Emperor replied, "Make him the instructor of two regiments. Let him be assisted by two well-drilled corporals. You will take fifty of the oldest recruits, and drill them twice a day; push them forward in tactics, and, in two months, I will see them. See that they are strong and capable of serving as officers." M. Belcourt came up to us: "Well, he has set us a task. We shall be confined for two months; but there is no need to throw yourself to the devil; you will come out all right in the end. Are you satisfied?" said he.—"I shall always remember the forest of Fontainebleau."

That evening, the quarry of the stag was held by torchlight in the court of honor, which was furnished with fine balconies, from which all the court looked on. It was a magnificent sight, that pack of two hundred dogs in line of battle behind a row of grooms, who held them, whip in hand. At the given signal, the man tore the skin from the stag; the horns sounded the pillage, and they all sprang upon their prey. Those two hundred famished creatures formed a mound, they were so piled up on one another.

At the end of a fortnight the hunts were over, the court returned to Paris, and we to Courbevoie. The barracks contained three battalions. Each month a battalion took its turn

to go on duty in Paris. And hard duty it was: eight hours on guard, two hours on patrol, and the grand rounds at night. The adjutant-major reported to General Dorsenne that the Emperor had appointed me instructor of two regiments of grenadiers, and I entered upon the duties at once. But this was not all. In the mornings those under arrest had to take brooms and sweep out the gutters, and then wash them down, and, worst of all, they were obliged to wash out the privies. As there was a bed of sand near the grating, if I had to punish many men, I made them haul sand, and they liked it better than going on drill. I went out with twenty or thirty of my men, and put them to work. Some dug up the sand, some rolled the wheelbarrows, others the tumbrel-carts, and so all the sand was carried into the courtyard. All this was done without a murmur. And even if I set them to pulling up grass, they grumbled a little, but they did it. I varied their punishments as much as I could. Those veterans were obedient enough considering they were men who were being turned out of the regiments, from the ranks of sergeant and even sergeant-major, and returned to the rank of simple grenadier. I had great trouble in managing some of the hard heads; but they would finally yield. I had the knack of controlling. All this took place within sight of the officers of the week, and I was firmly upheld by the two adjutants-major, who approved of strict discipline. It was in front of the officers' pavilion, and they could see all their movements. They had their boarding-house in our barracks, and passed from that into their garden. They sent for me to show me the plan of a large pleasure-ground, which they wanted to have prepared by the men under arrest. "We will give each of them," said those gentlemen, "a bottle of wine, if you will undertake to direct them." — "I will do so, very gladly." — "All right. We will go and draw a line on the terrace, and mark the places for some holes, where we wish to plant some acacias, forming two quincunxes in front of the barracks, and one on each side of the grating. Go call the roll of your prisoners, and tell them to be ready for this to-morrow."

After roll-call, I said to them, "You are not to drill any more; you are to plant trees to give you shade." — "Hurrah for our sergeant! that will be fun." — "You will not get tired. I will put four of you to dig each hole, and you shall have two hours to do it." — "We are satisfied." — "Go and rest; at six o'clock there will be a roll-call for the prisoners. One-half of you will do the sweeping, and the others will dig the holes."

The officers ordered a whole tun of Suresnes wine, which did not cost them ten cents a bottle, and gave a bottle of it to each man. All went right forward, the holes and the groups of trees; and the beautiful plantation of eight thousand seven hundred trees and shrubs was set out by the men under arrest.

"The Marshal said to the maid-of-honor, 'Give the prince to this sergeant.'" — Page 201.

It was complimented by my officers, and they appointed me to take charge of the non-commissioned officers' boarding-house. This was a laborious task, to see that the meals of fifty-four non-commissioned officers were well prepared and served. I was paid in advance. This brought me the sum of forty-five francs seventy centimes a day. The extras super-added each day were: first, bread (8fr. 10c.); wine (8fr. 10c.); dishes furnished from outside of the refectory (3fr.); wood (1fr.). On Sunday we went to Paris; this made 21fr. 20c. in addition to the 45fr. 70c., making 66fr. 90c. which I had to expend every day. I did it all, however, and they were pleased. At the end of a month, I showed my expenditures to the sergeant-major. "Why," said he, "you must be in debt." — "No, indeed, I have an extra allowance of 21fr. 20c. a day, which, added to my 45fr. 70c., makes 66fr. 90c." — "But what do you get?" — "I? I have 64fr. 50c. a month. That is enough. With the extras for three days, I pay my head man and two assistants; so don't worry, the boarding-house will get along."

The sergeants said at dinner, "You must be prompt in bringing on our meals. Give each of us a bottle of wine; the extras will be yours." — "Be prompt in seating yourselves at the table, four at a time. You shall be served at the appointed hour sharp, and I will see that your meals are well served."

The council (of administration) placed at my disposal a pleasure carriage and a soldier belonging to the train, so that I might send to Paris for provisions, and also four men for especial duty, and a corporal for the company. At two o'clock in the morning I went with this detachment to Paris, carrying a memorandum from my chief cook, and the purchases for the week were considerable. I paid five francs for the break-fast for my four men, and they were satisfied. At nine o'clock and at four I had to be on hand to preside over the meals. On Sunday there was an inspection of the refectory by the colonel or the general. The covers were laid with clean white napkins, and I received the commendation of my officers and even of General Dorsenne, before whom every one in the barracks trembled.

I have already said that, when this strict man went through our rooms, he passed his finger along the bread-shelves. If he found a speck of dust, the corporal, or the head man in charge of the rooms, was put under arrest for four days. He also ran his hand under our beds. And in our trunks he was never to find any soiled linen. He was a model in his own dress; he even rivalled Murat.

I was always ready to receive him,—always on the lookout, and never surprised. Once, however, I just missed receiving a severe scolding. We had saved up something on the food for the week, and it had been decided that we would buy some brandy with the amount saved. Well, in order that General Dorsenne's attention should not be attracted to the entry, I put it down in my account as "vegetable sundries," so much. The indefatigable general happened to light upon that very entry. "What is this?" he asked. "Vegetable sundries," I stammered, and finally acknowledged our peccadillo. At first he tried to be angry; but, seeing my confusion, and realizing our little strategy, he began to laugh. "This time," said he, "I pardon you; but I do not approve of your economizing on food in order to buy liquors."

I had a great deal to do: to exercise the prisoners, drill fifty recruits, and carry on my refectory. Every hour was occupied. By being very industrious, I proved myself worthy of my captain's good opinion. I can truly say that I owe to him whatever I may have won in the field of honor. Thus ended the year 1810.

In 1811 we had cause for great rejoicing. On the 20th of March a courier came to our barracks to announce the safe delivery of our Empress, and said that the cannons were about to fire. We were all excitement. As the first reports sounded from the Invalides, we counted in silence, but when we heard the twenty-second and twenty-third report, we leaped for joy, and all shouted at once, "Long live the Emperor!" The King of Rome was baptized on the 9th of June. We had holiday and fireworks. This darling child was always accompanied by the governor of the palace, whenever he went out to take the air, with his handsome nurse, and a lady who carried him. One day when I was at the palace of St. Cloud, Marshal Duroc, who was with me, signalled to me to approach, and this dear child held out his little hands for my plume. I stooped, and he began to pull at my plumes. The marshal said, "Let him do it." The child laughed with delight; but my plume was sacrificed. I looked a little upset. The marshal said to me, " Give it to him. I will give you another." The maid of honor and the nurse were much amused. The marshal said to the maid of honor, " Give the prince to this sergeant, and let him take him in his arms." Good Lord! how eagerly I stretched out my arms to receive that precious burden! Every one surrounded me. "Well," said M. Duroc to me, " is he heavy?" — " Yes, general." — " Come, walk him about; you are strong enough to carry him." I walked about with him awhile on the terrace. The child pulled away at my plumes, and paid no attention to me. His robes hung down very low, and I was afraid of stumbling; but I was proud to carry such a baby. I handed him back to the maid of honor, who thanked me, and the marshal said to me, " Come to my office an hour later." Accordingly, I appeared before the marshal, who gave me an order upon a merchant for a handsome plume. " Is this the only one you have?" said he. " Yes, general." — " I will give you an order for two." — " Thank you, general." — " You can go, my brave fellow; now you will have one for Sundays."

Meeting some of my officers, they said to me, " Where is your plume?" — " The King of Rome took it away from me." — " Oh! you are joking." — " See, I have an order from Marshal Duroc. Instead of only one plume, I shall have two, and I have held the King of Rome in my arms for nearly a quarter of an hour; he tore up my plume." — " Happy mortal!" said they; " such incidents are never to be forgotten." I never saw the child again. It was the fault of politics, which cut him down in his youth.

All the princes of the Confederation of the Rhine were assembled at Paris, and Prince Charles was godfather to the little Napoleon. The Emperor held a review for them after his own fashion in the Place du Carrousel. The regiments of infantry came up through the Rue de Rivoli, and formed their line on the square, in front of the Hôtel Cambacérès. The infantry of the guard was in two ranks in front of the Palace of the Tuileries. The Emperor came down the steps at noon, mounted his horse, reviewed his guard, and, returning, took his stand beside the sun-dial. He called our adjutant-major to him, and said, "Have you a non-commissioned officer whose voice is strong enough to repeat my commands? Mouton cannot repeat."—"Yes, sire."—"Send him here, and let him repeat word for word after me." M. Belcourt sent me to him. The general, the colonel, and the officers of the battalion all said to me, "Do not make a mistake. Try not to remember that it is the Emperor who gives command, and, above all, have self-possession."

M. Belcourt presented me. "Sire, here is the sergeant who commands best."—"Stand here on my left, and repeat my commands." The task was not a difficult one. I acquitted myself as well as possible. At each command from the Emperor, I turned round to repeat, and then turned round again, facing the Emperor, to receive another command. All the strangers on the balcony were watching me. They saw a non-commissioned officer with his gun, receiving commands, and immediately making an "about face" to repeat them, so that his body was in continual motion. All the officers of the corps repeated word for word, and, after making their men pass under the Arc de Triomphe, they drew them up in line of battle in front of the Emperor. He galloped past the regiment, and then returned to his post to put it through the manœuvres, and make it march off. This infantry drill occupied two hours. The guard closed up the march. Then the Emperor dismissed me, and my place was filled by a general of cavalry. It was high time; I was covered with perspiration. My officers congratulated me upon my strong voice. The sergeant-major took me by the arm, and led me to the *café* in the garden to give me something to drink. "Oh! I am so proud of you, my dear Coignet." The captain clapped his hands, saying, "It was I who forced him to be a corporal; it is all my doing. How well he gives command!"—"Thank you," said I; "but one feels very small beside his sovereign. I heard him, but I could not look at him: he would have frightened me; I only saw his horse."

After drinking our bottle of wine, we went back to the company. My captain grasped my hand, and said, "I am delighted." I was overwhelmed with praises. When we got back to Courbevoie, my comrades' table was ready. My head cook had neglected nothing, and the wine had been distributed: a litre and twenty-five sous for each man; the non-commissioned officers, one day's pay (forty-three sous); the corporals, thirty-three sous. Every face looked bright and happy.

The next day I resumed my tiresome duties. I encouraged my fifty recruits and my prisoners. I took my writing lessons in the evening, to say nothing of the superintendence of the refectory, and the care of the cleaning of the barracks. And never was any fault found with me. I said to myself, "I have got my marshal's bâton; I shall be the veteran of the barracks in my old age." But I was entirely mistaken. I had not gone through half my career. I was still sleeping on a bed of roses, and all the thorns were yet to be plucked out.

Some grenadiers arrived to fill up the regiments, and take the places of the veterans who could no longer go into the field. Two companies were formed of veterans of the guard, who were delighted to have such easy duty to perform. Every day splendid-looking men came in. I put them through the drill, and the adjutants-major attended to the tactics. They pushed the recruits forward so rapidly that the Emperor received them at the end of two months. It was charming to see them drill. They never made a mistake, and were all received as sub-lieutenants of the line, and went to join their regiments. The Emperor asked me, "Do they know how to give command?"—"Yes, sire, all of them do." —"Let the first one come forward, and go through the manual of arms." He was delighted. "Order the second one out." said he. "Let him order a charge in twelve time. Very well. Now, order out No. 10 from the first rank. Let him give the command to fire by two files. Make them carry arms. That will do."

I was very glad when this examination was over. He said to the adjutants-major, "You must push forward the newcomers, and make some cartridges for the grand drill. I will send you three tons of powder."

Then he started off for St. Cloud. For a fortnight a hundred men were at work making cartridges, and the adjutants-major superintended them. They had to wear shoes without nails, so as to avoid danger of accident. Every two hours they were relieved, and their feet examined. We made a hundred thousand packages. As soon as the required number was made, we had grand drills in the plain of St. Denis and reviews at the Tuileries, with parks of artillery in considerable force, and wagons and ambulances. The Emperor had them opened, and got up on the wheels to be sure that everything was in place. Sometimes M. Larrey received a reprimand. The engineer officers also trembled before him. It became more apparent every day that great preparations for war were being made; but we could not tell against whom it would be declared. But towards the latter part of April, 1812, we received orders to hold ourselves ready to march, and to have the linen and shoes inspected. Each soldier was to have three pairs of shoes, three shirts, and a dress uniform in his knapsack.

The day before the final review, I was called before the council, and appointed factor of the two regiments of grenadiers, and to have charge of the transportation of money and equipages: These consisted of four wagons: two for the officers' trunks, and two which were to be loaded at the Treasury, on the Place Vendôme. I was to show a letter, of which I was the bearer, and my two wagons were to be loaded immediately with casks containing twenty-eight thousand francs. The guard was kept in the day before we left, and I only was permitted to go out, so as to settle my accounts with the butcher and baker. I returned at two o'clock in the morning. The guard had started for Meaux at midnight on the 1st of May, 1812. An old sergeant, who was left at Courbevoie as keeper of the magazine, received my accounts, and handed me a "route," which authorized me to collect rations for eight men and sixteen horses. At noon I started from the

Place Vendôme with my four wagons, mounted on the first one, which had a pretty cabriolet on the front of it. I sat there, with my sabre at my side, like a man of great importance.

I reached Meaux at midnight, and went immediately to the

guard-room to learn the address of the adjutant-major. I was conducted to his apartment. "Who is there?" said he. —"It is I, major."—"You, Coignet, is it possible? Are your wagons all on the square ready loaded?"—"Yes, captain."—"You have flown, my brave fellow. I will see you to-morrow, before we set out. Here are your orders for rations of forage and bread. Take four men from the guard-room and four soldiers from the wagons; let them rouse the storekeeper. Your billets for lodgings are on my mantelpiece. Take them, and good-night." — "Good-night, captain. I will remain all night in the guard-room. It will be three o'clock by the time the horses and men are fed. The soldiers belonging to the trains shall sleep beside their horses, and I will be ready to start at seven o'clock."

M. Belcourt came to the post to see me, and assure himself that the rations for the men and horses had been furnished. He was pleased with my activity. "You are supplied for the whole route; you can follow us." — "If you will give me my 'route,' I will start every day two hours before you do, and then I shall be able to go and collect all the letters lying in the post-offices in the large towns. I shall be waiting for you with your letters." He went to see the colonel, who approved of my plan. Every day I went on ahead of the corps. Neither my men nor my horses suffered from the heat. When we came to the halting-places, I had all breakages which had taken place repaired.

The Emperor had left for Dresden, accompanied by the Empress. In this city there is the handsomest royal family in Europe. The father and son are not less than five feet ten inches tall. The Emperor remained here ten days to have an interview with the kings. After having given and received holy water in the courtyard, he bade farewell to his wife. Their leave-taking was a sad one. The splendid equipages set out for Paris, and the Emperor was left alone with his thoughts at the head of his grand army.

We reached Posen on the 3d of June, and Koenigsberg on the 12th, where he established his headquarters. There we had a brief season of repose, as he had gone to Dantzig, where he remained four days. This refreshed the old guard, who had made forced marches. We received orders to start for Insterburg, and, on the 21st of June, we reached Wilkowski. We left there on the 22d and 23d of June, and made our headquarters at a village a league and half from Kowno. The next day, at nine o'clock in the evening, we began the construction of three bridges over the Niemen. The work was completed at twenty-five minutes before midnight, and the army began to enter the Russian territory.

It was wonderful to see those bodies of men moving over those barren plains. Often they were without shelter and without bread; often in the wildest places, where we knew not where to turn to find necessary food. But Providence and courage never abandon a good soldier.

SEVENTH NOTE-BOOK.

THE RUSSIAN CAMPAIGN. — I AM APPOINTED LIEUTENANT ON THE MINOR IMPERIAL STAFF. — THE RETREAT FROM MOSCOW.

On the 26th of June, 1812, we crossed the Niemen. Prince Murat formed the advance guard with his cavalry; Marshal Davout, with sixty thousand men, marched in column, together with the whole guard and his artillery, on the high road to Wilna. It is impossible to give any idea of such a spectacle as those columns, moving over those arid plains, with no habitations except some wretched villages devastated by the Russians. Prince Murat caught up with them at the bridge of Kowno; they were obliged to fall back upon Wilna. The weather, which up to that time had been very fine, suddenly changed. On the 29th of June, at three o'clock, a violent storm arose, just before we came to a village, which I had had the greatest possible difficulty in reaching. When we reached the shelter of this village, we could not unharness our horses; we had to take off their bridles, cut some grass for them, and light our fires. The storm of sleet and snow was so terrible that we could scarcely keep our horses still; we were obliged to fasten them to the wheels. I was half dead with the cold; not being able to stand it any longer, I opened one of my wagons, and crept inside. Next morning a heart-rending sight met our gaze: in the cavalry camp near by, the ground was covered with horses frozen to death; more than ten thousand died during that dreadful night. When I got out of my wagon, all numbed with the cold, I saw that three of my horses were dead. After harnessing up my four wagons, I distributed all I had remaining. The unfortunate animals shook so that they broke the harness as soon as they were hitched; they threw themselves into their collars in desperation; they seemed perfectly wild, and plunged violently. If I had been an hour later, I should have lost them all. I must say, it took all our strength to manage them.

When we reached the highway, we found some dead soldiers, who had not been able to stand up against the terrible storm. This demoralized a great many of our men. Fortunately, our forced marches caused the Emperor of Russia to leave Wilna, where he had established his headquarters. In this large city it was possible to reduce the army to order. The Emperor arrived on the 29th of June, and immediately gave orders to deprive the stragglers of all their arms, and quarter them in an enclosure outside of the city. Here they were closely confined, and their rations were distributed to them. The gendarmes were sent out in every direction to pick them up. They numbered three battalions of seven hundred men, and had all preserved their arms.

After a short interval of rest, the army marched forward into immense forests, where it was necessary to be constantly on the watch, for fear of being surprised by the enemy in ambush. An army must march slowly when there is danger of being cut off. Before he started himself, the Emperor sent the chasseurs of his guard on ahead, and we remained with him. On the 13th of July, he issued an order for twenty-two non-commissioned officers to be sent to him, for promotion to lieutenancies in the line. As the chasseurs had all gone off, all the promotions fell to us. We had to be on the square at two o'clock to be presented to the Emperor. At noon I was passing by with my package of letters, for distribution, under my arm; Major Belcourt grasped my arm, and, pressing it heartily, said, "My brave fellow, you will be promoted to-day to be lieutenant of the line." — "I thank you; but I do not wish to return to the line." — "I tell you, you must this day wear the epaulets of a lieutenant; and I give you my word that if the Emperor puts you into the line, I will manage to have you returned to the guard. So not a word; be on the square at two o'clock, without fail." — "Very well, I will be there." — "I shall be there before you." — "All right, captain."

At two o'clock, the Emperor came to review us; all twenty-two of us were there, standing in line. Beginning at the right-hand man, and looking every one of those fine-looking non-commissioned officers all over from head to foot, he said to General Dorsenne, "These will make fine regimental officers." When he came to me, he saw that I was the smallest of them all, and the major said to him, "This is our instructor; he does not wish to go into the line." — "What! you do not wish to go into the line?" — "No, sire; I wish to remain in your guard." — "Very well, I will appoint you to my minor staff." Then, turning to his chief of staff, Count Monthyon, he said, "Take this little 'grumbler' as assistant in the minor general staff." How glad I was to remain near the Emperor! I did not suspect that I was leaving paradise for hell; but I learned it in time.

The brave General Monthyon came up to me; "Here is my address. Come to me to-morrow at eight o'clock, to receive my orders." That evening my comrades shot my knapsack to pieces.[1]

The next day, at the appointed hour, I went to see the general, who received me with the gracious smile of a man who loves his veterans. "Well," said he, "you are to do duty near the Emperor. If it will not be too much trouble, please cut off your long mustaches; the Emperor does not like mustaches on his staff officers. Come, now, make the sacrifice. If I were to send you on a mission, would you be afraid of a

---

[1] A symbolic ceremony in use in the old army. It proclaimed that the newly promoted man would have no more haversacks to carry.

Cossack?"—"No, general."—"I want two of your comrades, who know how to command, to lead three odd battalions. You will know which to select; send them to me. As for you, I have seen you command; you understand your business. I have three battalions of stragglers to send back to their army corps. To-morrow you shall command them in presence of the Emperor. So come here with your two comrades, and we will go at once to organize the three battalions."

On reaching the enclosure, the general called for the soldiers of the third corps, and placed them at one side, and soon for those of the other corps. When this was done, we returned to settle up our accounts with the quartermaster of the guard, and receive our certificates and our funds. Fortunately for me, the soldiers of the train had provided me with a fine horse, with saddle and portmanteau. So far, I was all right, but I had no chapeau, no sabre; I had only my foraging cap, and my chevrons had been taken off. I looked like a degraded non-commissioned officer. This hurt me.

I went to the quartermaster's office to get my pay and the certificate of my services, and then to take leave of my kind officers. They told me to take my choice of the horses belonging to my teams. "I thank you. but I am already well mounted. I had set aside a fine horse, with saddle and bridle, which did not belong to the equipages, and I leave everything in good condition."—"Farewell, my brave fellow, we will see one another often."—"If I had a chapeau, I should be content."—"Very well, come by this evening, and you will find one at the quartermaster's office; I will look out for it," said the adjutant-major. "Now I am all right."—"And if I can find a sabre for you, I will do it at once. You have a right to one."

I left them, quite overwhelmed; I went to see Count Monthyon, and tell him I had been discharged. "I will have your first pay as lieutenant given to you so that you can fit yourself out. Make haste and settle up your affairs; we must be off soon."—"To-morrow, general, all my accounts will be settled."

That night I went to the quartermaster's office, and found

a chapeau and an old sabre, and I felt as big again. The next morning, I presented myself with my long sabre at my side, and a three-cornered hat. "Ah!" said he, "you look nicely. I must find you some epaulets. We shall leave on the 16th of July. Come to me twice a day for orders."

On the morning of the 15th, I presented myself before Count Monthyon, who said, "We shall leave to-morrow. You will have seven hundred men to take back to the third corps. At noon we go to the castle and see the Emperor. I have just ordered your two comrades to be ready at eleven o'clock, to take command of their battalions. They must be reviewed at once; the muster-rolls are made out by regiments. My aide-de-camp has gone to have the roll-call; we must be ready."

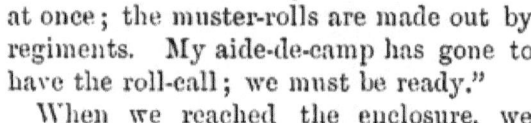

When we reached the enclosure, we found them all under arms, and forming three battalions. He placed us in command, and had us acknowledged as their commanders; he gave us our route-bills, and the rolls of the regiments. At six o'clock, on the 15th, I went into the enclosure to call them out, regiment by regiment. I first found a hundred and thirty-three Spaniards belonging to the regiment of Joseph Napoleon, and so on with the others. When my roll had been called, I made them arm themselves. I had had no sergeant given me; a drummer and one little musician was my whole staff with which to manage seven hundred men. I made them carry arms and stack arms. At nine o'clock we had soup, and at ten all was ready. My two comrades were equally energetic. At eleven o'clock Count Monthyon came up, passed on rapidly, and we started off. Fortunately, I had a drum; but for that, I should have marched like a mute.

My little musician marched at the right of the battalion with his little sword in his hand. We went to the palace. I placed my battalion on the right in line of battle, and in the front rank, with the others behind. I stationed guides on the line; as they knew nothing of the drill, I had to take them by the arm, and the Emperor was watching me from his balcony. I made them carry arms, and gave the command, "Dress up, in the centre! Guides to your places!" I corrected the dressing, and took my place at the right of my battalion. Count Monthyon went for the Emperor. They came out, and a sign was made for me to come to them. "How many cartridges do you need?" — "Three hundred and seventy-three packages, sire." — "Make out an order for your cartridges and one for two rations of bread and meat. Make them carry arms, by the right flank, and take them out on the square. I will have them guarded; and go at once for your bread, meat, and cartridges."

All the outlets from the square were guarded; my arms were stacked, and I took some men for special duty, went for the cartridges, and distributed them; then I went for the meat and bread. At seven o'clock all the distributions had been made. I was half dead of hunger, and went to get something to eat, and see about my fine horse. I chose a horseman who had been dismounted for my servant. I received an order to march at eight o'clock.

After leaving Wilna, we found ourselves surrounded by great forests. I left the head of my battalion, and went to the rear, making the stragglers keep up by placing my little musician on the right to mark the time. Night came on, and I saw my deserters steal away into the depths of the forest without being able to bring them back to the ranks on account of the darkness. I could do nothing but fret. What was to be done with such soldiers? I said to myself, "They will all desert."

They marched for two hours. The head of my battalion, coming to an open space where several roads met and where there were no woods, established themselves there. When the rear came up, the fires were already lighted. Imagine my surprise! "What are you doing there? Why do you not go on?" — "We have marched far enough; we need rest and food."

The fires were burning and the pots boiling. At midnight

the Emperor passed by with his escort. Seeing my bivouac all lighted up, he halted, and called me to the door of his carriage. "What are you doing here?" — "Please your Majesty, it is not I who command, but they. I came up with the rear-guard, and found the head of the battalion settled down and the fires lighted. A great many deserters have already returned to Wilna, taking their two rations with them. What can I do alone with seven hundred stragglers?" — "Do the best you can; I will give orders to have them arrested."

I departed, and I was left to spend the night with these unmanageable soldiers, and sigh for my sergeant's straps. But this was not the end of my troubles. At dawn I had the assembly beaten; at broad daylight I had the drummers beat to arms, and started once more on our route, telling them that the Emperor was going to have all the deserters arrested. I marched until noon, and, as we emerged from a wood, I came upon a herd of cows grazing in a meadow. My soldiers immediately took their bowls, and went off to milk the cows, and we had to wait for them. When the evening came, they would camp before nightfall, and every time we came across any cows, we had to stop. It may be imagined that this was not much fun for me. At last we came to a forest, very far away from the towns, a considerable portion of which had been destroyed by fire. This burnt forest extended along the way on my right, and I saw a party of my troops turn to the right into these charred woods. I galloped off after them, to make them come back to the road. To my surprise, these soldiers made an about face, and fired at me. I was obliged to let them go. This was a plot got up among the soldiers of Joseph Napoleon, who were all Spaniards. There were a hundred and thirty-three of them, and not one single Frenchman had joined the brigands. When I returned to my detachment, I made them form a circle, and said to them, "I shall be obliged to report this affair. Be Frenchmen, and follow me! I shall act as rear-guard no longer; that shall be your duty. By the right flank!"

That same evening, we emerged from the forest, and came

"They shot sixty-two of them." — Page 215.

to a village where there was a cavalry station, with a colonel who was guarding the forks of the road, and showing the troops which to take. I went to him, and made my report; he ordered my battalion to camp, and, upon suggestions from me, he sent for some Jews and his interpreter. He judged, from the distance, to which village my deserters must have gone, and sent off fifty chasseurs, with the Jews to guide them. About half-way they met some peasants who had been unjustly treated, and were coming to ask for protection. They reached the village at midnight, surrounded it, and surprised the Spaniards while they were asleep; seized them, disarmed them, and put their guns in a wagon. The men were tied and put into small wagons with a strong guard. At eight o'clock in the morning the hundred and thirty-three Spaniards arrived, and were set free from their shackles. The colonel ordered them into line, and said to them, "You have behaved very badly; I shall deal with you by lots. Are there any sergeants or corporals among you to form your lots?" At this two sergeants showed their chevrons, which had been concealed by their cloaks. "Stand aside, there! Are there any corporals?" Three came forward. "Stand there! Are there any more among you? All right! Now, the rest of you draw lots." Those who drew white tickets were placed on one side, and those who drew black ones, on the other. When all had drawn, he said to them, "You have run away, you have acted as incendiaries, you have fired upon your officer; the law condemns you to death, and you must submit to your punishment. I could have you all shot, but I will spare half of you. Let them serve as an example to you. Commander, order your battalion to load their guns. My assistant will give the command to fire." They shot sixty-two of them. My God! what a scene it was. I left the spot immediately with a bursting heart, but the Jews were highly delighted.[1] Such was my first experience as lieutenant.

I was anxious to reach the end of my journey; but the marshal was ahead of me. At Gluskoé, where I found the guard,

---

[1] They had the spoils of the men who were shot.

I put my soldiers into bivouac, and had provisions given them. The next day I started for Witepsk, where two severe battles had taken place. Oh, how I longed to get rid of my hateful burden! At last I reached Witepsk, full of joy, thinking I had come to the end of my march. But I was mistaken; the marshal's corps was still three leagues ahead. I went to get orders as to which road I should take, and, on returning, found only the drummer waiting for me. "Well, where are they all?"—"All run away," said my drummer and my soldier; "some one told them that the third corps was only one league off."

I started off with my drummer and my soldier. I had three leagues to go. At four o'clock I caught up with the marshal's staff. The aide-de-camp and the officers, seeing me alone with my drummer and solitary soldier, began to laugh. "It is not very becoming in you, gentlemen, to laugh at me. See, general, here is my route-bill; you will see what I have been doing since I left Wilna."

When the chief of staff had looked over my report, he took me aside. "Where are your soldiers?"—"They deserted me at Witepsk, just before we entered the town, when I galloped off to get orders for the route I was to take to join you. They all ran off in the joyful expectation of joining their corps more quickly. As for the sixty who were shot, there was not one Frenchman among them."—"How much you must have endured from these stragglers!"—"Ah, general, I have sweated blood."—"I want to present you to the marshal."—"I know him, and he knows me; he will not laugh at me as your officers did. They wounded me very much."—"Come, my brave fellow, think no more of it. Come with me; I will make it all right."

When he came where the officers were, he said, "Take this brave man to my tent, and give him something to drink. I am going to see the marshal, for he brings us news. See to this at once. I will rejoin you in a moment." He returned, and taking me by the arm before his officers, who were much confounded, he said, "Come, the marshal wishes to see you."

When the marshal saw my uniform, he said, "You are one

of my old grumblers." — "Yes, general. It was you who made me put the cards into my stockings so I should be tall enough to enter the grenadiers whom you commanded at that time." — "That is so; I remember. You had already received a gun of honor at the battle of Montebello, and you have since been decorated." — "Yes, general; the first one in 1804." — "This is one of my old grenadiers. You must not go away till to-morrow. I will give you my despatches. Which is your corps?" — "I am assistant at the Emperor's minor headquarters, under command of Count Monthyon." — "Ah! you have a good position. To-morrow, at ten o'clock, you will receive my despatches. Put this old soldier at the officers' table, and feed his horse." — "Yes, marshal." — "And hand over to him all the men who have returned and been received. Look over all the regiments, and see if they have re-entered, and report to me this evening at eight o'clock." To me, he said, "At ten o'clock to-morrow, you must start for Witepsk; you will find the Emperor there. I will give you a letter to Monthyon." Returning to his officers, the chief of staff said, "This officer is one of our oldest soldiers; receive him as he deserves; he is well known to the marshal. Let him dine with you, and after dinner my aide-de-camp will accompany him to the commanders of the corps, so that he can receive the men who have returned and been re-entered."

In a word, they sang low mass with me, and put water in their wine. I was most kindly received, and, after dinner, I was conducted to the camp, where I found my re-entered soldiers, who hastened to ask pardon for their ill-conduct to me. "I have no complaint against you, soldiers," said I; "it was your zeal which carried you away."

When we met the colonel of the Spaniards, who was a Frenchman, I asked him for my receipt. "But," said he, "half of them are missing." — "They are dead, colonel. Go and see the marshal." — "What, dead?" — "Half of them were shot." — "Then I will shoot the other half." — "You have no right to do it; they have been pardoned. They submitted to their punishment, and the Emperor must decide the matter." — "How many are killed?" — "Sixty-two, of

whom two were sergeants and three corporals." — " Give me
the details." — " I cannot; the marshal is waiting Let me
have my receipt, if you please; I must go at once." The aide-
de-camp took him aside, and, after a few words, we left. The
next day, at eight o'clock, I went to the marshal. " Here are
your despatches, march!"

By noon I reached Witepsk, and went to see Count Monthyon. I handed him my despatches and receipts. He had
learned all that had passed, and the Emperor was informed of
it. The marshal had said a word or two for me which pleased
the general. " You shall not go on duty again," said he,
" until we reach the suburbs of Smolensk."

Witepsk is a large town. There I met my old comrades
and my kind officers. We remained there waiting for supplies. The excessive heat, added to all our other privations,
brought on dysentery, from which our army suffered considerable loss. The Emperor left Witepsk during the night of the
12th of August. All the corps under his command went, by
forced marches, to Smolensk, a strong position about thirty-
two leagues off. The investment was completed on the morning of the 17th of August. Napoleon ordered the attack
along the whole line about two o'clock in the afternoon, and
the battle was a terribly bloody one. During the engagement
he sent for me. " Start at once for Witepsk with this order,
which enjoins upon every man, no matter to what branch of
the army he may belong, to give you assistance in unsaddling
your horse. At the relays, all the horses will be at your disposal in case of need, except the artillery horses. Are you
mounted?" — " Yes, sire, I have two horses." — " Take them
both. When you have ridden one down, take the other. Go as
fast as you possibly can. I shall expect you back to-morrow;
it is now three o'clock. Go!" I mounted at once; Count
Monthyon said to me, " There is need for haste, my veteran;
take your other horse by the bridle, and leave the first one on
the way." — " But they are both saddled." — " Leave your
best saddle with my servants. Do not lose a moment."

I flew like lightning, leading my other horse. When the
first one began to give way under me, I dismounted, with one

turn I changed the saddle to the other horse, and left my poor beast lying on the ground. I dashed on. When I came to a wood, I met some sutlers who were going to rejoin their corps. "Halt! a horse at once! I leave you mine ready saddled; I am in great haste. Unhitch and unsaddle my horse." — "Here are four fine Polish horses," said the sutler, "which will you have?" — "That one! quick, quick! I am in a hurry. I have not a moment to lose." Ah, that good horse, how far he carried me! I found in that forest a line of posts for the protection of the route. When I came to the officer of the post: "See, here is my order: a horse, quick! Keep mine!"

I did not lose an hour's time all the way to Witepsk. I gave my despatches to the general in command. After reading them he said, "Give this officer his dinner, let him lie down on a mattress for an hour, have a good horse ready for him, and a chasseur to escort him. You will find a regiment camped near the wood. He can change horses at the post in the wood." When the hour had elapsed the general came. "Your package is ready; start, my brave fellow. If you meet with no delay on the way, you will not have spent twenty-four hours on the road, even counting the loss of time in changing horses." I started off well mounted and escorted. I found the regiment camped in the forest. I presented my order to the colonel. As soon as he read it, "Give him your horse, adjutant-major, it is the Emperor's order. Unsaddle his horse. There is no time to lose."

I expected to find the cavalry stations in the wood; but I did not. They had all gone off, or been captured. I found myself alone without any escort. I wondered what I ought to do. I went along more slowly, and presently saw, some distance off on an eminence, some cavalry dismounted. I kept along the edge of the wood so as not to be seen, for they were doubtless Cossacks on the watch. I went closer into the wood. Suddenly a peasant came out, who said to me, "Cossacks!" I had seen them plainly enough. Without hesitating, I dismounted, and, seizing my pistol, I pointed it at the peasant, showing him gold in one hand and my pistol in the other. He understood, and said to me, "*Tac, tac*," which meant, "All right." Putting my gold back in the pocket of my waistcoat, and passing my horse's bridle over my arm, I took my loaded pistol in my left hand, and, with my right, I held on to the Russian who led me along a path. After following it for a considerable distance, he brought me back towards my route, saying, "*Nien, nien,* Cossacks!"

I then recognized my road, for I saw the birch-trees. Filled with joy, I gave three napoleons to the peasant, and mounted my horse. How I dug my spurs into his sides! The road disappeared behind me. I was fortunate enough to reach a farm before my horse began to stumble. I dashed into the courtyard, and, seeing three young physicians, I dismounted, and ran to the stable. "A horse at once! I will leave you mine. Read this order."

I mounted another good horse, which travelled well; but I should need one more, at least, to carry me to the end of my journey. The night was coming on, and I could no longer see my way before me. Fortunately, I met four officers well mounted. I began to go through the same ceremony. "See if you can read this order from the Emperor, requiring you to give me a fresh horse." A large man, whom I took to be a general, said to one of the others, "Unsaddle your horse; give it to this officer. His orders are pressing. Assist him."

This saved me. I reached the field of battle. I went around looking and asking for the Emperor. All answered me, "We do not know where he is." I went on, and leaving the route, I saw some fires on my left. I came to some small brushwood. I went forward and passed near a battery. Some

one called, "Who goes there?"—"An ordnance officer."—
"Halt! you are going towards the enemy."—"Where is the
Emperor?"—"Come this way; I will lead you near his post."
When I rode up to the officer, he said, "Conduct him to the
Emperor's tent."—"I thank you." I reached the tent, and
had myself announced. General Monthyon came out, and said
to me, "Is it you, my brave fellow? I will take you to the
Emperor at once. He thought you had been captured." Then
my general said to the Emperor, "Here is the officer who has
just come from Witepsk." I gave him my despatches, and he
saw my deplorable condition. "How did you get through the
forest? The Cossacks were there."—"With gold, sire; a
peasant took me through a winding path, and saved me."—
"How much did you pay him?"—"Three napoleons."—
"And your horses?"—"I have none now."—"Monthyon,
pay him for all the expenses of his journey: for his two
horses, and the sixty francs which the peasant well deserved.
Give my old grumbler time to remount himself. For his two
horses, sixteen hundred francs and expenses. I am well
pleased with you."

The next day we entered Smolensk. At daylight no one
could pass into the city. The Russians, from the other side
on the heights, riddled the town with shells and cannon-balls.
It was in a sad plight. About two o'clock in the afternoon,
a general attack was ordered. The battle was terribly bloody,
and the firing ceased only with the daylight. The city took
fire that beautiful August night. In order to get into it, we
had to cross a low ground, and then ascend to a gate, which
was barricaded with sacks of salt. Thousands of sacks barred
this handsome entrance. As for the street, we traversed it
between furnaces. All those fine storehouses were a solid
mass of embers, particularly the sugar depot. It is impossible
to describe the different colors of the blaze. It may be truly
said that Smolensk cost us dear, and the Russians dearer.
The loss on both sides was considerable. We were obliged
to move round the city in order to take possession of
the heights. Then we remained several days at Smolensk.
To go out of the city, we had to descend a very steep slope,

cross a bridge, and turn abruptly to the right. From Smolensk to Moscow is a distance of ninety-three leagues, and the whole way the road is through deep forests. On the 19th of August took place the battle which Marshal Ney fought at Valoutina. The Emperor received a report of the battle, and learned that Marshal Davout had gone three leagues beyond the line of battle. He had gone through a forest without searching it, and might be cut off by the Russians. The Emperor foresaw this, and sent me to order him to fall back.

On reaching the marshal, I handed him the despatches. He immediately ordered his reserve to wheel about, and his whole corps to retreat, and sent me back. I found his reserve division already in close columns, occupying the whole road through the wood. Not being able to pass them, I took a road to the left, which ran parallel with the route, and galloped off to get ahead of the retreating division, and so ran into the midst of a Russian column, which was going along this narrow road. Seeing that it was routed, I did not lose my presence of mind, but began to shout with the voice of a Stentor, "Forward!" And, turning back down the road, I passed those frightened fugitives, who stooped as they marched. I finally extricated myself, and, gaining the main road, I informed our officers that the Russians were in the wood.

I met the guard on the way, they having left Smolensk on the 25th of August to go to the outposts. I also saw the Emperor, and reported to him my adventure. "Did you see the battle-field?" asked the Emperor. "No, sire; but the road was covered with Russians and a great many Frenchmen."—"You cannot follow me; you must come on with the carriages to-morrow, and join me."

He said to his groom, "Take care of my old grumbler; he will follow you." I was kindly treated, and the next day a horse was furnished me, so that I could allow mine to rest. We rejoined the Emperor by forced marches. On the 29th, as the Russians were leaving a town on the banks of the Wiazma, they set fire to the storehouses, and a fourth of the town was burnt. For forty leagues they continued to do this, remorselessly burning the cottages filled with their own wounded, which we found reduced to ashes. Not a barrack remained along the route. As for their wounded, the amputations were skilfully performed, and bandages well applied; but they afterwards sent them into another world. And if they did not have time to bury them, they left them in piles for us to see. It was a heart-rending sight.

The Emperor, after having spent a part of the day of the 6th of September in reconnoitring the enemy's position, sent orders for the battle which was to take place the next day. It is known as the battle of the Moskwa. In order to pass into the plain occupied by the Russians, it was necessary to leave the wood. As soon as we emerged from it we saw, on the right of the road, a large redoubt which shelled us as we came out. We had to make unheard-of efforts to take it. The cuirassiers carried it, and then the columns spread out in the plain. The grand reserve was placed on the left of the main road, and we could not see the battle line of the columns; we could only see some coppices of willows and skirts of woods. We passed the night in getting ready; at break of day we were all on foot, and the artillery began on both sides. The Emperor made a great movement with his reserve, and ordered it over to the right side of the main road, flanked by a deep ravine, from which position he did not move all day. He had there with him twenty or twenty-five thousand men — the *élite* of France — all in full uniform. From time to time messengers came to ask him to order the guard to finish the battle, but in vain; he held out the whole day. Our troops made every possible effort to take the redoubts which were thundering upon our infantry on the right; they were always repulsed, and the victory depended upon this position. The general led me up to the Emperor. "Are you well mounted?" — "Yes, sire." — "Go at once and carry this order to Caulaincourt; you will find him on the right by the side of the wood. You will see the cuirassiers; it is he who commands them. Do not return till after the end."

I went to the general, and presented the order. He read it, and said to his aide-de-camp, "Here is the order which I have been expecting. Sound to horse! Send the colonels up for orders." They came up on horseback, and formed a circle. Caulaincourt read them the order to take the redoubts, and appointed to each the redoubt he was to attack. "I will reserve the second for myself. You, officer of the staff, follow me; do not lose sight of me." — "I shall not, general." — "If I fall, you, colonel, must take the command; those redoubts must be taken at the first charge." Then he said to the colonels, "You hear what I say: go take the head of your regi-

ments. The grenadiers are waiting for us. There is not a moment to lose! Trot when I give the command, and gallop as soon as you are within gunshot. The grenadiers will leap over the barriers."

The cuirassiers went along the edge of the wood and fell upon the redoubts directly in front, while the grenadiers attacked the barriers. Cuirassiers and French grenadiers struggled pell-mell with the Russians. The brave Caulaincourt fell stone-dead beside me. I followed the old colonel who took the command, and never lost sight of him. When the charge was over and the redoubts in our possession, the old colonel said to me, "Go tell the Emperor that the victory is ours. I shall send to him the staff-officers taken in the redoubts."

The Russians made every possible effort to save the redoubts, but Marshal Ney thundered upon their right wing. I started off at a gallop, and, as I was crossing the battle-field, I saw the ground ploughed up by cannon-balls, and thought I should not escape them. When I reached the Emperor I dismounted, and, loosing the string and taking off my hat, I saw that the hind corner was gone. "Well done," said he; "you have had a narrow escape." — "I had not perceived it before. The redoubts are taken; General Caulaincourt is dead." — "What a loss!" — "A good many officers are to be brought to you."

Everybody laughed at my hat with its one corner. I did not mind it; people laugh at everything. The Emperor called for his bear-skin. As he was occupying the sloping side of a ravine, he was almost in a standing position when lying down. Just at this moment the officers who had been captured in the redoubts arrived, escorted by a company of grenadiers. They were drawn up in line according to their rank. The Emperor reviewed them, and asked if his soldiers had robbed them of anything. They answered that not a single soldier had interfered with them in any way. An old grenadier of the company stepped from the ranks, and, presenting his arms to the Emperor, said, "It was I who captured that superior officer." The Emperor listened to all that the grenadier had to say, and took down his name. "And what did your captain do?" — "He was the first man to enter the third redoubt." The Emperor then said to the latter, "I appoint you chief of battalion, and your officers shall have the cross." And added, "Commander, order a movement by the left flank, and be off to the field of honor." Then they shouted, "Long live the Emperor!" and flew to rejoin their eagle. We passed the night on the battle-field, and the next day the Emperor had all the wounded taken up. This task made us shudder; the ground was covered with Russian muskets: near their field hospitals there were piles of dead bodies and heaps of limbs which had been amputated.

Murat pursued them so rapidly that they burned up their wounded men; we found them all charred skeletons. That shows how much they valued their soldiers. The Emperor left Mojaisk on the afternoon of the 12th, and moved his headquarters to Tartaki, a small village. Count Monthyon sent for me, and said, "You are very fortunate: the Emperor intends sending you to join Prince Murat, who is to enter Moscow to-morrow. Come, take the Emperor's orders." When I went into His Majesty's presence, he said, "I have appointed you to go and join Murat; take with you twenty gendarmes,

and when you reach the Kremlin examine the vaults, and post the gendarmes at all the entrances of the palace. Monthyon, give him your interpreter and my despatches for Murat. To-morrow morning you are to start." How proud I was of such a mission! At ten o'clock I had reached Prince Murat. I gave him my despatches. "We are to march," said he; "you will follow me with your gendarmes." — "Yes, prince." — "But you have only a piece of a hat." — "The Russians wanted the other part for touchwood." He burst out laughing. "You were formerly in the guard?" — "Yes, prince; in the foot grenadiers." — "You are one of our veterans.

Order your gendarmes to be on horseback at eleven o'clock to advance with us to the bridge."

We emerged from the forest. A dry and sandy plain sloped rapidly down in front of an immensely long bridge, built on piles, where there was no water; it was used only during the melting of the snows. When we reached the bridge, we found the city authorities there and a Russian general, who presented the keys to the prince. After the usual ceremonies, the prince gave the Russian general a casket richly studded with diamonds, and we entered the city by a broad and well-built street.[1] We were preceded by four pieces of cannon, a battalion, and a squad of cavalry; all the people came to the windows to see us pass, and the ladies presented us with bottles of wine, but no one stopped. We marched slowly. At the end of this immense street

we came to the foot of the Kremlin. The ascent to it is very steep. It is a strong castle overlooking the city, which is divided into two parts, and, consequently, two immense cities seem lying below it. On its summit to the right is the splendid palace of the Emperors. On the square of the Kremlin to the left is a large arsenal; to the right, the church, which has the palace at its back, and in front of the square is

---

[1] If the interest of Coignet's narrative depended upon the statement of facts, there would be here, as in other places, much to verify. The keys of the city were not presented; the "authorities" were only some foreign merchants, and the Russian general was only an officer, deputized to propose a sort of tacit armistice in order to facilitate the retreat through the city. As the advance-guard of the French almost touched the last ranks of the Russian rear-guard, Murat asked for the commander of the latter, and exchanged courtesies with him. He received from him a cloak of long fur, and offered him in exchange the Gourgand watch, which Coignet, stationed at some distance doubtless, took for a casket studded with diamonds. The watch was a very handsome one.

a magnificent public building. As we turned to the right we were assailed by a perfect hail of shot, fired from the windows of the arsenal. We wheeled about; the doors were burst open, and we found the ground floor and first story filled with drunken soldiers and peasants. A carnage ensued; those who escaped were put into the church. I lost my horse there. After this affray, Prince Murat continued his march, and descended into the lower town in order to pass out of the city and reach the road to Kalouga.

I left the prince at the Kremlin, and went to carry out my orders. My interpreter took me to the magistrates to have my gendarmes lodged, and afterward conducted me to the palace. The interpreter must have said very fine things to them about me, for refreshments were offered me immediately, and it was there that I drank tea with rum in it, for the first time. I was lodged in the house of a Russian general, and with me, four gendarmes and the interpreter. I went with the guards to examine the subterranean passages, and then went up again into the palace. One could easily get lost there. I posted my gendarmes, and had their food provided for them by the gentlemen who had received me so kindly. I and my guide were invited into a smoking-room. I do not know what effect my one-cornered hat had upon them, but they all gazed at it, and wanted to touch it.

I returned to the tomb of the czars. I was surprised to see at the foot of this gigantic monument a bell of immense size. I was told that it fell from the top of the framework, and was thus implanted here. The circumference of this bell has been decorated so as to mark it as an unusual monument; it is surrounded by bricks, placed so that it can be seen. I climbed up into the tomb of the emperors, and saw the bell which occupies the place of the one of which I have just spoken; it also is monstrous; the clapper is something unheard of. Thousands of names are inscribed upon this bell.

A beautiful street leading from the Kremlin opens upon a fine boulevard surrounded by handsome palaces. This part of the city was not burned, and became our place of refuge.

When I had fulfilled the duty which had been assigned me,

I waited for the Emperor, but in vain; he did not come. He had set up his headquarters in the faubourg; the guard took possession of the palace, and relieved my four gendarmes. As I was crossing the square of the Kremlin, I met some soldiers loaded with fur robes and bear-skins; I stopped them, and offered to buy their handsome sable robes. "How much is this one?" — "Forty francs." I took it immediately, and paid him the price he asked. "And this bear-skin?" — "Forty francs." — "Here they are." What good luck it was thus to obtain these two things of such inestimable value to me. I went off with my gendarmes to the house of my Russian general. The Emperor was obliged to leave his headquarters in the faubourg during the night, and establish himself in the Kremlin, in consequence of a fire which broke out in both of the lower towns. It must have required a great many persons to set fire to all parts of the town at the same time. It was said that all the galley-slaves took part in it; each man had a street, and went from house to house, setting them on fire. We were obliged to escape into the squares and large gardens. Seven hundred of these incendiaries were arrested, tinder in hand, and taken to the vaults of the Kremlin. This fire was rendered more frightful by the wind which blew the roofing of sheet-iron off the palaces and churches; all the people, as well as the troops, found themselves in the midst of the fire. The wind was terrible; the sheets of iron were blown two leagues through the air. There were eight hundred fire-engines in Moscow, but they had all been carried away.

About eleven o'clock in the night we heard screams in the gardens, and, going to see, found that our soldiers were robbing the women of their shawls and ear-rings. We hastened to put a stop to the pillage. Two or three thousand women were there, with their children in their arms, looking upon the horrors of the fire, and I am sure I never saw one of them shed a tear.

The Emperor was obliged to withdraw on the evening of the 16th, and establish himself at the castle of Petrowskoï, about a league from Moscow. The army also left the city, which was thus abandoned to pillage and fire. The Emperor remained four days at Petrowskoï, awaiting the end of the burning of Moscow; he re-entered that city on the 20th of September, and again took up his quarters in the Kremlin, and the minor-staff, to which I belonged, was stationed near the ramparts at a short distance from the Kremlin. I was employed as assistant, with two of my comrades, to a colonel of the staff, who had charge of the clearing of the hospitals.

We were lodged in the house of a princess, all four of us, with our horses and our servants; the colonel had three servants of his own, and he kept them well employed. He used to send us into the hospitals to have the sick discharged, but never went himself. He stayed to attend to his own affairs. He would go out in the evening with three servants furnished with wax tapers; he knew that the pictures in the churches were all in relief on plaques of silver, so he took them down, in order to get this silver plate; put the saints into a crucible, and reduced them to ingots, which he sold to the Jews for bank-notes. He was a hard-looking man with a base countenance.

We had thousands of bottles of Bordeaux wine, champagne, and thousands of pounds of white and brown sugar. Every evening the old princess sent us four bottles of good wine and some sugar. Her cellars were full of casks. She came frequently to see us, and consequently her house was respected. She spoke good French. One evening the colonel showed us his purchases, or, rather, his stolen goods, for he was always going around with his three servants. He showed us some beautiful fur robes made of the skins of the Siberian fox. I had the imprudence to show him mine, and he compelled me to exchange it with him for one of the Siberian fox. Mine was of sable, but I had to submit. I feared his vengeance. He was rascal enough to take it from me, and sell it to Prince Murat for three thousand francs. This robber of the churches was a disgrace to the name of Frenchman. I saw him afterwards at Wilna, frozen to death. God punished him. His servants robbed his body.

All the hospitals in Moscow were under round vaults.

Russians and Frenchmen died together in these infected places. Every morning the wagons were loaded with the dead; and I had to see that they were buried, having them dumped from the wagons into holes twenty feet deep. It is impossible to describe such a sight. After the fire was over, a list was made out of the burned houses; it numbered ten thousand; and the palaces and churches burned were more than five hundred. All that remained of them were the chimneys and the stoves, which were very large. They looked like a forest which had been lopped off, and only the stumps left. The ground might have been ploughed up, for there was not one stone left upon another.

The palaces filled the city with parks, brooks, and conservatories, so large as to contain trees of considerable height, and bearing fruit in winter. This was one of the luxuries of Moscow. The losses could not be estimated. No one can imagine a sadder scene.

When my wretched task was completed, I had a few days' rest. My general said to me, "I shall keep you near me; you shall not leave me any more, and you shall eat at my table. You have suffered a great deal in the service of the evacuation of the hospitals. Now you shall rest." I was fortunate to be under such a general. I had nothing to do but to see that our horses were provided for, and seat myself at the table. My general had twelve covers; and, as his aide-de-camp was a little lazy, I said to him, "Do not worry yourself; I will attend to everything." Thus all went well at our quarters. We had provisions enough for the winter, both for ourselves and our horses. I was not exempt from the duty of carrying despatches, however, when my turn should come. The Emperor held reviews every day. He sent off trophies from Moscow, among them the cross from the tomb of the czars. It was a sight, that scaffolding erected to take down the cross. Men on it looked like dwarfs. This cross was thirty feet high, and was of solid silver. All the trophies were packed in large wagons, and sent to General Claparède with a battalion of men as escort, and he consequently was the first to start out on the retreat. The Jews informed our soldiers of the hiding-places dug in the ground. Their cupidity caused great wrong to be done to the unfortunate people. No one in the army put any stop to the robbery. It was dreadful to see it.

I was sent to a village, eighteen or twenty leagues from Moscow, to carry orders to Prince Murat. I came upon a body of cavalry in retreat,—our men, on bare-back horses. They had been surprised while grooming their horses. I could not find Prince Murat; he had run off in his shirt. It was pitiful to see those fine cavaliers running for their lives. I asked for the prince. "He is captured," they replied; "they took him in his bed." And I could learn nothing further.[1]

The Emperor heard of it at once through Nansouty's aides-de-camp, and on my return from this miserable mission, I found the army *en route* to aid Murat. I was half dead, and my horse could no longer walk. Fortunately, my servant procured me two more very good ones, and I was remounted. The Emperor had ordered that his household and all his bureaus should be sent from Moscow on the 23d of October, and join him at Mojaïsk. It is impossible to give any idea of the rapidity of the execution of his orders. The preparations for this move were completed in three hours. We went to the house of our princess, and there we found some good horses, which had been concealed in a cellar. We mounted two superb ones, and immediately hitched them to a fine carriage. While this was being done, I got the provisions ready: about ten loaves of sugar, a good-sized box of tea, some elegant cups, and a boiler. We had a carriage-load of provisions.

---

[1] On the 18th of October a Russian attack did in fact endanger our cavalry reserve, and Murat came near being captured. Next day the French army began to evacuate Moscow.

At three o'clock we left Moscow. It was scarcely possible to make our way, for the road was blocked up with carriages, and all the army plunderers were there in great numbers. When we had gone about three leagues from Moscow we heard a tremendous report.[1] The shock was so terrible that the earth shook under our feet. It was said that there were sixty tons of powder[2] under the Kremlin, with seven trains of powder, and some sort of contrivance fixed on the casks. Our seven hundred brigands, who had been captured with tinder in their hands, met their just punishment. They were all galley-slaves.

There was a line of carriages on the road twelve leagues long. By the time I had reached our first halting-place, I had had carriage enough. I had all our provisions put on horses, and burned up the carriage. After that we could pass everywhere. It was with the greatest possible difficulty that we at last reached the headquarters beyond Mojaïsk. The next day the Emperor went over the battle-field of the Moskwa, and groaned at seeing the dead still unburied. On the 31st of October, at four o'clock in the afternoon, he reached Wiazma. The Russian winter set in with all its severity on the 6th of November. The Emperor made frequent marches in the midst of his guard, following his carriage on foot, with an iron-shod cane in his hand; and we went along the side of the road with the cavalry officers. In a dispirited condition we reached Smolensk on the 9th of November. The halting-places were miserably supplied; the horses died of hunger and cold, and when we came to any cottages, they devoured the thatches. The cold was already intense, seventeen degrees below zero. This occasioned great losses to the army. Smolensk and the environs were filled with the dead. I took every possible care of myself. Our horses fell down upon the ice. As we were passing a camping-place, I got hold of two axes, and took the shoes off my horses, and they did

---

[1] There were at least five reports. Mortier had been left at Moscow with instructions to blow up the Kremlin. The despatch announcing the execution of this order reached Napoleon on the 27th of October.

[2] There were much more than sixty tons — 180,000 pounds. (See the Itinéraire of Baron Deniée.)

not slip any more. I had furnished myself with a little pot for making tea. When we reached the place where the Emperor stopped, I built a good fire, put my general in front of it to thaw himself, and then put the boiler on the fire to melt some snow. What bad water snow makes when melted in the midst of smoke! When my water was boiling, I put in a handful of tea. I cut up the sugar, and then the pretty cups did service. We had our tea every day. All the way to Wilna I did not want for friends; they followed my boiler, and I had ten loaves of sugar. They were three captains, and death only separated us, which means that I alone am left alive.

I followed my general, always as near as possible to the old guard and the Emperor. When we were attacked by the Russians, it was necessary to concentrate as much as possible. Every day the Cossacks burst out with shouts on the road, but, as our men were armed, they dared not approach us; they merely stationed themselves along the road to see us pass. But they slept in good quarters, and we on the snow. We left Smolensk with the Emperor on the 14th of November. On the 22d he learned that the Cossacks had just seized upon the *tête de pont* at Borisow, and that we should have to effect the passage of the Beresina. We came out past the great bridge which the Russians had half burned; they were on the other side waiting for us in the woods and in the snow. Though we had not exchanged fire once, we were already in great destitution. At one o'clock in the afternoon of the 26th of November the right-hand bridge was finished, and the Emperor immediately ordered the Duke of Reggio's corps and Marshal Ney with the cuirassiers to cross over before him. The artillery of the guard went over with their two corps, and crossed a marsh, which was fortunately frozen. In order to be able to reach a village, they drove the Russians back into the woods on the left, and thus gave the army time to cross, on the 27th. The Emperor crossed the Beresina at one o'clock in the afternoon, and took up his headquarters in a little hamlet. The army continued to cross the river during the nights of the 27th and 28th. The Emperor sent for Marshal Davout, and

I was appointed to guard the head of the bridge, and allow only the artillery and ammunition to go over. The marshal was on the right side and I on the left. When all the ammunition had gone over, the marshal said to me, "Come on, my brave fellow; come, let us rejoin the Emperor." We crossed the bridge and the frozen marsh; it was strong enough to bear our ammunition, without which all would have been lost.

During our wearisome watch, Marshal Ney had driven off the Russians, who came back again in order to cut off our route. Our troops had surprised them in the midst of the wood, and that battle cost them dear. Our brave cuirassiers brought them back all covered with blood; it was pitiful to see them. We came to a beautiful plateau. The Emperor reviewed the prisoners. The snow fell so heavily that every one was covered with it; we could not see one another.

But behind us a frightful scene was being enacted. After we had left the bridge the Russians directed the fires of their batteries upon the crowd[1] which surrounded the bridges. From our position we could see these unfortunate creatures rush for the bridges; then the wagons overturned, and all were swallowed up under the ice. No one could give any idea of this sight. The bridges were burned the next day at half-past eight o'clock. Immediately after reviewing the prisoners, the Emperor sent for me. "Start at once; carry these orders by the road to Wilna; here is a guide upon whom you can rely. Make every effort to get there by daybreak tomorrow." He had my guide questioned. A reward was given him in my presence, and to each of us was given a good Russian horse. I set out on a fine road, white with snow, but where there was scarcely anything else: our horses did not slip. At night we came to a wood, and, as a precaution, I tied a strong twine string around my guide's neck, lest he should get away from me. He said to me, "*Tac. tac*," which meant "That is a good idea." At last I had the good fortune to

---

[1] This crowd was composed of stragglers who had refused to cross on the preceding days, and who were bivouacking on the bank. It took the Russian cannon to make them start. The precise details of the passage are to be found in the very interesting narrative of Colonels Chappelle and Chapuis. (Versailles, 1844.)

reach my destination without any mishap. I dismounted, and my guide introduced me to the mayor, who had our horses put in a barn. I gave him my despatches; he offered me a glass of schnapps, and, first tasting it himself, he said, "Drink," in French. He broke the seal of my package, and said to me, "I could not possibly collect the immense quantity of provisions which your sovereign demands of me within three leagues of this city. There is a great deal in my diocese, but it would require a month to do it." — "That is none of my business." — "All right," said he, "I will do my best."

But he had no time to say more. The man who had taken my horse to the barn began to scream, "Cossacks, Cossacks!" I expected to be captured. The worthy mayor led me out of his cabinet into an ante-chamber, turned suddenly to the right, and, taking me by the shoulders and telling me to stoop, pushed me into the oven. I had no time for reflection. The oven was close to the ground under a vault, very long and deep; it was already lighted, but was not too warm, and so I could stand it. I had no time to go back. I knelt down on my right knee, and stayed. I was in a state of great anxiety. This kind mayor had had the presence of mind to take some wood and put it in front of the entrance to the oven, so as to conceal me. This was no sooner done than some officers entered the mayor's house; but they passed by the door of the oven where I was awaiting my fate. The minutes seemed ages; my hair stood on end; I thought I was lost. How long time seems when one is in suspense!

At last I heard all the officers leave the cabinet, and pass by my place of refuge. A terrible shuddering seized me. I thought I was lost; but Providence watched over me. They had seized upon my despatches, and had gone to join their regiment at the end of the village so as to go to the place indicated in my despatches. (I learned afterwards that the Emperor had sacrificed me in order to have my despatches captured and deceive the enemy.) The worthy *maire* came to me: "Come out," said he, "the Russians have gone off with your despatches, and to stop the advance of your army. Your road is open."

When I got out of the oven, I threw my arms around that generous man's neck, and said to him, "I shall inform my sovereign of your conduct." After having taken a glass of schnapps, he gave me some bread, which I put into my pocket. I found my horse at the gate, and, starting off at a gallop, I flew like the wind for a league. At last I began to go more moderately, for my horse was giving out. I thought no more of my guide who was left in the village. What joy when I came in reach of our scouts! I began to breathe freely, and cried out, "Saved, saved!" and then I felt for my piece of bread, and devoured it. The army was marching silently; the horses slipped, for the roads had been made smooth by the tramping of the troops. The cold became more and more intense. At last I came up to the Emperor and his staff; I went up to him, hat in hand. "So here you are! And your mission?"—"It is accomplished, sire."—"What! they did not capture you? And your despatches, where are they?" —"In the hands of the Cossacks."—"What! Come nearer. What do you say?"—"I have told you the truth. When I reached the mayor's house I gave him my despatches, and a moment after the Cossacks arrived, and the mayor hid me in his oven."—"In his oven?"—"Yes, sire; and I was not very comfortable; they passed right by me when they went into the mayor's cabinet; they took my despatches, and ran off."—"It is strange, my old grumbler, how you escaped being captured."—"The brave mayor saved me."—"I shall see him, this Russian."

He related my adventure to his generals, and said, "Set him down for a week's rest, and pay his expenses double." I rejoined General Monthyon, and found my horses and sugar safe. I was half dead of hunger. That night we came to a place about a mile from where my despatches had been taken by the Cossacks. He sent for the mayor, and had a conference with him. The mayor conducted him to within a league of his village, and I gave him, as he passed me, a good grasp of the hand. "I love the French," said he. "Farewell, brave officer." To this day I bless that man who saved my life.

The cold continued to grow more intense; the horses in the bivouacs died of hunger and cold. Every day some were left where we had passed the night. The roads were like glass. The horses fell down, and could not get up. Our worn-out soldiers no longer had strength to carry their arms. The barrels of their guns were so cold that they stuck to their hands. It was twenty-eight degrees below zero. But the guard gave up their knapsacks and guns only with their lives. In order to save our lives, we had to eat the horses which fell upon the ice. The soldiers opened the skin with their knives, and took out the entrails, which they roasted on the coals, if they had time to make a fire, and, if not, they ate them raw. They devoured the horses before they died. I also ate this food as long as the horses lasted. As far as Wilna, we travelled by short stages with the Emperor. His whole staff marched along the sides of the road. The men of the demoralized army marched along like prisoners, without arms and without knapsacks. There was no longer any discipline or any human feeling for one another. Each man looked out for himself. Every sentiment of humanity was extinguished. No one would have reached out his hand to his father; and that can be easily understood. For he who stooped down to help his fellow would not be able to rise again. We had to march right on, making faces to prevent our noses and ears from freezing. The men became insensible to every human feeling. No one even murmured against our misfortunes. The men fell frozen stiff all along the road. If, by chance, any of them

"On the retreat from Moscow we marched more than forty leagues without knapsacks or guns." — Page 239.

came upon a bivouac of other unfortunate creatures who were thawing themselves, the new-comers pitilessly pushed them aside, and took possession of their fire. The poor creatures would then lie down to die upon the snow. One must have seen these horrors in order to believe them. I can certify that on the retreat from Moscow we marched more than forty leagues without knapsacks or guns. But it was at Wilna that we suffered most. The weather was so severe that the men could no longer endure it; even the ravens froze.

During this fearful cold, I was sent to the general who had charge of the trophies taken at Moscow, with an order to have them turned over into the lake to the right of our route. At the same time the treasure was abandoned to the stragglers.[1] Those miserable creatures seized upon it, and burst open the casks. Three-fourths of them were frozen to death beside their plunder. Their burdens were so heavy that they fell. I rejoined my post after the greatest possible difficulty, and that I did so was owing to my unshod horse, which did not slide. I am sure that a man reduced to the same condition of weakness could not have been able to carry five hundred francs. I had seven hundred francs of my savings in my portmanteau. My horse was so weak that he began to go to sleep. I perceived this, and, taking my bag, I went to see my old grumblers in their bivouac, and proposed to them to rid me of my seven hundred francs. "Give me twenty francs in gold, and I will give you twenty-five francs." They all did so with pleasure, and I was unburdened, for I would have left them on the spot. All my fortune now consisted of eighty-three napoleons, and this saved my life.

At Smorgoni the Emperor bade farewell, before leaving the army, to such of the general officers as he could gather around him. He left at seven o'clock in the evening, accompanied by Generals Duroc, Mouton, and Caulaincourt. We remained under the command of the King of Naples, disconcerted enough,

---

[1] At Krasnoë the enemy had already captured twelve hundred and ninety-four thousand francs. At Wilna nothing would have been saved but for the energy and honesty of a German officer (of Baden or Württemberg), who put four hundred thousand francs in gold on his sleigh, and came and honestly deposited them, on the 24th of December, at Koenigsberg, with the paymaster of the army.

for, though he was always the first to draw a sabre or brave danger, he may truly be said to have been the executioner of our cavalry. He kept his divisions constantly mounted all along the route; but our cavalry were dying of starvation, and when night came, the unfortunate soldiers were not able to use their horses to go for forage. For himself, the King of Naples had twenty or thirty relays of horses, and every morning he started out on a fresh one. He was, indeed, the handsomest horseman in Europe; but without foresight, for it was not a question of being an intrepid soldier, but of being able to economize his resources. He lost for us (I heard him say so to Marshal Davout) forty thousand horses through his mismanagement. It is always wrong to blame one's officers; but the Emperor could have made a better selection. There were among our leaders two warriors, rivals in glory, Marshal Ney and Prince Beauharnais, who saved us from the greatest perils by their coolness and courage.

The King of Naples went on to Wilna; he arrived there on the 8th of December, and we with the guard, on the 10th. It was night when we came to the gates of the city, which were barricaded with pieces of wood. We had the greatest difficulty in entering. I and my comrade were lodged in a college, well warmed. When I went to my general for my orders, he said, "Be ready at four in the morning to leave the city, for the enemy is now arriving on the heights, and we shall be bombarded at daylight. Do not lose any time." As soon as I returned to my lodgings, I made my preparations to leave. I awoke my comrade, who would not listen to me. He had got thawed, and preferred to remain in the enemy's hands. At three o'clock I said to him, "Let us go." "No," said he, "I shall remain." — "Very well, I shall kill you if you do not follow me." — "All right; kill me." I drew my sabre, and gave him some stout blows with it, thus forcing him to follow me. I loved my brave comrade, and would not leave him to the enemy.

We had scarcely got ready to leave when the Russians forced the Witepsk gate; we had barely time to get out. They committed the most horrible acts in the town. All the unfortunate soldiers, who were asleep in their lodgings, were murdered, and the streets were strewn with the dead bodies of Frenchmen. Here the Jews were the executioners of our Frenchmen. Fortunately, the intrepid Ney put a stop to the confusion. The right and left wings of the Russian army had passed by the city, and saw us go by; they were stopped by a few rounds from our guns, but the rout was complete. When we reached the mountain of Wilna the confusion was at its height. All the ammunition of the army and the Emperor's carriages were on the ground. The soldiers helped themselves to gold and silver plate. All the chests and casks were burst open. What a quantity of plunder was left on that spot! No, a thousand times no; never was there such a sight!

We marched on to Kowno, which place the King of Naples reached on the 11th of December, at midnight; he left there on the 13th at five o'clock in the morning, and went to Gumbinnen with the guard. In spite of the efforts of Marshal Ney, seconded by General Gérard, Kowno at once fell into the hands of the Russians. A retreat was urgently necessary; Marshal Ney effected it at nine o'clock at night, after having destroyed all that remained of our artillery, ammunition, and provisions, and having set fire to the bridges. It may be said in praise of Marshal Ney that he kept the enemy at bay at Kowno by his own bravery. I saw him take a gun and five men and face the enemy.[1] The country ought to be grateful for such men. We had the good fortune to be under the command of Prince Eugene, who made every effort to reunite our scattered forces. At Koenigsberg we came upon some Prussian sentinels, who insulted our unfortunate soldiers, who were without arms; all the doors were closed against them, and they died on the pavement of cold and hunger. I went at once with my two comrades to the town-hall. No one was allowed to approach. I showed my decoration, my epaulets, and was allowed to enter through a window. Three billets

---

[1] It is a fact that Ney and Gérard, musket in hand, ensconced behind a palisade with a handful of men, for several hours prevented the passage of the bridge of Kowno.

for lodgings were given me, and we had the best apartments. No one spoke to us; they only stared at us. They were at dinner. Seeing this indifference on their part, I took out twenty francs, and said, "Have something got for us to eat; we will give you twenty francs a day."—"All right," said the host. "I will have a fire made in the stove in this room, and give you some straw and some coverings."

Some broth was served us immediately, and we were fed for thirty francs a day, not including the coffee (a franc for each man). This Prussian was kind enough to stable our horses and feed them. The poor beasts had had no hay and oats since they left Wilna; how glad they were to bite into a bundle of hay! And we, so happy to sleep on some straw in a warm room.

I sent at once for a physician and bootmaker to examine my left foot, which had been frozen. I had to consult a physician, so as to have a boot made. It was decided to have one made lined with rabbit skin and to leave my foot a prisoner in it, after having cut my boot open to dress my foot. "Make the boots this night," said I. "I will give you twenty francs."— "To-morrow, at eight o'clock, you shall have them." So then I kept my boots on. The next day the doctor and bootmaker came; the former cut open my boot, and there was my foot, looking like a new-born baby's,— no nails, no skin, but in a perfect condition. "You are all right," said the doctor.

He had the host and his wife called up. "Come," said he,

"see a chicken's foot. I must have some linen to wrap it up." They gave me very willingly some fine white linen. My foot was put into my boot, and tightly laced. I asked the doctor how much I owed him. "I am paid," said he. "This service is free." — "But" — "No buts, if you please."

I held out my hand to him. "I will tell you," said he, "how to make it well. Your foot will be very sensitive to heat and cold; do not expose it to the air; let it remain a long time just as it is, but when the season for strawberries comes, take and mash up a plateful of them, at least two or three pounds, and make a compress, and bind it to your foot. Continue to do this during the strawberry season, and you will never feel any pain." — "Thank you, doctor. And for you, Mr. Hatter, here are twenty francs." — "Not so," said he. "My expenses only, if you please." — "How much?" — "Ten francs." — "Why, you two have conspired together." — "Well," said two of my comrades, "let us have a rum punch." — "No," said they, "time is precious, we must return. Farewell, brave Frenchman."

I followed the physician's directions, and have never felt any inconvenience from my injury; but it cost me twelve francs' worth of strawberries.

I went to the palace to take Count Monthyon's orders; there I found Prince Eugene and Prince Berthier. Count Monthyon said to the minister of war, "I wish to have baggage-officer Coutant for my aide-de-camp, and to have his place filled by Lieutenant Coignet; he is a good business man. I need him to rid the army of all the vehicles which are needless and in the way."

The minister immediately appointed me baggage-master at headquarters, December 28, 1812. I no longer feared to enter the line. We remained at Koenigsberg a few days to reunite all the remnants of that grand army, now reduced to a small corps. We started on the march to Berlin, which had to be promptly evacuated so as to fall back upon Magdeburg. There the army became stationary for a while. On the Elbe, Prince Eugene reunited the army in a fine position. Provisions were distributed every night; he looked after everything, and never allowed three days to pass without going to the out-posts to reconnoitre the enemy, and greeted them, every morning for three months, with eight pieces of cannon, fifteen or sixteen thousand infantry, and eight hundred cavalry. This little affair over, he ordered a retreat, always bringing up the rear himself; he never left one man behind him. Yet he was always pleasant. A fine soldier on the field of honor. He held his position for three months without falling back.

I received the following letter:

> I send you enclosed a copy of the *Moniteur*, which contains the conditions prescribed by the Emperor with regard to equipages in the army. The prince viceroy intends to issue an order for the day on the subject, but, in the mean time, you are to notify those persons who are not to have carriages hereafter, that, on the 15th of this month, their carriages are to be burned.
>
> Signed: The general of division, chief of the major-general's staff.
> Cte MONTHYON.

I went to the general's office, and said to him, "This is a strict order, general." — "I am going to rid the army of its incumbrances. No exceptions are to be made. I shall give you some gendarmes, and all the carriages which are not marked with plates you are to have burned. I have got them — those army plunderers; I shall take away their stolen horses, and turn them over to our artillery." — "You have the authority to do this, but it will be a stormy duty for me." — "I shall be with you to uphold you. Let them come and complain! I will receive them. Leave them their pack-horses, and give the rest to the artillery. Go! the prince depends upon you."

I received orders to have plates of steel with escutcheons on them made for those who had a right to keep their carriages; their names and titles were engraved on the plates, and also their rank in the order of march. These plates cost three francs. The viceroy himself was not exempt from this order. I had barely time enough to give out my plates before I started off. I said to myself, "I am going to have a jolly time disencumbering the army."

EIGHTH NOTE-BOOK.

I AM APPOINTED CAPTAIN. — CAMPAIGNS OF 1813 AND 1814. — THE FAREWELLS AT FONTAINEBLEAU. — MY VISIT TO COULOMMIERS.

The general bulletined every day the news from Paris and from the army which was being organized. The Emperor arrived in order to effect a junction with the viceroy, but his plans miscarried: the Russians and Prussians had got ahead of him by forced marches, leaving us quiet in our camp. They passed along on our left without being perceived, overtook the Emperor, and offered him battle. When he found himself attacked, he made his arrangements for defence, and at the same time sent one of his aides-de-camp galloping as fast as possible to inform Prince Eugene that he was in close combat. The latter attacked the enemy's flank, and forced him to fall back upon the road to Lutzen. The army continued its march on Leipzig, the corps of Marshal Ney forming the advance guard. On the 2d of May the memorable battle of Lutzen took place, the success of which was due to the French infantry, and chiefly to the valor of our young conscripts, entirely unsupported by cavalry. It is impossible to give any idea of the desperate valor of our troops. Before Lutzen all the wounded were carried off by young girls and boys. Thirty couples at least went from the city to the field of battle, and returned with their miserable burdens, only to go back again immediately. I saw this done, and it ought not to be left unremarked; those boys deserved laurels and the girls crowns.

As for the army equipages, I had them collected together according to orders, with a strong guard of picked gendarmes and all the grooms. The Emperor warned me to come back at night. I had them all placed in a square, with the horses inside of it, and the wagons touching one another so that it would be impossible for the enemy to penetrate it.

On the 8th of May, about noon, the army entered Dresden. On the 12th the Emperor went to meet the King of Saxony, who was returning from Prague, to which he had retired, and conducted him to his palace amid the ringing of bells and firing of cannon. Before reaching Dresden, I received an order to go with my gendarmes and guard the bridge, allowing no equipages to pass but those of the staff and the canteens belonging to the corps. All the rest were unhitched at once, and the horses put aside. The most curious thing was to see the sergeants-major on horseback. I made those gentlemen dismount. Consequently, I had some horses ready harnessed, not to speak of wagons drawn by oxen. I turned over two hundred horses to the artillery, who had first choice; the cavalry took the rest of them; the oxen were sent to the great pen. The Jewish gentlemen offered me gold for them, but I gave them some blows on their backs with my sabre-blade, and said, "Go take that to the kitchen."

I performed my duty so well that it was spoken of in the cabinet of the minister of war, Prince Berthier and General Monthyon being present. He said, "This old grumbler is making everybody go on foot." — "True, my prince; but he turned all the horses over to the artillery." — "Very well, I appoint him captain in the general staff of the Emperor, and he will continue his duties."

That night I returned with my gendarmes to the hotel

"Napoleon spent the rest of the evening seated on a stool in front of the tent." — Page 248.

where my general was. He began to laugh. "Well," said
he, "have you done a good day's work?" — "Yes, general;
I have sent some good horses to the artillery." — "Let us go
to dinner." When we were seated at table, he said, "Captain,
we shall mount our horses to-morrow." — "But, general, you
said 'captain.'" — "Yes, here is the minister's letter; he has
appointed you on account of what I have told him of you.
Come, embrace your general. And here is your nomination
awaiting your certificate of service." — "How glad I am!"
— "You will be always near the Emperor. Try to procure
some captain's epaulets at once." — "But, general, how can
I?" — "I have given a lace-maker permission to set up her
shop on the principal street." — "I will go and see her, if
you will permit me." — "Go, my brave fellow." — "General,
in my joy at being made captain, I have forgotten to tell you
that I sent home two peasants from Lutzen, with their wagons
and horses. They got on their knees to me, and I asked them
from what country they came; they answered, 'From Lutzen.'
Then I said to them, 'Very well, I grant you your request as
a reward for the good deeds of the young men and girls of
your town, who took up all our wounded men. You can
choose the best wagons in place of your own, and go along the
cross-roads to your homes. You owe this to the good conduct
of your young people.' Did I do right, general?" — "I shall
report the fact to the minister. I approve of what you have
done. But about the other wagons?" — "I did not have
them burned; I left them for the use of the town. Now,
general, that is what I did. I did it on my own responsibility." — "You have done well."

The next day I appeared at table with my fine epaulets, which
cost me two hundred and twenty francs, and also some beautiful tassels on my hat. "Ah, how handsome they are!"
people said. "They are actually the epaulets of the guard."

On the 19th of May the Emperor appeared before Bautzen,
and prepared for a battle there. On the 20th of May the
cannonading began at noon and lasted until five o'clock without interruption. Two hours after, the battle began again on
a larger scale. The next day, the 21st of May, the enemy

effected a retreat about six o'clock in the evening. On the 22d of May, four o'clock in the morning, the army began to march in pursuit of the enemy. The Russians were overwhelmed by Latour-Maubourg's cavalry, after a bloody battle. The cavalry general, Bruyère, had his legs carried off by a cannon-ball. As we were in pursuit of the Russians along the highway, we received two shots from a cannon on our right. The Emperor stopped, and said to Marshal Duroc, "Go and see about that." They reached an eminence, and the marshal was struck by a ricochet-ball. The general of engineers who was with him was killed on the spot. Duroc lived a few hours. The Emperor ordered the guard to stop. The tents of the imperial headquarters were set up in a field on the right side of the road. Napoleon went inside of the square of the guard, and spent the rest of the evening seated on a stool in front of his tent, his hands clasped and his head bent down. We all stood around him motionless; he preserved the most mournful silence. "Poor man," said the old grenadiers, "he has lost his children."

When it was quite dark the Emperor left the camp accompanied by the Prince of Neuchâtel, the Duke of Vicenza, and Dr. Ivan. He wanted to see Duroc, and embrace him for the last time. When he returned to the camp he walked up and down in front of his tent. No one dared go near him; we all stood around him with bowed heads.

Peace was concluded on the 4th of June. The Emperor set out immediately for Dresden, where he occupied himself in active preparations for a new campaign. On the 10th of August the armistice was broken. The allied armies formed an effective force of eight hundred thousand combatants. The forces which were to oppose them did not number more than three hundred and twelve thousand men. Several engagements, in which the enemy lost seven thousand men, took place in the three days of the 21st, 22d, and 23d of August.

At this time the Emperor received news from Dresden, which compelled him to return there in great haste. Marshal Gouvion St.-Cyr's corps had been left alone in charge of the defence of Dresden. The allies, who were ignorant of Napoleon's return, made an attack on the 26th of August, at four o'clock in the afternoon. The enemy was repulsed. He lost four thousand men and two thousand prisoners on the first day. The French had about three thousand men unfit for service; but five generals of the guard were wounded. The next day, the 27th, an attack was ordered. The rain fell in torrents; but the enthusiasm of our soldiers was unabated. The Emperor directed all our movements. His guard was on a street to our left, and could not go out of the city without being riddled by a redoubt defended by eight hundred men and four pieces of cannon.

There was no time to lose. Their shells were falling in the midst of the city. The Emperor called up a captain of fusileers of the guard named Gagnard (of Avallon). This brave soldier presented himself to the Emperor with his face a little askew. "What have you in your cheek?"—"My quid, sire."—"Ah! you chew tobacco?"—"Yes, sire."—"Take your company, and go and take that redoubt which is doing me so much harm."—"It shall be done."—"March along the palisades by the flank, then charge right on it. Let it be carried at once!"

My good comrade set off at a double quick by the right flank. Within a hundred feet of the barrier of the redoubt his company halted; he ran to the barrier. The officer who held the bar of the two gates, seeing him alone, thought that he was going to surrender, and so did not move. My jolly soldier ran his sabre through his body, and opened the barrier. His company made two leaps into the redoubt, and forced them to surrender. The Emperor, who had watched the whole affair, said, "The redoubt is taken." The rain was falling in torrents. They surrendered at discretion, and my jolly soldier brought them to the rear, surrounded by his company.

I hastened to my comrade (for we had belonged to the same company), I embraced him, and, taking him by the arm, I led him to the Emperor, who had made a sign to Gagnard to come to him. "Well, I am well pleased with you. You shall be put with my old grumblers: your first lieutenant shall be made captain; your second lieutenant, lieutenant; and your sergeant-major, second lieutenant. Go, guard your prisoners." The rain was falling so heavily that the Emperor's plumes drooped upon his shoulders.

As soon as the redoubt was taken, the old guard went out of the city, and formed a line of battle. All our troops were in line in the low grounds, and our right wing rested on the road to France. The Emperor sent us off in squads of three, to carry orders for the attack all along the line. I was sent to the division of cuirassiers. On my return from my mission, I went back to the Emperor. He had in his redoubt a very long field-glass on a pivot, and he looked through it every moment. His generals also looked through it, while he, with his small glass in his hand, watched the general movements. Our right wing gained some ground; our soldiers became masters of the road to France; and the Emperor took his pinch of snuff from the pocket of his vest. Suddenly, casting his eye towards the heights, he shouted, "There is Moreau! That is he with a green coat on, at the head of a column with the emperors. Cannoneers, to your pieces! Marksmen, look through the large glass! Be quick! When they are half way up the hill, they will be within range." The redoubt was mounted with sixteen pieces of the guard. Their round made the very earth shake, and the Emperor, looking through his small glass, said, "Moreau has fallen!"

A charge of the cuirassiers put the column to rout, and brought off the general's escort, and we learned that Moreau was dead. A colonel, who was made prisoner during the charge, was questioned by our Napoleon in the presence of Prince Berthier and Count Monthyon. He said that the emperors had offered to give the command to Moreau, and he had refused it in these words: "I do not wish to take up arms against my country. But you will never overcome them in mass. You must divide your forces into seven columns; they will not be able to hold out against them all; if they overthrow one, the others can then advance." At three o'clock in the afternoon the enemy made a hasty retreat through the cross-roads and narrow, almost impracticable, by-ways. This was a memorable victory; but our generals had had enough of it. I had my place among the staff, and I heard all sorts of things said in conversation. They cursed the Emperor: "He is a ——," they said, "who will have us all killed." I was dumb with astonishment. I said to myself, "We are lost." The next day after this conversation, I made bold to say to my general, "I think our place is no longer here; we ought to go on to the Rhine by forced marches." — "I agree with you; but the Emperor is obstinate: no one can make him listen to reason."

The Emperor pursued the enemy's army as far as Pirna; but just as he was about to enter the town, he was seized with vomiting, caused by fatigue. He was obliged to return to Dresden, where a little rest soon re-established him. General Vandamme, upon whom the Emperor relied to keep in check the remnant of the enemy's army, risked an engagement in the valleys of Toeplitz, and was defeated on the 30th of August. This defeat, those of Macdonald on the Katzbach and Oudinot in the plain of Grosbeeren, destroyed the fruits of the victory of Dresden. On the 14th of September we received the news of the defection of Bavaria, which caused our forces to be sent on to Leipzig. The Emperor arrived there on the morning of the 15th. On the 16th of October, at nine o'clock in the morning, the army of the enemy began the attack, and cannonading immediately commenced all along the line. The first day's fight, though marked by bloody engagements, left the victory undecided.

All through the day of the 17th of October the two armies remained, facing each other, without any hostile demonstrations. On the 17th, at noon, the Emperor sent his aide-de-camp to me with an order to start with his household establishment, consisting of seventeen equipages and all his grooms, with the treasure and the charts of the army. I went through the city, and came to the battle-field, near a large garden, which was well concealed. I had orders not to move. So there I established myself, and put our pots on the fire. The next day, 18th of October, early in the morning, the allied army again took the initiative. From where I was, I saw the French divisions fall into line on the battle-field. The whole battle-front was before me. The heavy columns of the Austrians came out from the woods, and marched in columns upon our army. Seeing a strong division of Saxon infantry marching upon the enemy with twelve pieces of cannon, I ordered all my men to eat their soup, and hold themselves ready to start. I galloped over towards the line, following the centre of this division; but they turned their backs upon the enemy, and sent a volley of shot upon us. I was so well mounted that I was able to get back to my post, which I ought not to have left. By the time I got back, I had recovered my presence of mind, and I said to the grooms, "Mount at once to return to Leipzig." Two minutes after, an aide-de-camp galloped up, and said, "Start at once, captain. Go across the river; it is the Emperor's order. Follow the boulevards and the great causeway."

I started off, putting the head groom at the head of my equipages. As we came near the boulevard, I came upon a piece of cannon drawn by four horses and two soldiers. "What are you doing there?" I cried to them. They answered me in Italian: "They are dead" (the gunners).—"Take your place there in front of my wagons. I will save you. Now go on, gallop, take the lead!" I felt very proud to have this piece to open the way. Once on the first boulevard, I gave orders not to allow the train to become separated; but here a great danger awaited us. When we reached the second boulevard, I went to get a light from a bivouac fire on the lower side of the promenade, and had scarcely lighted my pipe when a shell burst near me. My horse reared. I did not lose my balance, but the balls went through my wagons. A terrible wind was blowing. I could not keep my hat on my head. I took it and threw it into the nearest wagon. Drawing my sabre and riding along the train, I shouted, "Grooms, keep your postilions in place; the first who dismounts, blow out his brains. Have your pistols ready, and I will split the head of the first man who moves; a man must learn how to die at his post, if need be. Save your master's wagons." Two of my grooms were struck; the grape-shot cut off two buttons for one, and went through the coat of the other, and I received ten cannon-balls in my wagons. But only one of my horses was wounded, and I found myself entirely out of danger when we came to the opening of the ravine which runs along the promenades and receives the waters of the marshes on the right side of the city. Here there was a small stone bridge, and we had to cross it in order to reach the great causeway which ends at the long bridge. I saw in front of me a park of artillery which was just going over the small bridge. I galloped up, and found the colonel of artillery who was taking his park over. I went up to him. "Colonel, in the name of the Emperor give me your protection, and let me follow you. Here are the Emperor's wagons, the treasure, and the charts of the army. I have orders to take them over the river." — "Yes, my brave fellow, as soon as we have crossed, be ready, and I will leave you twenty men to assist you in crossing the bridge." — "Here," said I, "is a piece of cannon which had been abandoned. I turn it over to you ready hitched." — "Go bring it here," said he to two gunners; "I will take it along."

I then galloped back to my train. "We are all right now," said I to the grooms. "We shall be able to cross. Hitch up." I took my stand beside the little bridge, and my wagons came up. As soon as the first wagons had gone over the bridge, I said to the gunners, "Go back now to your pieces." I am thankful to those brave soldiers.

When we came to the great causeway, I found no artillery there; it had all gone galloping off to fall into position. But I met the ambulances of the army, commanded by a colonel of the Emperor's staff, who occupied the middle of the causeway. My head groom said to him, "Colonel, be so good as to let us have a part of the road." — "I have no orders to receive from you." — "I will inform the officer in command," replied the groom. — "Let him come to me. I will wait for him." He came and told me; I galloped off. When I reached the colonel, I begged him to give me half of the road. "Just as you did for the park of artillery," said I; "you can easily move to the right, and we will double." — "I have no orders to receive from you." — "Is this your final answer, colonel?" — "Yes." — "Well, then, in the name of the Emperor move to the right, or I shall hustle you off." I pushed him along with the breast of my horse, repeating, "Move to the right, I tell you." He took hold of his sword. "If you draw your sword, I will blow out your brains." He called some gendarmes to

his aid, but they said, "Settle it with the Emperor's baggage-master yourself; it is no concern of ours." The colonel still hesitated. Turning towards his ambulance, I had it moved aside. As I passed the colonel, he said to me, "I shall report your conduct to the Emperor." — "Make your report. I shall wait for you, and go in after you; I give you my word for that."

I crossed the long bridge; on the left of it was a mill, and between that and the bridge there was a ford where the whole army could cross without any danger. But this river is walled in and very deep; the banks are perpendicular. I mounted the plateau with my seventeen vehicles, and took a position behind that fine battery which protected me. When night came on, the armies were in the same position as at the commencement of the battle, our troops having valiantly repulsed the attacks of four united armies. But our ammunition had become exhausted. We had fired off, during the day, ninety-five thousand cannon-shots, and we had left only about sixteen thousand. It was impossible to hold the battle-field much longer, and we had to resign ourselves to retreat.

At eight o'clock in the evening the Emperor left his bivouac to go down into the city, and established himself in the inn of the "Prussian Arms," where he spent the night in dictating orders. I waited for him; he did not come till the next day; but Count Monthyon was despatched to give orders to the artillery and the troops. He sent for me. "Well, how about your wagons? How did you get through with that job?"—"Very well, general; all the household establishment of the Emperor is safe, the treasure and the charts of the army. Nothing was left behind; but I have had ten balls go through my wagons, and two grooms slightly wounded." And I related to him my adventure on the causeway with the colonel. He told me that he should report it to the Emperor. "Do not disturb yourself," he added. "I will see the Emperor to-morrow morning. Let him show himself; he should have been on the battle-field, picking up our brave wounded men who were left in the hands of the enemy. He will get his deserts from the Emperor. You were at your post, and he was not."—"But, general, I treated him severely. I threatened to blow out his brains. If he had been my equal in rank, I should have sabred him; but I was certainly wrong to be so disrespectful to him."—"Never mind; I will attend to it all. Go, my brave fellow, you shall not be punished. You were under the authority of the Emperor, and not his." One may imagine how relieved I was.

About two o'clock in the morning we saw a fire on the battle-field; all the wagons were being burned and the caissons blown up. It was a frightful sight. On the 19th of October, Napoleon, after a touching interview with the King of Saxony and his family, withdrew from Leipzig. He went by way of the boulevards which lead to the long bridge of the faubourg of Lindenau, and ordered the engineer and artillery officers not to have the bridge blown up until the last platoon had left the city, the rear-guard being obliged to remain twenty-four hours longer in Leipzig. But Augereau's sharpshooters on one hand, and the Saxon and Baden troops on the other firing upon the French, the sappers thought that the enemy's army was coming, and that the moment had come to fire the mine. The bridge was destroyed, all means of retreat was cut off from the troops of Macdonald, Lauriston, Régnier and Poniatowski. The last mentioned, though wounded in his arm, attempted to swim across the Elster, and met his death in a whirlpool. Marshal Macdonald was more fortunate, and reached the opposite shore. Twenty-three thousand Frenchmen who escaped the slaughter which was carried on in Leipzig till two o'clock in the afternoon were made prisoners. Two hundred and fifty pieces of artillery fell into the hands of the enemy.

The Emperor reached his headquarters greatly fatigued; he had passed the night without sleep, and was utterly worn out. "Well, Monthyon," said he, "where are my wagons and the treasure?" — "All are safe, sire. Your 'grumbler' stood a volley on the promenades." — "Send him here; he had a serious affair with a colonel." — "I know it," said the general. "Send them both here; let them explain the matter." I went into the presence of the Emperor. The general related the affair. "Where is your hat?" — "Sire, I threw it into one of the wagons, and could not find it again." — "So you had some trouble on the causeway?" — "I wanted to share the road with the ambulances, and the colonel told me he had no orders to receive from me. I said to him, 'In the name of the Emperor, move aside to the right.' He had done this for the artillery, and he was not willing to give me half of the road. Then I threatened him; if he had been my equal, I should have sabred him."

The Emperor, turning to the colonel, said, "Well, and what have you to say? You have barely escaped being degraded. You shall be put under arrest for fifteen days for having started without my order, and, if you are not satisfied, my grumbler will make it all right for you. As for you," said he to me, "you have done your duty. Go and look for your hat."

After the Emperor had collected the shattered remnants of his army, he crossed the Saale on the 20th of October. The Emperor spent the night in a little pavilion on a hill planted out with vines. On the 23d, at Erfurt, King Murat parted from Napoleon to return to Naples. During that first day's march the remnant of the Saxons deserted[1] in the night, and also the Bavarians; only the Poles remained faithful to us. The army left Erfurt the 25th of October, and went first to Gotha and then to Fulda. The Emperor, having been informed of a manœuvre of the Bavarian general, Wrede, marched hastily to Hanau. On reaching the forest through which the road passes to the entrance of the city, Napoleon spent the night in making his arrangements. The next morning he walked in front of his guard with his arms folded, and said, "I count upon you to make a road for me to Frankfort. Hold yourselves in readiness; you must crush them to the earth. Do not encumber yourselves with prisoners; drive ahead, and make them repent of barring the road against us. Two battalions will be enough (one of chasseurs and one of grenadiers), two squadrons of chasseurs and two of grenadiers. You will be commanded by Friant." And he walked around, talking to everybody; but the stragglers met with a rough reception from him. All this took place in a thick pine forest, which concealed us from the enemy; but we had to deal with a force stronger than our own. The Bavarian army, which was opposed to us at this place, numbered more than forty thousand men. The Emperor gave the signal: the chasseurs started off first, the grenadiers following. The enemy formed an imposing body. As I saw my old comrades start out, I trembled. The horse grenadiers, with all the cavalry, began to move forward. I rode up to the Emperor. "Would your Majesty permit me to follow

[1] An exception should be made in the case of the Saxon cavalry, who left our army in this campaign only after having expressed their regrets at being forced to go. They came and solemnly shook hands with ours. Commander Thirion was a witness of this, and related it in his Souvenirs. (Published in 1851, in a journal at Metz, *Le Vœu national*.)

the horse grenadiers?"—"Go," said he; "there will be one more brave fellow."

How thankful I felt for my boldness! I had never asked anything of him before; I was too much afraid of him. Our old infantry grumblers went to meet that great body of men, who were resolutely awaiting them on the opposite side of a stream which crossed the highway, and into which emptied the waters of some large marshes. For a moment we were between two fires. If the enemy had taken advantage of his opportunity, we should have been compelled to surrender. It was impossible to manœuvre, and we were plunging about in mire up to our knees. But we managed to turn the position. The chasseurs rushed upon the frightened Bavarians, who were unable to resist them for a moment, and were cut to pieces. We rushed in like lightning when the cavalry opened its ranks, and the most fearful carnage ensued that I ever saw in my life. I found myself at the extreme left of the horse grenadiers, and I was anxious to follow the captain. "No," said he; "you and your horse are too small; you would impede the manœuvre."

I was provoked, but I controlled my temper. Looking round on my left, I saw a road which ran along the city wall. Hanau is surrounded on the side next to where I was by a very high wall which conceals the houses. I galloped forward. A platoon of Bavarians came up with a fine-looking officer at their head. Seeing me alone, he rode up to me. I stopped. He attacked me, and tried to stick his long sword into me. I parried his blow with the back of my great sabre (which I still have at my house). I fell aboard of him then, and cut his head half off. He fell down in a heap. I took his horse by the bridle, and galloped off, and his platoon fired on me. I rode like the wind up to the spot where the Emperor was, with this beautiful Arab horse which had a tail like a plume. The Emperor seeing me near him, said, "So you have come back. Whose horse is this?"—"Mine, sire" (I still had my sabre hanging); "I have cut off a fine officer's head. And I was fortunate to do it, for he was a brave fellow. He attacked me."—"Now you have a good horse to

"I fell aboard of him then, and cut his head half off." — Page 258.

ride, get all my carriages ready; you will leave for Frankfort to-night, as soon as the road is open." — "We cannot pass: they are piled upon one another." — "I will have the road cleared immediately." The aides-de-camp arrived, and said to his Majesty, "The victory is complete." Then he took some big pinches of snuff. He enjoyed one more day of happiness.

He sent out all the stragglers to clear the high-road, so that his train could pass. I received orders to start with a sufficient escort. It was so dark that we could not see our way; and we reached Frankfort late in the night of the 1st and 2d of November. On a large square there were some piles of nice wood, which furnished us with good fires. The army made its entrance into Mayence on the 3d of November, with the miserable remnant of that once magnificent corps. They were lodged in the convents and churches. They were attacked by the yellow fever, and the dead were to be found lying around in great confusion. In their frightful paroxysms they called for their relatives, their animals. I again had this sad duty to perform, for I was appointed to have all the bodies of those men who died during the night taken away. We had to make the convicts put them into the big wagons, where they were packed away like wagon-loads of hay. At first the convicts refused, but they were threatened with being shot. The dead were turned out by tipping up the wagons. As at Moscow, this sad duty fell upon me. All the Emperor's equipages had gone on. I trust never to see such horrors again.

The minor headquarters were moved to Metz, and we remained a long time in that large city. All the troops went into encampments, and we spent two months in inactivity.

The enemy's columns reascended the Rhine so as to reach Champagne and Lorraine. On the 27th of January, 1814, the battle of St. Dizier took place. It was not an ordinary fight, but one of the most fearful and bloody battles. The town was riddled by the discharges of musketry, and one could count thousands of bullets in the shutters of the doors and windows; the trees on a small square were cut to pieces; all the houses were robbed, and not one of the inhabitants could remain in the town.

The allies lost heavily, and were obliged to fall back to a position on the heights of Brienne. From this position they could send thunder-bolts upon us. All the efforts of our troops, made in several charges, were repulsed by their artillery. From the constant manœuvring the earth had become softened. The day was drawing to an end, and we could not get out of those mucky places. Meantime the Emperor, who was on horseback near a garden, was preparing to attempt another attack. Prince Berthier saw some Cossacks on our right, who were carrying off a piece of cannon. "Follow me," said he, "gallop." He started off like lightning; the four Cossacks fled, and the unfortunate soldiers of the train brought back their piece. At this moment the Emperor said, "I am going to sleep to-night in the château of Brienne. I must put an end to this business. Put yourself at the head of my staff, and follow me."

Then he rode out in front of his first line, and, halting before the central regiment, he said, "Soldiers, I am your colonel; I shall lead you. Brienne must be taken." All the soldiers shouted, "Long live the Emperor!" Night was coming on; there was no time to lose; each soldier became equal to four. Our troops were so transported that the Emperor could not control them; they rushed past the staff. At the foot of the mountain which faces the château and the main street of Brienne the slope is steep. Almost superhuman efforts were required to reach the spot; but all obstacles were surmounted. The darkness had fallen, and the combatants could no longer distinguish one another. They fell upon each other, charging bayonets. The Russians, massed in the principal street, were driven out. Our troops came up so rapidly on the left that they dashed against General Blücher's staff. He lost several officers. Among the prisoners was a nephew of M. de Hardenberg, Chancellor of Prussia. He told me that the field-marshal had been several times surrounded by our sharpshooters, and owed his escape only to his own bravery in self-defence and the fleetness of his horse.

The Emperor then ordered a "left-wheel." did not halt at the château, and pursued the enemy as far as Mézières. It was pitch dark, and a band of Cossacks who were prowling around in search of booty heard the tramping of the horses of Napoleon and his body-guard as they passed along. This made them run out. They rushed first upon one of the generals, who shouted, "Cossacks!" and defended himself. One of the Cossacks seeing, a few steps from him, a horseman in a gray coat, fell upon him. General Corbineau first threw himself in the way, but without success. Colonel Gourgaud,

who was at that moment talking with Napoleon, came to his defence, and, with a pistol-shot, at close aim, he struck down the Cossack. At the sound of the pistol, we fell upon the marauders. It was, indeed, time to halt. We were all worn out, and ready to drop from hunger. Twenty-four hours in the saddle without anything to eat. I can truly say the soldiers had overtaxed their strength: they fought one against four.

From Brienne the Emperor went on to Troyes, keeping along the left bank of the Aube, and we halted three days for rest and refreshment. On the 1st of February we met the enemy at Champaubert. They received a good drubbing, and we were obliged to fall back upon the right bank of the Aube, at the village of La Rothière. The fight at La Rothière was the first drawn battle of the campaign. We kept the battle-field, but nothing more. We were not able to renew the fight the next day. However, the allies could not boast of having defeated us. On the 11th of February a battle was fought at Montmirail.

Everywhere where the Emperor commanded, the enemy was defeated. On the 12th there was a battle at Château-Thierry; on the 15th, at Gennevilliers. On the 17th we reached Nangis, after making forced marches at night through by-ways, in order to get ahead of the enemy's column. We drove before us some heavy columns as far as Montereau. Here the Emperor had stationed an army corps to receive them. But they were not there; a mistake had been made by whoever had allowed them to pass on, and the burden fell upon us alone. This battle took place on the 18th. Montereau was reduced to ruins; cannon-balls fell all over the town from every direction. The Emperor, furious at not hearing the cannon of his army, gave the command, "Gallop." We were on the road to Nangis, to the left of the road to Paris. When we reached an eminence to the left of this road, he could see the enemy crossing over the bridge of Montereau. Furious at this disappointment, he said to Marshal Lefebvre, "Take all my staff. I will keep with me Monthyon, and such and such a one; go at a gallop; go seize the bridge. The affair has miscarried. I will fly to your aid with my old guard."

So we started off. After descending to the foot of the mountain with this intrepid marshal, we reached the spot without any halting. We turned to the left, and rode at the utmost speed, by fours, upon the bridge. The whole of the rear-guard had not gone over. As we rode over the bridge, a large gap in it was no obstacle to us, on account of the rapidity with which we came. Our horses flew. I was mounted on the fine Arab horse captured at the battle of

Hanau. An incident occurred here which deserves to be mentioned. As we were crossing the arch of the bridge which had been destroyed, I saw a man lying on his stomach alongside of the parapet, and pushing over some pieces of plank so as to assist us in crossing.

At the end of the bridge, which is long, there is a street to the left. This faubourg being blocked up with the wagons belonging to the rear-guard, we had to fight our way through with our sabres. We swept everything before us. Those who escaped our fury did so by dragging themselves under the wagons. Our marshal fought so hard that he foamed at the mouth.

When we came to a fine causeway which led to St. Dizier, in front of an immense plain, the marshal ordered us to follow up our charge; but the Emperor, seeing us engaged in certain peril, ordered a battalion of chasseurs to put down their knapsacks, and go to our assistance. This battalion saved us. We were driven back by a body of cavalry. The chasseurs lay down on their stomachs alongside the causeway, and the enemy's cavalry, after having passed by them, were surprised by a file-fire. The ground was strewn with horses and men, and we were enabled to reach the faubourg. During the charge, the Emperor, with his old guard and his artillery, mounted the hill which faces Montereau. In front of the bridge, on a wall surrounding a space of circular form and filled with beautiful yoke-elms, our pieces were in battery, and thundering upon the masses in the plain. Here it was that the Emperor did duty as a gunner; he himself directed the pieces. They tried to make him go to the rear. "No," he said, "the bullet which is to kill me is not yet moulded." Why did he not meet death gloriously there after being betrayed by the man whom he had raised to such high rank! He was furious at this miscarriage. We recrossed the bridges, and again ascended the eminence where the Emperor was. "The rapidity with which you made that charge," said he, "has given me two thousand prisoners. I feared you would all be captured." — "Your chasseurs saved us," said the marshal.

I was so delighted with my part in the affair, that I got down off my horse, and embraced him. Thanks to him, I had been able to use my sabre freely.

On the 21st there was a battle at Méry-sur-Seine; on the 28th, one at Sézanne; on the 5th of March, at Berry-au-Bac, where the Poles defeated the Cossacks; on the 7th, at Craonne. This last was terrible. Some considerable heights were carried by the foot chasseurs of the old guard and twelve hundred foot gen-

darmes, who came from Spain, and performed prodigies of valor. On the 13th of March, at night, we arrived at the gates of Reims.

A Russian army was occupying the city, intrenched in redoubts made of rubbish and well-filled casks. The gates of the city were barricaded. Near the gate which faces the road to Paris, there was an elevated piece of ground surmounted by a windmill. Here the Emperor established his headquarters in the open air. We made him a good fire. We could not see two steps before us, and he was so overcome by the day's work at Craonne, that he called for his bear-skin, and stretched himself out near the nice fire, while we watched him in silence. The Russians began to advance about ten o'clock at night. They made a sortie with a fearful discharge of musketry on our left. The Emperor rose to his feet in a fury. "What is that going by?"—"It is a hurrah, sire," answered his aide-de-camp. "Where is so and so?" (He referred to a captain commanding a battery of sixteen pieces.) "Here he is, sire," some one replied. He approached the Emperor. "Where are your pieces?"—"On the road."—"Go bring them here."—"I cannot pass," said he, "the artillery of the line is ahead of me."—"You must throw all those pieces over into the ditches. I must be in Reims by midnight. You are a . . . if you do not go through those gates! Go," said he to us, "turn them all over into the ditches."

We all started off. When we reached the pieces and the caissons, instead of throwing them over, we moved them to one side, with all the gunners and the soldiers of the train. All this was done in a moment, and the sixteen pieces passed along under the Emperor's eyes, as he stood watching them with his back to the fire. They were placed in battery on the right of the road in a fine position, facing the gateway. We could not see a step before us, and the misfortune was that there were two pieces in battery near the gates exposed, in case of a sortie from the Russians; we did not see them at all. Our pieces in battery let loose their volleys on the gates and redoubts; the shells fell in the very centre of the city. During the cannonading the Emperor gave orders to the cuirassiers to hold themselves in readiness to enter the city, stating to them the streets he wished each squadron to take. Then he gave the signal; the cuirassiers dashed forward to form a line of battle behind the pieces; the order was given to cease firing, and all rushed into the city. This charge was so terrible that they carried everything before them, and the people, shut up in their houses, hearing such an uproar, put lights in their windows. Every place was lighted: one could have picked up a needle. The Emperor, at the head of his staff, was in Reims by midnight, and the Russians utterly routed; their "hurrah" had cost them dear. Our cuirassiers cut the soldiery down with their sabres as they liked. If the Emperor had been seconded in France as he was in Champagne, the allies would have been lost. But what was to be done? They were ten to one of us. We had the courage, but not the strength; we were compelled to give up.

Our misfortunes ended at Fontainebleau. We wanted to make a last effort, and march upon Paris; but it was too late. The enemy was on the edge of the forest, and Paris had surrendered without resistance. We had to return to Fontainebleau. The Emperor was treated falsely by all the men whom he had raised to prominent positions; they forced him to abdicate. I wanted to follow him. Count Monthyon sent to him, and asked him to let me go. "I cannot take him; he is not one of my guard. If my signature could do him any good, I would appoint him chief of battalion, but it is now too late." Six hundred men were granted him for his guard. He made them take their arms, and asked them to volunteer. Every man walked out of the ranks, and he was obliged to make them go back. "I will choose. Let no one move." And, passing in front of the rank, he himself designated each one, saying, "You come," and so on, for the whole number. This occupied a long time. Then he said, "See if I have made up my number." — "You need twenty more," said General Drouot. — "I will pick them out."

When he had made his selection, he chose his non-commissioned officers and officers, and then re-entered the palace, saying to General Drouot, "You will take my old guard to Louis XVIII. at Paris after my departure."

When all the preparations had been made, and all the equipages were ready, he, for the last time, gave the order to take up arms. All his old warriors having assembled in the grand courtyard once so brilliant, he came down the stairway, accompanied by his staff, and presented himself before his old grumblers. "Bring me my eagle!" And, taking it in his arms, he gave it a farewell kiss. Oh, how touching it was! Groans could be heard all up and down the ranks, and, I must say, I cried to see my dear Emperor start for the island of Elba. One great cry rose up, "We are then left to the mercy of the new government." If Paris had held out twenty-four hours, France would have been saved. But at that time the people of Paris did not know how to build barricades; they have only learned how to erect them against their own fellow-citizens. We had to wear the white cockade; but I kept my old one as a souvenir.

After the tricks we played upon the officers of the allies at Paris, my brother made me keep in. "Do not go out," said he to me, "you will be arrested." I promised him I would not.

However, I often thought of my old master and mistress, who had been so kind to me, and I was very anxious to hear from them. Now, one day, having my brother's permission to go out, I went to the Faubourg St. Antoine, and, as I came near the Bastile, a big man, dressed in a blouse, who was going by, stopped me suddenly, and said, "Here is a man who ought to be acquainted with Coulommiers, if I am not very much mistaken." — "You are not mistaken," I replied, staring at the man with wide-open eyes. "I knew M. Potier at Coulommiers very well." — "So it is really you, M. Coignet?" — "Yes, it is I, M. Moirot;[1] for I think I also recognize you. How are M. and Madame Potier?" — "Very well. They have long feared you were dead, for we speak frequently of you." — "However, here I am, and, as you see, jolly and in good health." — "I see you have a cross." — "Yes, my friend; and also the rank of captain. It has been a long time since we have seen each other; will you let me embrace you?" — "Very willingly. I have not yet recovered from the surprise of seeing you again, my dear Coignet. We had all so long believed you to be dead. But where are you staying?" "With my brother at the Aguesseau Market." — "I sell my flour to a baker at the corner of the market." — "My brother

---

[1] Moirot had been a servant in the employ of M. Potier at the same time that Coignet was.

supplies him." — "Now that you know my address, you must be so good as to come and dine with me this evening, and we will have a long talk together." — "I will do so with great pleasure."

I went early, and Moirot told me that he no longer lived with M. Potier; he had set up in business on his own account. He had earned in that house sixty thousand francs, and, thanks to his good conduct, he had married a cousin of M. Potier. When we parted he grasped my hand with emotion, and said, "Ah, how happy I shall make them to-morrow when I tell them that I have seen you!"

He had scarcely returned to Coulommiers when he flew to the mill in the meadows. "What extraordinary thing has happened, Moirot, that you are running so fast?" M. Potier called to him from a distance as soon as he saw him. "Ah, sir, I have found M. Coignet, the lost child!" — "What? What do you say?" — "Yes, M. Coignet. He is not dead, but very well — decorated — a captain!" — "You must be mistaken; he did not know how to read or write; he could not possibly occupy such a position. It is doubtless some other Coignet, whom you have taken for ours." — "It is he himself. I immediately recognized him by his big nose, his size, and his voice. He is a fine soldier. He told me that he had three horses and a servant. He is very anxious to see you. He has kept his word, for he has won the silver gun which he promised you he would bring back with him when he left your house." — "But it seems incredible. All this overwhelms me with astonishment. I must see him before I can believe it." Then M. Potier went to tell the good news to Madame, who was none the less surprised and happy to learn that Jean Coignet, her faithful servant, was found again; and that, decorated and an officer, he had a servant and three horses of his own. "We must send for the dear child," said she to her husband.

But the allied forces still occupied Paris, and I had to get a special permit from the prefect of police in order to leave the city. Through the intervention of the king's procurator, to whom he made known his wishes on the subject, M.

Potier succeeded in having his request granted, and the next day his son came to Paris for me. I was very, very glad to see this young man, who said to me, "Papa and mamma sent me for you. Here is the permit of the prefect of police. We will start for Coulommiers to-morrow, servant, horses, and all. I am to bring everything: papa says so." My brother insisted upon his remaining until after dinner. No, it was impossible. By four o'clock he was up and hastening our departure. "We have fifteen long leagues to go," he kept saying, "and they expect us early."

We travelled rapidly, and I arrived, wearing my undress uniform, for my servant carried the regulation dress. Pride of heart goes before a fall. But I had to make a good appearance. I dismounted at the mill gate. I, an old "grumbler," felt a quivering at my heart at the sight of all the people I used to know. My limbs trembled. I ran towards the house of my good master and mistress, ready to throw my arms around their necks. Madame Potier was in bed. I asked permission to see her. "Come in," she called to me, her voice trembling with emotion, "come right in. Poor child! Why did you not let us hear from you, and send for some money?" — "I have done very wrong, madame, but you see that at this moment I need nothing. You made me what I am. I owe my life and my fortune to you. You and M. Potier made a man of me." — "Have you suffered much?" — "I have endured everything that it is possible for a man to endure." — "I am glad to see you with such a uniform on. You have a high rank?" — "Captain on the Emperor's staff, and the first man decorated with the Legion of Honor. You see you have bestowed good fortune upon me." — "You won it yourself; your courage carried you through. My husband has ordered a feast, so he can present you to our friends." M. Potier, on his part, welcomed me as if he had been my own father. He wished to see my horses. After examining them all, he said, "Here is one which is particularly handsome; he must have cost you a great deal." — "He cost me nothing but one sabre cut, which I gave to a Bavarian officer at the battle of Hanau. But I will tell you that story while we are at dinner." — "All right. After dinner we will go and see my children; and to-morrow we will go out on horseback, and take your servant along, for your position is altered. You are no longer our little Jean of old times; you are the distinguished captain. I expect a great deal of pleasure in presenting you to my friends. They will not recognize you."

So we went round to see the stout farmers, and were received everywhere with open arms. "I have come," said M. Potier, "to ask you to invite my escort and me to dine with you. Allow me to present a captain who has come to visit me." — "You are very welcome," they replied. And as I was a soldier, they talked a great deal about the ravages made by the enemy then occupying the environs of Paris. Until dinner time M. Potier said nothing about me; and it was not until after the first course that he asked our hosts if they did not know the officer he had brought with him. They all stared at me, but no one recognized me. "You have all seen him at my house, ten years ago," continued M. Potier. "He is the lost child whom I found at the fair at Entrains, twenty years ago. It is he whom I present to you to-day. He has not wasted his time, as you see. He said to me when we parted, 'I shall try for a silver gun.' He has fulfilled his promise, for he won it the first time he stood fire; and, as you see, he has the cross of honor and the rank of captain, and was attached to the person of the great man, now fallen. . . . Here is my faithful servant of fifteen years ago, let us drink his health."

We drank together, and everywhere I was overwhelmed with attentions and kindnesses. I had to tell them my adventures; and many a time we spent whole hours and days, I telling stories and they listening, pleased and happy in one another's society. Those were pleasant days which I spent thus among all those old friends who had formerly seen me carrying sacks of three hundred and twenty-five pounds and managing the plough.

After having made, among the stout farmers and millers of

the neighborhood, a sort of progress which I can compare only to that of the "*bœuf gras*" at the time of the carnival, I took leave of all M. Potier's friends. I embraced my benefactors, and returned to Paris, where I received orders to start immediately for my department.

NINTH NOTE-BOOK.

ON HALF-PAY. — THE HUNDRED DAYS. — TEN YEARS OF SUPERINTENDENCE. — MY MARRIAGE. — THE REVOLUTION OF 1830. — I AM APPOINTED AN OFFICER IN THE LEGION OF HONOR.

The government sent us off to plant cabbages in our departments, upon half-pay — seventy-three francs a month. We had to be resigned to it. I set out for Auxerre, chief town of my department, and vegetated in that town the whole of the year 1814.

I knew no one; at last I was invited to the house of M. Marais, a lawyer in Rue Neuve, a true patriot. He offered me a home at his house. He was carrying on a suit in the name of my brother, against my family, who had cheated us out of the small property inherited from my mother. It was the father-in-law of M. Marais who had begun the accursed suit, which lasted seventeen years.

I endured my misfortune patiently, and awaited my fate under the laws of man. I took up my abode in a moderate-sized lodging which I got rent-free; I hired a cot-bed and a mattress. In this inhabited house, fortunately, there was a small stable for my horse. I went to see the general, and from there to see M. Goyon, the paymaster. On the first of the month we had to go and receive our seventy-three francs. Two and a half per cent. was deducted in advance on our crosses. Then they gently struck the final blow. A hundred and twenty-five francs a year was deducted from our Legion of Honor, besides the two and a half per cent., so that the half-pay was reduced to a third.
This life lasted seven years.

I took it patiently. I used to go to the Café Milon. One day I found some groups of old frequenters who were talking politics; they came up to me to ask if I had heard any news. "None at all," I said. — "You do not want to talk: you are afraid of compromising yourself."—"I swear to you I know nothing." — "Well," said a fat old papa, "they say that a Capuchin has come over in disguise, and also another distinguished personage whom the prefect wanted to have arrested." — "I do not understand you." — "You are pretending to be ignorant." — "This is the reason he kept his horse," said one of them; "he was expecting the *gray coat*." I withdrew, overwhelmed with joy, I can truly say, and I felt as if my Emperor was already back again.

It was reported on the streets of Auxerre, that the Emperor had landed at Cannes, and was marching on to Grenoble and Lyons. Every one was filled with consternation; but the report was made a certainty when, early in the morning, a fine regiment of the line, the 14th, arrived with Marshal Ney at its head. It was said that he was going to arrest the Emperor. "It cannot be possible," said I to myself, "that the man whom I saw at Kowno take a gun, and with five men keep back his enemies — this marshal whom the Emperor called his lion — can lay hands on his sovereign." The thought of it made me tremble. I went everywhere where I could hear without being seen; I was restless. At last the marshal went to the office of the prefect. A proclamation was made and published throughout the town. The commissioner of police, accompanied by a full escort, advertised that Bonaparte had returned, and that it was the order of the government that he should be arrested. And there were cries of "Down with Bonaparte!" — "Long live the King!" My God! how I suffered! But this fine 14th of the line put the shakos on their bayonets, and shouted, "Long live the Emperor!" What could the marshal do without soldiers? He was obliged to yield.

That evening the advance guard returned to the hotel, but not as it had left it: white cockades in the morning and tri-colored ones in the evening. They took possession of the town-hall, and by torchlight the same commissioner went through the town to publish another proclamation, and shout at the top of his voice, "Long live the Emperor!" I must say that I about ruptured my spleen.

The next day everybody assembled on the road to St. Bris to see the Emperor come by in his carriage with his fine escort. The snowball had grown; seven hundred of his old officers formed a battalion, and troops came in from every direction. On reaching the Place St. Étienne, the 14th of the line formed a square, and the Emperor reviewed it. Afterwards he formed a circle of his officers, and, seeing me, he called me to him. "So you are here, old grumbler?" — "Yes, sire." — "What rank did you hold on my staff?" — "Baggage-master of the headquarters." — "Very well; I appoint you quartermaster of my palace, and baggage-master-general of the headquarters. Are you mounted?" — "Yes, sire." — "Then follow me, go and join Monthyon at Paris."

The next day I set out for Joigny, and the day following I embarked with ten officers in a vessel bound for Sens. The river was covered with boats filled with troops, and we found some submerged at the bridges, for they had tried to proceed at night; the shores were covered with snow. We landed, and took public coaches for Paris. I stopped at my brother's to make my toilet, and went to see General Monthyon. I informed him that the Emperor had appointed me baggage-master-general to the headquarters. "How glad I shall be, my brave fellow, to have you near me! I shall take out your commission; that is my business." I went to the Tuileries, and had myself announced. "I wish to speak to General Bertrand." — "I will call him," said General Drouot. The general came.

"Already, my brave fellow? You took the post, then?" — "I came as quickly as possible; I ask leave for six days, general." — "Granted. Go."

That same evening I left Paris for Auxerre, and reached there Saturday morning. In those days people walked out to the Arquebuse on Sundays. About four o'clock I went out, dressed in full uniform, to show myself as though I had not gone away from Auxerre. On Monday I went to see my lawyer, who said to me, "Your suit is suspended, like many others." — "But I must go away; I must be in Paris in six days." — "Well, it will have to remain suspended." I set off to go to my post. I went to my brother's house. The next day I went to see my general. "Here you are, my brave fellow! And here is your commission; you have a right to lodging with your servant and horses. You must go find the mayor of your brother's *arrondissement*, so that you can be near the Tuileries. You must be mounted; you must have two horses, and then you have the right, as one of the 'sacred battalion,' to three hundred francs, which will be paid you at No. 3 Place Vendôme. Every day you will come to take my orders, and go on to the Tuileries at noon."

The next day I went to No. 3 Place Vendôme to get my three hundred francs gratuity of the "sacred battalion." When I went to the captain who commanded the third company of officers, for the inferior officers were only soldiers (it was necessary to be a superior officer to be captain of a company of a hundred officers): "I have come, captain, to claim the three hundred francs due me." — "What is your name?" — "Coignet." He looked over his book, and found my name. "I have no more money; you must do as the rest have done." — "But you have my money." — "I tell you the pay has been stopped." — "All right, captain, I will see about that."

This man was an old *émigré* who had offered to take a position under the Emperor, and who had been granted one. I informed General Bertrand of my disappointment. "Is it possible that that old cavalier would not pay you?" — "He would not, indeed, general." — "Very well, I will give you a *billet-doux (poulet)* for him."

I went back to him with the letter. "Captain, you will not need a spit to roast this chicken (*poulet*); it is ready picked." His aide-de-camp was near him; he read the letter, and, turning to me said, "Why did you go to the Tuileries? It was not your place." — "Pardon me, captain, I am baggage-master-general and quartermaster of the palace; I have charge of the quartering of the army. I promise to lodge you as you have received me. My three hundred francs, if you please." I was paid immediately, and carried my money to my brother. I went for my coupons, so that I could draw my rations of forage from the contractor, who cashed them for me. I had a right to three rations a day; this, added to my monthly allowance of three hundred francs, made me in this short while worth eight hundred francs. Then I had to be mounted, so I set out to look for some horses. I found two near the Carrousel, at the house of a royalist who had run away. I bought them for two thousand seven hundred francs, and they were very handsome. My brother lent me two thousand five hundred francs.

I went immediately to my brother's notary, who made out a contract by which I acknowledged that I owed my brother two thousand five hundred francs. While the contract was being drawn up, I made my will, which I placed in the hands of the notary. My brother scolded me when he saw the copy of the contract. "That's all right," said I, "and if I die in this campaign, you will find my will in the hands of your notary."

I busied myself in looking up a good servant, and having harness made for my two horses. When all this was done, I went to see my general on horseback, with my servant riding behind me, like a commandant going his rounds. I entered Count Monthyon's hotel, and said, "General, see, I am mounted." — "Already!" said he, "that is the way you do things; and two fine horses!" — "My war-horse cost me eighteen hundred francs, and my servant's horse nine hundred francs." — "You are better mounted than I am. I am very glad, my good fellow; now you are ready to start on a campaign. Are they paid for?" — "Yes; my brother lent me the money."

The good general frequently came to my brother's to take me out for an airing, either on horseback or in a carriage, and invited me to dine at his house. He remembered the good fires I made for him on the retreat from Moscow.

All my own preparations for the campaign being made, I set to work to arrange the order of march for the equipages according to their rank, so as to avoid confusion on the marches, as well as in the distributions. This precaution was useful to me, and I was congratulated upon it later on.

Preparations for the Champ de Mai were going on in the Champ de Mars in front of the façade of the École Militaire. The Emperor, in full dress, surrounded by his staff, came out to receive the deputies and the peers of France. When the reception was over the Emperor descended from his royal amphitheatre to go to another in the centre of the Champ de Mars. We had the greatest possible difficulty in getting through the crowd, which was so great that it had to be driven back in order to allow us to pass. And there, with his staff all standing round him, the Emperor made a speech. He had the eagles brought to him to distribute to the army and the national guard. With that stentorian voice of his, he cried to them, "Swear to defend your eagles! Do you swear it?" he repeated. But the vows were made without warmth; there was but little enthusiasm: the shouts were not like those of Austerlitz and Wagram, and the Emperor perceived it.

On my return from this grand ceremony, I made my preparations for the departure of the army. I left Paris on the 4th of June, for Soissons, and from there I went to Avesnes, where I was to await new orders. The Emperor arrived on the 13th, and only remained there a short time. He was to sleep at Laon. On the 14th of June he ordered forced marches. When we had entered the fertile country of Belgium, the columns were obliged to clear roads for themselves through the high rye. The front ranks could not advance. After being trodden down, it was only fit for straw, in which the cavalry stumbled. That was one of our misfortunes.

In order to gain a footing in the plain of Fleurus, the Emperor went on in advance, following the main road with his staff, and a squadron of horse-grenadiers. He talked awhile with an aide-de-camp. He looked over to his left, took his small glass, and examined attentively a perpendicular eminence far off from the road, in an immense plain. He saw some cavalry dismounted, and said, "That is not my cavalry, is it? I must find out. Send me an officer of my body-guard, and let him go at once and reconnoitre that troop." A sign was made to me to come to the Emperor. "It is you, is it?" — "Yes, sire." — "Gallop off, and reconnoitre the troop on that mountain. Do you see them from here?" — "Yes, sire." — "Do not get caught." I galloped off. When I reached the foot of the steep mountain, I saw three of the officers mount their horses, and I thought I saw lances; but I was not sure. I continued to ascend slowly, and I saw that their soldiers were going round the mountain to cut off my retreat. Half-way up the mountain I saw my three jolly fellows coming down corkscrew fashion. They jostled against each other, and could only come very slowly. I stopped short. I saw they were enemies. Then I saluted them politely, and began to descend. All three of them also came on down the mountain. I was not afraid of them, but I was of the others, who had gone round the road to cut me off. I looked to my left, but saw no one. I reached the foot of the mountain, the officers following me.

When I had fairly reached the plain, I turned towards them, and made them a low bow, seeing that my road was open. I said to my fine war-horse, "Gently, Coco" (that was the name of the beautiful animal). I was ahead, when one of them undertook to follow me; the other two stood still. He gained on me, and this encouraged him. When I saw that he had gone over half the distance between the mountain and the staff of the Emperor (who was watching my movements, and, seeing me so closely pressed, sent two horse-grenadiers to my assistance), I patted my horse to put him in a good humor. I looked behind, and saw that I had time enough to make a left-wheel, and attack him. He shouted to me, "Surrender." And I to him also, "Surrender." Wheeling to the left, I fell upon him. Seeing me make this sudden wheel-about, he yielded, but it was too late; the wine was poured out, and he had to drink it. He had scarcely turned to gallop off in retreat, when I was at his side, dealing him a blow with the point of my sabre. He fell head foremost to the ground, stone dead. Leaving my sabre hanging at my wrist, I seized his horse, and rode proudly back to the Emperor. "Well, old grumbler, I thought you would be captured. Who showed you how to make such a turn?" — "One of your picked gendarmes, in the Russian campaign." — "You have done well, and you are well mounted. Did you see that officer?" — "He seemed to be a blond man." — "He was a coward, whoever he was: he came out to fight, and allowed himself to be killed like a baby. One sabre-cut like that is no credit to any one. You grumble over it, I know." — "Yes, sire; I ought to have been able to take his horse by the bridle, and lead him to you." He smiled at this, and I led the horse forward. (Some one said) "It was such and such an English regiment." All praised my horse, and an officer begged me to let him have it. "Give fifteen napoleons to my servant, twenty francs to the grenadiers, and take it."

The Emperor said to the marshal, "Make a note of this old grumbler. After the campaign I will see about him."

It was, I believe, on the 14th that we met a large body of the Prussian advance-guard beyond Gilly. The cuirassiers went through the town at such speed that the horses' shoes flew over the houses. The Emperor watched them go through before leaving. It was a steep ascent, but it is impossible to imagine the rapidity with which that body of cavalry could go over a mountain. Our intrepid cuirassiers fell upon the Prussians, and sabred them without taking any prisoners. They were driven back upon their front with considerable loss. The campaign had begun.

Our troops encamped at the entrance to the plain of Charleroi, which is called Fleurus. The enemy could not see us, and did not think that the army had become united. Our Emperor also thought that they had not collected their forces, and on the 15th, during the night, he took command of the army in person. Early in the morning he sent in every direction to reconnoitre the enemy's position. Only the grand marshal, Count Monthyon, and I remained with him. He was at a village on the left of the plain, at the foot of a windmill, and the Prussian armies were mostly on his right, concealed by gardens, skirts of woods, and farms. "Their position is concealed; we cannot see them," said all the officers when they returned. The order was given for a general attack. The Emperor went up into the windmill, and, looking through a hole, watched all the movements. The grand marshal said to him, "There goes the corps of Marshal Gérard." — "Send Gérard up here." He came up to the Emperor. "Gérard," said he, "your Bourmont, for whom you said you would be answerable to me, has gone over to the enemy." And pointing through a hole in the mill to a steeple on the right, "You must go toward that steeple, and drive

the Prussians to extremities. I will sustain you. Grouchy has my orders."

All the officers of the staff started off, and did not return. Then the Emperor sent me to General Gérard. "Go to the steeple and find Gérard. Wait his orders to return." I galloped off. This was not an easy task; I had to take many turns. The space was covered with gardens. I did not know which way to go. However, I found the brave general at last, fighting hand to hand, covered with mud. I went up to him. "The Emperor sent me to you, general." — "Go tell the Emperor that if he will send me re-enforcements, the Prussians will be beaten. Tell him that I have lost half my soldiers, but that, if I am sustained, the victory is assured."

This was not a battle, it was a butchery. A charge was beaten on all sides. There was but one shout, "Forward!" I carried the report of it to the Emperor. After hearing me, he said, "Ah! if I had four lieutenants like Gérard, the Prussians would be lost." I had returned long before those whom the Emperor had sent off before he sent me. Some came back in the evening, after the battle was won; six did not appear at all. The Emperor rubbed his hands after I made my report, and made me describe all the places through which I had passed. There were only orchards, big trees, and farms. "Is that so?" said he. "We thought there were woods there." — "No, sire; the roads are only concealed by the foliage." All our columns were now advancing; the victory was decided. The Emperor said to us, "To horse, and gallop! there are my columns coming up the hill." So off we started. Across the plain there was a ditch three or four feet wide. The Emperor's horse halted for a moment, my horse leaped over, and there I was in front of his Majesty, carried on by his fleetness. I feared I should be scolded for my boldness, but I was not. When we reached the top of the hill the Emperor looked at me, and said, "If your horse were a stallion, I should take him."

Some cannon-balls were still falling at the foot of the hill, but our columns defeated the Prussians in the low ground on the right. This was kept up till night. The victory was complete. The Emperor retired at a very late hour from the battle-field, and returned to the village near the windmill. Thence he sent out officers in every direction. Count Monthyon dictated the despatches by order of the major-general, and the officers on duty started out at once. We were all on duty that night; no one had any rest.

The next day, June 17, 1815, at three o'clock in the morning, orders to advance were sent out. At seven o'clock our columns had come up. At that hour there were only the English in front of us. The Emperor sent an officer of the engineer corps to reconnoitre their position on the heights of Belle-Alliance, and to see if they were fortified. He returned, and said that he had seen nothing. Marshal Ney came up, and was rebuked for not having followed up the English, for there were only some "sans-culottes"[1] at the Quatre Bras. "Go, marshal, and take possession of the heights; the enemy are backed up against the woods. When I receive news from Grouchy, I will give you the order for the attack." The marshal started, and the Emperor went up on an eminence near a château by the roadside. From this point he uncovered his right wing just at the strongest part of the English army. I was sent for, and orders given me to go a little to the right of the road to Brussels, to make sure of the position of the left wing of the English which rested on the wood. I was obliged, in descending, to go alongside of the road on account of a broad and deep ravine which I could not cross, and a hill where the artillery of the guard was in battery. I must mention that we were drenched with rain, and the ground was very muddy; our artillery could not manœuvre. I passed near them, and when I came in front of that immense ravine, I saw some columns of infantry closely massed in the lower part of it. I crossed it, going a little to the right, and came upon an isolated barrack, a little way from the road. I stopped to look. On my right I saw some large rye-fields and their pieces in battery, but no one was moving. For a moment I did a little swaggering. I went near the rye-fields, and saw a body of cavalry behind them. I had seen enough of them. It appeared that it did not suit them to see me come near them: they saluted me with three shots from their cannon. I went back to tell the Emperor that on the right their cavalry was concealed behind the rye-fields, their infantry masked by the ravine, and that a battery had fired on me.

The Emperor gave orders for a general attack. Marshal Ney performed prodigies of courage and daring. This intrepid marshal had in front of him a formidable position. He could not take it. Every few moments he sent to the Emperor for re-enforcements so as to finish the work, he said. At last, in the evening, he received some cavalry, who put the English to rout, but without positive success. One more effort, and they would have been overthrown in the forest. Our centre

[1] The Scotch, thus called on account of their naked legs.

was making progress. They had passed the barracks in spite of the grape-shot which fell into the ranks. We knew not the misfortunes which awaited us.

An officer came up from our right wing. He told the Emperor that our soldiers were sounding a retreat. "You are mistaken," said he, "it is Grouchy coming." He sent off immediately in that direction to assure himself of the fact. The officer returned, and confirmed the report. There was no means of holding out. The Emperor, seeing himself out-flanked, took his guard, and marched it forward to the centre of his army in close columns. Followed by his whole staff, he formed the battalions into squares. Having gone through this manœuvre, he spurred his horse forward so as to enter the square commanded by Cambronne; but all his generals surrounded him. "What are you doing?" they cried. "Is it not enough for them to have gained the victory?" His design was to have himself killed. Why did they not allow him to accomplish it? They would have spared him much suffering, and at least we should have died at his side; but the great dignitaries who surrounded him were not willing to make such a sacrifice. However, I ought to say that we all surrounded him, and compelled him to retire.

We had the greatest possible difficulty in getting away. We could not make way through the panic-stricken multitude. And it was still worse when we arrived at Jemmapes. The confusion lasted a considerable length of time. Nothing could calm them: they would listen to no one; the horsemen shot their horses; the foot-soldiers shot themselves to avoid falling into the hands of the enemy; everything went pell-mell. I found myself taking part in another rout as complete as that of Moscow. "We are betrayed," they cried. This great blow came upon us on account of our right wing being broken in. The Emperor did not know the extent of the disaster till he reached Jemmapes.

The Emperor left Jemmapes, and rode to Charleroi, where he arrived between four and five o'clock in the morning. He left orders that all of his equipages should fall back, part by way of Avesnes, part by way of Philippeville, to Laon, which

"I ought to say that we all surrounded him and compelled him to retire." — Page 284.

he reached about ten o'clock. Officers were also sent to Marshal Grouchy with orders for him to come on to Laon. The Emperor dismounted at the foot of the city.

After he had given his orders, and made out his bulletin for Paris, an officer arrived who announced a column. The Emperor sent to reconnoitre it. It was the old guard returning in good order from the battle-field. When the Emperor heard this news, he no longer wished to start for Paris; but

he was compelled to do so by the majority of his generals. An old open carriage had been got ready for him, and some carts for his staff. One of his superior officers came, and gave orders to Colonel Boissy to take command of the place, and collect all the stragglers. The national guard was coming in from every direction. At last the Emperor came out into the great court where we were all together in the greatest state of anxiety. He asked for a glass of wine; it was handed to him on a large plate; he drank it, then saluted us, and started off. We were never to see him again.

We remained standing in the courtyard without speaking to one another. We reascended that steep hill in profound silence, worn out with hunger and fatigue. Our poor horses could scarcely go up, having galloped for twenty-four hours. Men and horses fell from want of food, not knowing what would become of them. No one took any account of us. We were, indeed, miserable. A few brave soldiers, who had not thrown away their arms, were gathered together. The greater portion of the soldiers had abandoned them in order to save their lives, leaving the main roads, and running across the fields. When the officers of the headquarters were collected together with Count Monthyon at their head, they started for Avesnes in a dispirited condition. By forced marches we reached the forest of Villers-Cotterets. We spent the night at the house of a physician on the edge of the forest. Count Monthyon said to me, "My good fellow, you must not unsaddle your horses, for the enemy may surprise us during the night. I am sure they are in pursuit of us, and we must not undress." I put up all our horses. Fortunately, I found some hay in the house. The servants were stationed in the stable with the bridles on their arms. I set one on guard to warn the general, and returned to his side. After supper I begged the general to take off his boots to rest himself. "No," said he. I pulled out a mattress, "Lie down there; you will rest better than on a chair. I will go and watch with the servants. Do not worry, and I will call you in time." At three o'clock in the morning the Prussians attacked Villers-Cotterets. They came out upon the main road, having turned suddenly to the right so as to shut us up in the city. This was what saved us. They fell upon our train, and made fearful havoc. At this noise I ordered the horses to be bridled and brought out, and ran to inform the general: "To horse, general! the enemy is in the city."

That time the servants did their duty quickly, I assure you. The horses were at the door as soon as I was. The general came down the stairs, and mounted his horse as I did mine. "This way," said he to us, "follow me." He went to the left into a narrow road, concealed from view, which ran along the edge of the forest and the beautiful plain. Three minutes later and we should have been captured. Two gun-shots behind us were platoons of foot-soldiers, placing sentinels everywhere. When we reached the end of the grand avenue, the general dismounted to breathe and think. After that we started for Meaux. Desolation reigned everywhere. Our deserters were coming in, most of them without arms. It was a heart-breaking sight. Meaux was so filled with troops that we had to go on to Claye; there we found the country deserted. All the inhabitants had moved out. It seemed as though the enemy had passed through it. Every one was on the way to Paris with his valuables. The roads were blocked up with carriages. They had turned their houses upside down. The enemy could not have caused greater destruction. We reached Paris at the gate of St. Denis. All the barriers had been barricaded. The troops were encamped in the plain of Les Vertus, and at the hills of St. Chaumont. The head-quarters was at the village of Villette, where Marshal Davout was stationed.

Our whole army was then reunited on the north of Paris, in that plain of Les Vertus, and there Marshal Grouchy arrived with his army corps, which had not suffered. We were told that he had thirty thousand men. The chief head-quarters had been established at Villette, near Marshal Davout. As I was baggage-master, I had the right to present myself every day to receive orders, and be present at the distributions. Consequently, I saw all the deputations arrive: generals and great personages in citizens' dress. Grand conferences were held night and day. I ought to say, for the credit of the Parisians, that we lacked for nothing. They sent everything, even Bologna sausage and white bread for the staff. About four or five o'clock in the morning I saw the brave national guards mount the walls which enclose Paris, turn to the left of the village so as not to be stopped, and advance to the line to exchange fire with the Prussians. Every day I witnessed this same movement. On the 29th or 30th of June, I said to my servant, "Give my horse some hay, and saddle him. I am going to see the national guards." I started off well armed. I had two pistols in my holster. They were rifled. A wooden hammer was necessary in loading them, and they shot at long range. They had cost me a hundred francs.

When I reached the plain of Les Vertus, I had the old guard on my right, and the national guards on my left. I went as far as the last of our sentinels who were in the first line supporting arms. I spoke to them. They were furious at their inaction. "No orders," they said; "the national guards do the firing, and we, we support arms. We are betrayed, captain." — "No, my children, you will receive your orders; have patience." — "But we are forbidden to fire." — "See here, brave soldiers, I want to pass the line. I see down there a Prussian officer who is taking on great airs; I should like to give him a little reproof. If you will permit me to pass, you need fear nothing from me; I am not going over to the enemy." — "Pass, captain."

I saw behind me four fine-looking men, who were approaching me. One of them came near me, and said, "Are you going over to the line for the fun of it?" — "Just as you are doing, I think." — "That is true," said he to me, "you are well mounted." — "So are you, sir." The other three turned to the right. "What are you looking at over there on the Prussian line?" said he to me. "See that officer down there who is making his horse prance. I want to make him a special visit; he displeases me." — "You cannot approach him without danger." — "I know my trade. I shall make him cross his line, and make him angry, if possible. If he gets angry, he is mine. I beg you, sir, not to follow me; you will spoil my manœuvre. Fall back farther." — "Very well, let us see."

I started off, having thoroughly determined what to do. When I reached the centre of the space between the two lines, he saw that I was advancing upon him. He thought that I would doubtless cross over to his side, so he crossed the line so as to get ahead of me. A hundred paces from his own lines he stopped and awaited me. Having gone the same distance, I also halted, and, drawing out my pistol, I sent a ball past his ears. He got angry, and started in pursuit of me. I wheeled about. He was no longer following me, but was returning. Then I made my left-wheel, and rushed upon him. Seeing me again, he came towards me. I sent him a second pistol-shot. He became more angry, and charged me. I wheeled about and ran off. He pursued me to the centre of the space between the lines, in a fury. I made an about-face, and fell upon him. He came close to me, and tried to stick his sabre into me. I struck his sabre up above his head, and, by the same movement, I brought my sabre down upon his face with such force that his nose went down to find his chin. He fell stone-dead.

I seized his horse, and proudly returned to my private soldiers, who crowded round me. The fine-looking man who had watched all my movements came galloping up to me, and said, "I am delighted; this is one of your tricks; you know how to do it well; it is not your first trial. I beg you to tell me your name." — "For what, if you please?" — "I have friends at Paris; I should like to tell them about this little play that I have seen. To what corps do you belong?" — "To the Emperor's staff." — "What is your name?" — "Coignet." — "And your Christian names?" — "Jean Roch." — "And your rank?" — "Captain." He took out his memorandum-book, and wrote it down. He told me his name: Boray or Bory. He went over to the right of the St. Chaumont hills where the old guard was stationed, and I returned to headquarters, leading my horse, and very proud of my capture. Every one stared at me. An officer asked me where I got my horse. "It is a horse which deserted and came over to our side; I caught him as he was going by." — "Good capture," said he.

When I reached my lodgings, I had some hay given to my horse, and examined my prize. I found a small portmanteau with some fine linen and other things necessary to an officer. I had the saddle taken off the horse, and sold him; as I had three horses, they were sufficient. I went to headquarters to resume my office manners. I found a great many people with the marshal, some going, some coming. There were conferences all night long. The next day, July 1, we received orders to move to the south of Paris, behind the Invalides, where the army was reunited and well intrenched. I went there after having gone to receive my general's orders. He sent me off with his aide-de-camp and his horses. "Go," said he; "Paris has surrendered. The enemy is about to take possession of it. Lose no time; all the officers are to leave Paris; you will be arrested. Go join the army which is collected on the side next the Barrière d'Enfer, and there you will receive orders to cross the Loire at Orleans."

When I reached the Barrière d'Enfer, where the army had collected, I found Marshal Davout on foot, his arms folded, gazing at that splendid army, who were shouting, "Forward."

He, silent, not speaking one word, walked up and down along the fortifications, deaf to the supplications of the army who wished to advance upon the enemy. The movement began, our right wing moving toward Tours, and our left wing toward Orleans. The enemy immediately became our rear-guard, and they had the cruelty to seize some men who were rejoining their corps, and rob them, as well as the officers. At our first halting-place they pressed so closely upon us that the army wheeled about, and attacked their advance-guard; they were driven back. After this they were not so insolent, and followed us only at a distance.

We reached Orleans without being pursued. We crossed the bridge over the Loire, and established the headquarters in a large faubourg which seemed to be almost entirely deserted. The inhabitants had gone into the city, and we suffered for everything. When we were installed, we undertook to barricade the bridge in the centre, with enormous posts and two gates to resist a heavy attack; then the *tête-de-pont* was put in a condition of defence, and made to bristle with pieces of artillery. We remained quiet for several days; the two enormous gates opened voluntarily to those who went in search of provisions, and we were obliged to go to the city for them. We found a boarding-house at the entrance of the principal street, and every day the gates had to be opened; but this did not last long. The great marshal was seen behind his batteries, his arms behind him, and his face anxious. No one spoke to him. He was no longer the same grand soldier whom I had formerly seen so brilliantly daring on the field of battle; all the officers left him alone.

One morning, as usual, we started out at nine o'clock to go to our boarding-house for breakfast. The rascal came to us, and said, "I cannot serve you. I have orders to be ready to receive the allies who are at the gates and are about to enter; the authorities have sent them the keys of the city." At the same moment there was a shout of "The Cossacks!" We went out with empty stomachs, and had scarcely got into the streets, when we saw the cavalry marching slowly in line of battle, and an immense crowd of people of both sexes, men and women. This sight made us tremble. All the women, richly dressed, with little white flags in one hand and white handkerchiefs in the other, formed the van, shouting, "Long live our good allies!" But the crowd was driven along by the cavalry close to the bridge and past our gates. Then the enemy stationed sentinels; the gates were closed, and each party was left to itself on either side of the palisades. As for the white handkerchiefs and little flags, our soldiers seized them all. The marshal did not utter a word; everything went off as quietly as you please. Pains and pleasures are all over in time.

We received orders to move the headquarters to Bourges, and Marshal Davout established himself there; but we did not remain there long. Marshal Macdonald arrived with a brilliant staff, the chief of which was Count Hulot, who had only one arm. I went every day to the marshal for his orders, and then to the post to carry the despatches. I always went late, and found the marshal at table. One of his aides-de-camp came out, and asked me for my package of despatches. "I do not know you," said I; "tell the marshal that his baggage-master is waiting for him at the door." — "But the marshal is at table." — "I tell you I do not know you." He went to inform the marshal of my refusal to deliver the papers. "Send him in." I went in, hat in hand. He rose to receive his package, and said to me, "You know your duty; you were perfectly right to answer my aide-de-camp as you did. I thank you, my good fellow; this shall not happen again. Let him come in whenever he brings my despatches; he should deliver them only to me."

In 1815 each day was only a repetition of the last. The army was disbanded and new regiments formed which bore the names of the several departments. I was appointed to have the rations distributed each day, and during the time I stayed at Bourges I had two hundred thousand rations distributed to the different ranks. Often I could only give out half rations. Then I had to call out some gendarmes to keep order.

The marshal kept me with him as long as he could; but it was intimated to him that an order would be sent to retire me on half-pay. On the 16th of January, 1816, the marshal sent for me. "I was told to come; that you wished to speak to me." — "Yes, my brave fellow. I am obliged to send you home on half-pay. I sincerely regret to part with you, but I have received orders to do so. I have put it off as long as possible." — "I thank you, marshal." — "If you wish to rejoin the depot (of the regiment) of the Yonne, and go into service again, I will see that you have a company of grenadiers." — "I thank you; but I have some business to attend to at Auxerre, and then I have three horses which I wish to get rid of. I shall ask leave of you to go to Paris to see them." — "I grant it with pleasure." — "I shall only need a furlough of a fortnight. My horses are valuable; I can sell them well only in Paris." — "You can start from here." — "I should like to go by Auxerre." — "I give you full permission to do so."

On the 4th of January I left Bourges; on the 5th I reached Auxerre with my three fine horses. At the town-hall I got a billet for five days at the Pheasant. There I found a *table d'hôte* at which the Marquis of Ganay, colonel of the regiment of Yonne, took his meals. I was asked to his table for three francs a meal; this was too much for my small purse. With seventy-three francs a month one cannot afford to spend ninety francs for dinners, not counting anything for my servant and my three horses. I could not begin life over again, and so I was obliged to be very economical. I wrote to my brother in Paris to send me two hundred francs to pay for the feeding of my horses, telling him that as soon as they were sold, I would return him the amount. I received the two hundred francs immediately, and set out for Ville-Fargeau to purchase a wagon-load of hay, straw, and oats, for the inn had ruined

me. In six days my three horses and my servant had cost me sixty francs. I went to see Carolus Monfort, an innkeeper near my hotel, who offered to serve me. "Come to my house," said he to me; "I will lodge you and your horses, and only ask you sixty francs a month; your horses shall have separate stalls, and you shall eat at the *table d'hôte*." — "It is a bargain," said I. "I will go and send all my horse-feed over to you." — "I remember you; you boarded at my father's house in 1804." — "That is true, my friend; but sixty francs is very dear. I have only seventy-three francs a month." — "You can send away your servant; my boy will groom your horses, and you can get along on three francs a month." — "Thank you," said I; ",I agree to that." So I established myself at the house of that excellent man.

On the 7th of January I went to see General Boudin. "General, I am again subject to your orders. Marshal Macdonald has given me a furlough of a fortnight to go to Paris to sell my horses." — "I forbid you to leave Auxerre." — "But, general, I have the permit." — "I repeat that I forbid you to leave the city." — "But, general, I have no money. How can I feed them?" — "That is none of my business." — "What must I do?" — "Let me alone. If you cannot sell them, you must blow out their brains." — "No, general, I will not do that; they shall eat so long as I have an old coat, and I will never harm them. I would rather make a present of them to my friends." I took leave of him, and withdrew, greatly cast down, but made no boast of what I would do, and kept perfect silence on the subject. When I returned to my lodgings I at once dismissed my servant. This was only the beginning. I did not suspect that I was watched by the devotees of the old monarchy. Once established at the house of Carolus Monfort, I became the nucleus of his *table d'hôte*. The regiment of Yonne was quartered at the insane-hospital at the Paris gate; sixteen or seventeen officers came and put up at the house on account of the cheapness of the board, and I was then the oldest hand at the table. I was obliged to make the acquaintance of the new-comers. Among them was an old captain with gray hair, who sat opposite me at the table every day. I saw that he wanted to become acquainted with me, and was not at his ease with the young officers. One of them, named Tourville, a second lieutenant from the life-guardsmen, and another, named St. Leger, formerly sergeant-major in the line, who had been to see the King at Ghent, told a fine story of the part they had played in the Marshal Ney affair. They boasted of having been disguised as veterans to shoot him in the Luxembourg. I could stand it no longer. I felt ready to jump over the table. I, however, restrained myself, and said to myself, "I will catch you the first opportunity."

On Friday Madame Carolus Monfort served us for vegeta-

"I received orders to ride at the right coach door of the princess, sabre in hand." — Page 297.

bles a plate of lentils. This threw my antagonists into a violent rage. They wanted to take the dish, and throw it out of the window. I said to them quietly, "Gentlemen, we must let your old captain decide. I refer the question to him." The old captain tasted the lentils. " I think, gentlemen, they are good." — " We do not want them." — " All right," said I, "suppose I should chase you round the town with a whip? That would not suit you either, would it? But you must submit to it, however. You understand me. I have no more to say. I shall wait for you a long time." But

I waited in vain. I was dealing with pewter plates which would not stand fire. The old captain pressed my hand.

Every day I went to the Café Milon to spend the evening and see the old habitués play cards. I made the acquaintance of M. Ravenot-Chaumont. That excellent man became very friendly to me. After having taken his cup of black coffee, he said to me, "Come, captain, let us take our little walk." We went out by the Temple gate and through some unfrequented paths to look at the vines. I believed myself to be alone with my friend, but this was not the case. We saw a man lying flat on his stomach under the vine branches, listening to our conversation. The police was then watching me, and it was not long before I had evidence of this. I was sent for to come to the town-hall, and present myself before the mayor, M. Blandavot, a big, good-natured magistrate. I had reason to congratulate myself upon his reception, which was exceedingly pleasant. " Information is lodged against you," said he. " You must look out. You are accused of having designs against the government." — " I swear to you, upon my honor, that it is false. I deny the accuser and the accusation. Allow me to justify myself before the rascal. Bring me into his presence. I ask neither pardon nor protection. If I am guilty have me arrested: you are the mayor." — " Go; I believe you, but look out."

Lovers of fine horses came to see mine. At last a man named Cigalat, a veterinary, persuaded me to sell my fine war-horse for nine hundred and twenty-four francs to his son Robin, who was on the diligence route. He had cost me eighteen hundred, but I had to submit to it. I had still two left. When the 60th (of the Yonne) had orders to leave Auxerre and go into garrison at Auxonne, I received the following letter from the surgeon-major: " My good captain, you can bring your two horses. I think I have sold them, if the price suits you (twelve hundred francs, and eighty francs for travelling expenses). If this suits you, you will find us at Dijon. We are to be there to escort the Duchess of Angoulême. The major will take one of them and the commandant the other. Come down to the Red Hat. We are putting up there."

How should I manage to go to Dijon? If I asked permission to go, I should be told, " I forbid you to leave the city." The devil! that would spoil it all! I had to start at three o'clock in the morning. I was sleepless, just as if I was about to do something wrong. The next day, at eight o'clock, I was at the hotel of the Red Hat. At eleven o'clock the regiment of the Yonne came to escort the duchess. I had had time to have my horses watered and fed. The gentlemen were informed of my arrival; they came. When the big major saw me, he said, " The owner of these horses has not yet come, has he?" — " You take me, no doubt, for a servant; but you are mistaken. I am the owner of those horses. Neither do I look like a servant. I am decorated, and received my decoration before you did, begging your pardon. Which of these two horses will you take?" — "The Normandy horse." — "You can have it for six hundred francs paid down, and eighty francs on time." — "It is a bargain."

The next day no one knew that I had been absent from Auxerre. I moved to the house of Father Toussaint-Armansier, on the square of the Marché-Neuf. There my board and lodging cost me only forty-five francs a month, with a little stew of a pound and a half every two days. I used to go to the Café Milon to see the old customers enjoy themselves, without ever taking a cup of coffee myself. From there I always went with my friend, Chaumont-Ravenot, to take our usual walk, and then I returned to the café to stay till ten o'clock. This was the life that I led during the time I was a bachelor. Scarcely a fortnight passed without my being accused of something. Then the accusations became less frequent. The commissioner of police was interrogated as to my conduct. I must say, for his credit, that I owe my liberty to him. He became responsible for me during the whole time that I was being watched. He kept his eye upon me without saying anything to me.

The Duchess of Angoulême was about to pass through Auxerre, and great preparations were made to receive her. Some men of the marine corps, all dressed in white, were ordered to unhitch her horses under the gate of the Temple. As for me, I received orders to appear in full uniform at the gate of the Temple, to ride at the right coach-door of the princess, sabre in hand. I went. Orders are not invitations, and must be obeyed.

When I went to my post, I took my stand near the doorway, and the poor fools dressed in white dragged the carriage slowly by. I, with my old mouth, never uttered a word. She might have been sure, if she had known me, that I would not have allowed her to be insulted. I always respect the unfortunate. On reaching St. Étienne square, the carriage stopped near the cathedral, and the clergy, with the cross and the great crucifix borne by the Abbé Viard and M. Fortin, the vicar, appeared at the left doorway. The Abbé Viard presented his crucifix, and poor Fortin, with his head bowed upon Abbé Viard's shoulder, was crying bitterly. The tears flowed so plentifully over his fat cheeks that I almost felt like crying too. One may imagine how much fun there was for me in all this. When all the benedictions were over, the princess's carriage, drawn by the jackasses of the port, entered the courtyard of the prefecture. At the foot of the stairway she was received by the authorities, and slowly mounted the steps. She looked pale, thin, and careworn. She was conducted to a large hall which could hold three hundred people. There a throne had been prepared to receive her. When my duty was done, I joined the corps of officers on half-pay, and went to make a visit to this unfortunate princess, the daughter of Louis XVI. Our turn came; we were announced, and formed a circle in that immense hall. She did not address a word to us, and looked cross.

About this time we were told to look out for some place to live, which meant, "You are thrown overboard." All the officers, who could not remain in the city, went off into the country to live among laborers, on consideration of a pension of three hundred francs a year. As for me, I determined at once what I should do. I went to Mouffy to stay for a month, so as to get my little vineyard in good condition, feeling sure that by using economy there, I could manage to live comfortably on my seventy-three francs a year. I, as well as my two laborers, made the handle of my pickaxe move. In a month's time my little vines were in excellent condition. I did not leave the care of them to my two vine-dressers. I showed them that the soldier could resume the plough. My poor hands had great blisters on them; but I went to work with all my might, saying, "I have gone through many trials; I will show you, my children, that the earth must yield a living to its master."

I went back to Auxerre on more serious business. I had said to myself, "You must settle down, and marry. You must not remain a bachelor any longer, when you have the opportunity to make a home for yourself." But the important part was to find the lady. Whom should I consult? I went to see M. More, who was one of my best friends. I had visited him since 1814, and had always been kindly welcomed. He had a relative employed in his shop, whom he always addressed as "my cousin." I had been particularly struck with her business energy, but I had not spoken of it. This amiable young woman found a small business, and, without saying anything to her relatives, she purchased it. I had lost sight of her. Happening one day to go to see M. Labour, the confectioner, Madame Labour said to me, "Do you know a decorated captain who lives at Champ?" — "No, madame." — "He is the one who wanted to marry a girl, one of our friends, who lived with M. More for eleven years, and who has just set up in business for herself." — "Where has she established herself?" — "At the corner of the Rue des Belles-Filles. She paid cash for the house and

business, with a good personal property." — "Well, madame, I have no acquaintance with the captain further than having seen him at public ceremonies. I cannot give you any positive information about him." I bade farewell. "Ah," said I to myself, "somebody's going to forestall me with this girl. I must not lose any time."

That same day I went to Mademoiselle Baillet's house: that was her name. "Mademoiselle, I should like some coffee and some sugar." — "You shall have it, sir," said she. — "I should like to have the coffee freshly ground." — "I will grind you some. How much do you want?" — "A pound will be enough." And so I made her turn her mill.

When this operation was over, and my two packages were tied up, I paid her. "I have not taken much?"—"So much the worse, sir."—"That's not what I came for; I want to speak to you."—"Very well; speak, I am listening."—"I came to ask for your hand. I make my petition myself, without preamble and without subterfuge. I do not know how to make speeches. I ask you this with a soldier's bluntness."—"And I answer you as frankly,—perhaps I will give it."—"Well, mademoiselle, when shall I come to speak with you seriously on the subject?"—"At six o'clock."

At six o'clock exactly I presented myself. "You have not got your permit?"—"I am going to ask for it; but first we must come to an understanding about our ways and means. In order for me to receive a permit, my future wife must bring a dowry of twelve thousand francs."—"I can do that," said she, "counting my house and furniture. So far we are all right."—"As for me, I have nothing but a few acres of ground and some vines, but I have no debts. All my little savings have been spent in getting my vines in good order; I did not expect to marry so soon."—"Very well, ask for your permit; I agree to your proposal."—"And I, mademoiselle, pledge my word to you. To-morrow I will make my petition to the general." I was kindly received by the general. "I will send off your petition at once, and I shall add a postscript also."—"Thank you, general."

Eight days after I received my permit. I hastened to Mademoiselle Baillet's house. "Here is my permit; we must set the day for the signing of the contract. If you are willing, we can also fix the day for our marriage."—"You are in such a hurry; I ought to tell my relatives about it."—"Take your time, and we will settle upon any day that suits you." We fixed upon the 10th for the contract, and the 18th for our marriage. The contract was signed. M. Marais was my witness and M. Labour was witness for my future wife. My dowry in hard cash was of the smallest. I said to her, "My whole fortune consists of four francs and fifty centimes; you will be so good as to add the rest. I offer you a repeater watch, a beautiful chain, and two silver knives, forks, and spoons. As for my wardrobe, I need nothing; forty shirts and other things in proportion; also seventy-three francs a month, a hundred and twenty-five francs a year from the Legion of Honor, and four casks of wine. But I do not owe a sou." — "All right, sir; we will do our best." Everything was settled. I went at once to see M. Rivolet to ask him to lend me eighty francs to buy a shawl, which I carried immediately to my future wife. She was delighted. I went afterwards to see M. More, and inform him of our expected marriage. "Whom are you going to marry?" — "Your cousin, Mademoiselle Baillet." — "She is the very woman I should have chosen for you, my good fellow. I shall be glad to do anything I can for you." — "I may have to call on you." — "You may rely upon me."

Then I went to see M. Labour. "It is to you that I owe my marriage with your friend; you gave me the hint. But for you some one else might have secured her." — "How fortunate it was that we spoke to you." But this was not what gave me most trouble. I had to go to confession. I made some inquiries, and was told that I had better apply to M. Lelong, who was a fine man. I went immediately to see him. "Sir," said I, "I have chosen you to marry me." — "But have you been to confession?" — "No, indeed; and it is for that purpose that I have come to you. What can be required of a soldier? I have done my duty." — "Very well, then I will do mine." Then he knelt with both knees on the edge of a chair, mumbled a short prayer, and, rising from the chair, he gave me his blessing (which was as good as another) with my card of confession. "Tell the Abbé Viard that I am to marry you. Whom are you to marry?" — "Mademoiselle Baillet." — "Ah," said he, "I studied with her father. Has she been to confession?" — "No, sir." — "Send her to me."

— "All right. I should like to be married on the 18th, at four o'clock in the morning." — "The church is not open till five o'clock, but I will be at the door with the keys at half-past four." — "Thank you; I will go and send my future wife to you at once." — "I will wait here for her."

I was ready to jump for joy at having got rid of that duty. I went to see my *fiancée*. "Mademoiselle, I have been to confession. M. Lelong is now waiting for you." — "Very well; I will go." — "You must go to his house. He is an old friend of your father, so he told me." — "All right; you stay here with these girls. I shall not be gone long." Everything was settled in half an hour, and the next day we carried our three francs to Abbé Viard.

I had got everything ready for our departure. I had hired a four-seated carriage, which was to wait for us at the Champinot gate as we came out of the church. At six o'clock we were seated in the carriage after having taken a cup of coffee. No one in the neighborhood was up. It was like a runaway match. I had informed them at Mouffy that I should bring my wife on the 18th, and that they must have ready for four of us a good stew. I would attend to everything else. I took a three-franc pie, and we started off to dine at Mouffy.

The next day we went to Coulanges to dine with M. Ledoux, who was expecting us, and had ordered a handsome dinner. His daughter was one of my wife's shop-girls. We returned to Auxerre at nine o'clock in the evening. I am sure that, including the carriage, I spent twenty francs in two days for my bridal expenses. One could not have been more economical. No one in the neighborhood had any suspicion of it. The next day I rose at five o'clock to open my shop, and my neighbors, seeing me so early, said, "The lover is an early riser." The next day the same thing occurred. They never suspected that I was married.

On Sunday we went out to make some visits. Everywhere we were reproached for not having invited any one to our wedding. "Do not bear me any grudge. I could not do so. I should have been obliged to send you off as soon as we left the church. We could not receive you; there are too many of you. I desire, however, your friendship." The ladies said, "If we could only have been present at the benediction!"—"It was too early in the morning to disturb you." Everywhere we met with the same reproaches. The family was so large that we heard the same thing for three days. When these tiresome visits were over, I put on the harness at once. I did everything. At four o'clock in the morning I was up and attending to our little household affairs. I helped my amiable wife with everything. We were not able to keep a regular servant, but only a charwoman at three francs a month. I put on a coarse cloth apron when I roasted the coffee; but, as I was on half-pay, I was forbidden to wear it. I had to submit.

I went to see M. More, and asked him to furnish me spices on credit. "I will let you have all you want."—"But no notes. All on my word of honor, and I will keep only a little pass-book."—"You can get all you want."—"Very well, we will begin to-day. I shall not buy everything from you. M. Labour will have to furnish me certain things, such as oil, chocolate, and wax-tapers."—"Everything you want you can have."

My purchases amounted to a thousand francs. He wanted me to buy more. "If I want more, I will come again." I went to see M. Labour, and made the same request of him. "You can get anything you want at my store on a pass-book." —"It is a bargain. I shall divide my custom between you and M. More."—"That's right, that's all right."—"Come, then, let us begin. Here is the memorandum that my wife gave me. Put all these articles on my pass-book. The first month I will pay M. More, and the next month I will pay you. Does that suit you?"—"Any way that suits you suits me." His memorandum amounted to eight hundred francs.

When all this was settled I had to go back to M. More. He gave a little toss of his cotton cap on seeing me enter. "Here is a memorandum."—"All right, my good fellow; you shall have the things this evening." I made quite as large an account with M. Labour. The four bills amounted to three thousand five hundred francs. This seemed a frightful amount to me; but my dear wife said, "Do not be worried. We shall succeed with industry and strict economy. We shall come through all right." How fortunate I was to have found such a treasure!

When we got our business well arranged, customers came from every direction, and the amount of our sales was as much as we could possibly have expected — fifteen hundred francs a month. I was greatly pleased to be able to take a thousand francs to M. More and five hundred francs to M. Labour. I gladly made fresh purchases from them.

I was constantly tormented with fears of being informed against. When I saw a police agent I always thought he was coming for me, and frequently I was not mistaken. My wife said to me, "My dear, you must look for a garden where you can amuse yourself." — "I should like to have one," said I. So I looked around, and spoke to M. Marais about it. He said, "I will find one for you. There are plenty of them to be had." One day he came to see me, and said, "I have found just the thing you want, near me on the promenade. Go

see Father Chopard, the cooper and wooden-shoe dealer. He wants to sell his garden." I went to see Chopard. "You wish to sell your garden?" — "Yes, sir." — "Will you show it to me?" — "Certainly, sir." — "Come along then. If it suits me, and the price is not too high, I will buy it."

After I had seen it, I said, "How much do you ask for it?" — "Twelve hundred francs." — "If you will come to my house, you can take my wife to look at it. If she likes it, we can determine about it." My wife went to see it, and said, "It suits us. You can buy it." I went to see those poor people, and concluded the purchase for twelve hundred francs. Oh, how glad I was to have a garden! It was a barren spot, but in a year's time it looked altogether differently. I spent six hundred francs on it, and I made my pickaxe and spade fly in it. I made it my Champ d'Asile.[1] In my garden I was sheltered from spies. It was the delight of both my wife and myself, and to it I owe all my good health. I abandoned all the rest of the world (I ought to say that I saw persecutors everywhere). For thirty years I cultivated my sweet retreat, never passing two days without going to look at it, and during all that time always accompanied by my wife.

When I got possession of my garden, people came to see me. They came to see the "old grumbler," always at work with his coat off and his pickaxe in his hand, and so happy to own a little piece of ground. In 1818 I made a good crop on my vines at Mouffy. I sold the wine for a thousand francs, which stopped a hole in my debts. I was very proud to be able to carry two thousand francs to M. More and M. Labour in addition to my monthly receipts.  But the spies were always after me. About the end of September, 1822, at ten o'clock in the morning, a fine-looking man with full black whiskers, and handsomely dressed in a blue coat and pantaloons of the same color, came to my house. He had the scar of a sabre-cut from his ear to his mouth, and looked every inch a soldier. I could not resist asking him into my little chamber.

---

[1] There was much talk at that time of the colony founded under that name in Texas by old soldiers of the Empire, under General Lallemand.

"Pray be seated, and take a glass of wine." My wife said, "If you would like it, I will give you a cup of bouillon." — "I cannot refuse it," said he.

After taking some refreshment, he showed me a list of all the officers who remained in the town. "Who gave you that list?" — "I do not know who he was." — "Have you found out anything?" — "Oh, yes," said he. I said to my wife, "Give him three francs." — "Certainly, dear."

I asked him where he came from. "I came from Greece." And he drew some papers from his pocket, and read me the names of the principal officers who commanded in Greece. "Permit me to ask you this question, Why did you go down there?" — "My commander took me there with him." — "And why have you come back here?" — "Because I saw my commander impaled, and that frightened me, and I left the country immediately." — "What are you going to do?" — "I have protectors in the office of the minister of war." I took leave of this fellow, who went straight to the mayor's office, and brought accusation against me.

I was summoned before the mayor without delay. At noon the agent of police informed me that I was sent for. I went with my cap on, without even changing my dress. "What do you want with me, M. Mayor?" — "You are accused." — "I protest. I ask neither pardon nor protection. I am innocent. I know the rascal. He has a sabre-cut on his face, and he told me he came from Greece. I gave him three francs, a cup of bouillon, and two glasses of wine. He is the very one who has informed against me. If you will permit me, I will go to see the general." — "He knows all about it." — "What, already? It was only ten o'clock when the rascal left my house. He travelled rapidly; he went in two hours. Will you allow me to go and explain the matter to the general?" — "Go, and come back and tell me what he says to you." — "All right."

I went to the Rue du Champ. I found the general in his chamber, beside a bright fire, in a handsome dressing-gown. "Good-morning, general." — "Good-morning, sir." — "I am not sir, general. I am Captain Coignet, who has just been accused; but this time I know the rascal who informed against me. He is a police-spy from Paris. He came to my house with a list of all the officers on half-pay. I would like very much to know who was mean enough to give all our names. I would take his life, or he should take mine. I gave him three francs, two glasses of wine, a cup of bouillon, and, in return for my hospitality, he has just accused me of ill-conduct. You ought to have kept him here, I think, so that I could have seen him in your presence. If you have let him go off, it is high time to put an end to this business. For the past six years I have been kept under surveillance by you, without deserving it. To-day, general, I have determined to die, or have my liberty, which I demand of you. You can decide which it is to be. I do not ask pardon of you. I swear upon my honor that I am innocent, and my word ought to be sufficient. This is all I have to say. I will come to-morrow at three o'clock to hear what you have decided. You can have me arrested, if you choose. If you permit me to withdraw, I will take my gun, and go up and down the streets, and, if I find the rascal, I will shout to the citizens, 'Get out of the way, while I shoot this mad dog.'" — "Come, captain, restrain yourself." — "General, if your police-spy has not told the truth, have a hundred blows laid on him with a good stick, and you will not be deceived any more." — "You can go."

He went with me to the door. I had hit the nail on the head. The next day, at a quarter to three o'clock, I stood on my doorstep waiting for the hour to come when I should go to see the general. M. Ribour came up, and said, "Captain, I have come to tell you that all the accusations filed against you have been burned before my eyes; there were forty-two of them. You can speak now, and say anything you like; you will not be accused again."

On the 8th of May the hail injured my garden. I lost my little crop. Those who did not suffer from this disaster at Auxerre made good wine. I made eighteen casks of it from my small vines at Mouffy, which helped me out for the year 1822. In 1823–1824 I made a tolerable crop, but in 1825 I made some excellent wine. I sold it to liquidate my indebtedness to MM. More and Labour, and I had three hundred francs left, which I immediately laid out in groceries, buying not a sou's worth more. When I went home I said to my wife, "I am the happiest of men. I no longer owe anything, and here are three hundred francs of fine groceries, for which I paid cash." The king was not happier. My little establishment was nicely kept up. I gave up visiting entirely. In summer my wife and I started out at three o'clock in the morning; I went back from the garden at six o'clock to open my little shop, and returned at once. At nine I went home for breakfast.

This was the life my dear wife and I led for thirty years. May the earth rest lightly upon her! She was always kind to the poor. Every Monday she distributed a wooden bowl full of big sous, and she used to knit stockings for the blind. She laid by for this purpose twelve francs a month. I said to her, "That is too much, dear." — "It will bring us good luck," she answered. I have continued to do the same; but I have lost two, which has lightened it by six francs a month.

Every fortnight my wife had some poor people at our table. I have laid aside this habit since I have lived alone. I only go myself, and take to them the money that my wife was accustomed to give. All her wishes are sacred to me. She asked me in a paper, which is in my desk, and which has neither date nor signature, to give a hundred francs to her brother, Baillet, who is in Paris. That I pay every three months from my pension, and also seventy-two francs for her poor people, making a sum of one hundred and seventy-two francs a year.

I have involuntarily fallen into a sad train of thought, which is, perhaps, out of place here. I will now return to my subject. The years from 1826 to 1829 passed without any changes for me. My thirty years of service had expired. I had been looking forward to it a long time. I held the rank of captain fifteen years eleven months and nine days. My services for thirty years amounted to twelve hundred francs; for twelve campaigns, to two hundred and forty francs; for six months, ten francs: total, fourteen hundred and fifty francs. I was retired on the 23d of August, 1829, the date of the expiration of my thirty years of service. A friend went to Paris, and attended to my business for me through his cousin, M. Martineau des Chesnez, who had charge of personal affairs in the office of the minister of war. I received this fine pension in the Rue des Belles-Filles. A good many persons were present when I received my pension, which amounted to fourteen hundred and fifty francs instead of nine hundred and thirty francs, as I had expected. I uttered an exclamation of joy, and said, "So much the better! My poor people shall profit by it." I kept my word. I doubled my charities. There was in my neighborhood the widow of a soldier, who had two sons and a daughter. I put the two sons to school, which cost me eighty francs a year. I gave them all my old clothes. One of them I must notice particularly; his name was Choude. He made such progress in his studies that he entered a small seminary in Auxerre, and now he is a curate in a country parish. I have never seen him since; but I did good, and that is enough for me.

There was great commotion in France in 1830. The people were much excited against the old monarchy, and wanted to get rid of it forever. Paris revolted; she always gives the start to the revolutions. Paris would like to change government as often as we change our shirts. Auxerre also joined the movement. There was great excitement there. Fortunately, however, it was confined within the town-gates. The people contented themselves with having small gatherings at the Temple gate, the town-hall, the prefecture, and on the road to Paris, in order to intercept the despatches. They took good care not to go beyond Mount St. Simeon; but they escorted the mail. Ah, those brave defenders of their country! I watched them slyly, and followed all their movements.

The authorities hastened to restore order. A national guard was formed immediately, and the elections took place as soon as possible. To my surprise, I was appointed ensign without my permission. I had the law on my side. I was at liberty to join the national guard or not. The ensign's commission was brought to me. "Who gave you permission to appoint me without my knowledge?" — "Everybody voted for you; you were unanimously elected; you must not refuse." — "So you are the masters, are you? Who is your chief of battalion?" — "M. Turquet." — "You have chosen a good man. I will give you my answer to-morrow. If I accept your ensign, I will be at the town-hall at noon."

I consulted my wife. "You must not refuse," said she. — "But it will be an enormous expense, and a heavy task for me." — "Do not refuse, I beg you; they will think you have

a grudge against them." — "But they have made me suffer a great deal by their tale-bearing. They deserve to have me send them off." — "No," said she; "do not remember that against them." — "But this will inconvenience us very much. It will cost me two hundred francs." — "Do not refuse, I beg you."

At noon I took my answer to them. "Here comes our ensign," they shouted. — "You don't know that, gentlemen; I belong to myself, and not to you. You have no right over me; there is the law. If you think you are doing me a favor in giving me this heavy burden, you are mistaken; but I will

"You are giving this standard into the hands of the soldier who was the first man decorated on the 14th of June, 1804." — Page 312.

bear it." — "We will give you an aide." — "And this expense which I must incur? You are all rich; but I am not." — "Come, my good fellow; you are one of us." — "I promise you to enter upon my duty at once. But I do not see your mayor; he must be restored to his position. The police-spies drove him away, and you have no right to administer justice. If he does not agree to return, he must be replaced. You must immediately appoint an officer at the prefect's house to protect him; the spies pointed their bayonets at his breast to make him give up his despatches."

They followed all my advice. Authority was restored to its proper channels, and the mayor returned to his post. The national guard, numbering from fifteen to eighteen hundred men, all dressed in blouses (the tailors had not sufficient time), were called together to go to Arquebuse. I received orders to go there in order to be received. A standard had been hastily prepared to make the first proclamations. Every day they sent me up and down the streets with my heavy burden.

But later it was still worse. The town had a standard made which cost six hundred francs; it was magnificent. The flag was as large as the sail of a seventy-four. It hid my face. I bent under it. When I came in, all my clothes were wet with perspiration. One may imagine how amusing all this was for an old captain who had seen battles enough. It took me two hours to go over the town; then, when I got back to the town-hall, I had to carry it to the house of Commandant Turquet at the port. If it had been kept there, I should have been thankful. I went beyond my strength. I gave it one day to M. Mathieu to take it down. He could not carry it to its position.

Fortunately, the Queen had embroidered one, so it was said, for the national guard of Auxerre; the Duke of Orleans brought it. All the national guards of the country districts assembled on this occasion. The Prince dismounted at the Leopard, and we had to furnish him a body-guard: the firemen, the chasseurs, the grenadiers, and the ensign (this was indispensable). We had to spend the night with our feet in water, and have a stable for our guard-room. No one thought of us. We spent the night shivering, lying on a dunghill. This was all the consideration the authorities of Auxerre had for the citizens. If a battalion of troops of the line had been in our place, the officers would not have left us in such a condition. The next day I had to carry the standard to the town-hall. I took advantage of the opportunity to go by my house, and take my breakfast as quickly as possible, so as to get back to my post. I had plenty of time to look about me. All the national guards from the country had to be stationed on the right of the broad walk of Éperon. When all were stationed the duke was informed. I was at my post to receive the standard. The Prince came on horseback, bearing it himself. He halted in front of me. I said to him, "Prince, you are giving this standard into the hands of the soldier who was the first man decorated, on the 14th of June, 1804, in the dome of the Invalides, by the hands of the First Consul." The Prince replied, "So much the better, my good fellow; that is one more guarantee for its being well defended." These words and mine were reported in the newspapers. I carried the standard for three years, and I cannot tell what I suffered. All the quartermasters and corporals trod on my feet, having taken too much wine three-quarters of the time. Fortunately, they gave me an aide named Charbonnier, an old decorated gendarme. Without his assistance I could not have served my term.

The Duke of Orleans, on returning to his hotel, made inquiries about me. The next day we went to escort him, carrying the flag. When he reached Paris he gave an account of his mission, and spoke of me. The King, wishing further information concerning me, had the muster-rolls in the office of the minister of war examined, and found that I had gone through all the campaigns. He sent to the chancellor's office to make sure that I had really been the first man decorated, as I had told his son. All I had said was confirmed. He saw that I had been appointed an officer in the Legion of Honor, on the 5th of July, 1815. by the provisional government. I did not know that the Duke of Orleans was interested in my favor, and I did not find it out till 1847.

On the 31st of January of that year I received a letter, and, to my astonishment, I saw that it was addressed to "M. Captain Coignet, officer in the Legion of Honor." I said to myself, "They are mocking me; they are gilding my pill."

I broke the seal, and read as follows: —

Sir, — You were appointed on the 5th of July, 1815, by the provisional government, and again on the 28th of November, 1831, by the King, an officer in the Legion of Honor. Consequently, you ought not to be receiving a hundred francs; you should receive two hundred and fifty francs, which will be paid you annually.

(Signed) Secretary-general of the Legion of Honor,
VISCOUNT DE ST. MARS.

So I was appointed for the third time. But who could have had me appointed by the provisional government? Turning over in my head the memories of past days, I recalled the plain of Les Vertus, the 30th of June, and the handsome superior officer who took down my name and my Christian names. Perhaps it was he; he told me his name also when he saw me cut off the Prussian officer's nose. Ah! now I remember it. His name was Bory de St. Vincent. What a fortunate thing for me to be able to recall the name of such a man!

I received my commission, and letters from all who were interested in me: Count Monthyon, M. Larabit, and my sister-in-law Baillet, superintendent of a branch establishment of the orphans of the Legion of Honor, in Rue Barbette.

On the 16th of August, 1848, the anniversary of my birth, the greatest of all misfortunes befell me. I lost my dear companion, after thirty years of happy days. I was left alone, crushed with sorrow. What could I do at seventy-two years of age? I could not undertake anything. My little business was not sufficient to rouse me from my deep dejection. For a long time I thought over the events of my earlier life, which now seemed so far away. I said to myself, "If I only knew how to write well, I could undertake to write the story of all my fine campaigns, and the tale of the saddest childhood that a child of eight years ever suffered.

Well, I think God will help me." My resolution taken, I bought some paper and other necessary things. I set to work. What made it most difficult for me was, that I had no memoranda or any document to assist me. No one can imagine how much thought and worry I went through in order to be able to retrace the whole of my military career. I can give no idea of the trouble I had in portraying myself. If I have succeeded, I shall consider myself sufficiently rewarded; but it is time for me to come to an end. My memory is failing. It is not the history of others that I have written; it is the story of my own life, which I have told with all the sincerity of a soldier who has done his duty, and who writes without prejudice.

And now let me speak to the fathers of families who may read this. Let them use every effort to have their children taught to read and write, and to train them well. This is the best inheritance, and is easily supported. If my parents had bestowed this precious gift upon me, I might have made a distinguished soldier. I had courage and intelligence. I was never punished, always present at roll-call, untiring in marches and counter-marches, and I could have gone round the world without complaining. In order to make a good soldier, one must have courage in adversity, obedience to all officers, no matter of what rank. He who is a good soldier will make a good officer. I end the story of my life July 1, 1850.

Written by me,

JEAN-ROCH COIGNET.

DOCUMENTARY EXTRACTS.

STATEMENT OF THE MILITARY SERVICES OF COIGNET (JEAN-ROCH), CAPTAIN ON THE GENERAL STAFF, BORN AT DRUYES, IN THE DEPARTMENT OF THE YONNE, MARCH 16TH, 1776, RETIRED AT AUXERRE, CHIEF TOWN OF THE AFORESAID DEPARTMENT OF THE YONNE.

Entered the service as a soldier in the 1st auxiliary battalion of Seine-et-Marne, the 6th Fructidor, year VII. (23d of August, 1799).

	YRS.	MOS.	DAYS.
Incorporated in the 96th half-brigade, the 21st Fructidor, year VII. (September 8, 1800)	1		12
Entered the guard the 2d Germinal, year XI. (March 23, 1803)	2	6	15
Corporal, July 14, 1807	4	3	21
Sergeant, May 18, 1809	1	10	4
Lieutenant in the line, July 13, 1812	3	1	25
Captain on the general staff, September 14, 1813	1	2	1
Retired to his home, by virtue of the letter of the Duke of Tarento to the camp-marshal, chief of the general staff, dated Bourges, October 31, 1815.	2	1	16
Total of years of service	16	2	4

NOTE.—The effective service should be added to what is contained in this paper, counting from the 31st of October, 1815, the date of the letter of the camp-marshal, chief of the general staff, Count Hulot, who ordered the retirement to his native place.

Collated conformably to the original as shown to us and immediately copied by us, mayor of the town of Auxerre, December 2, 1816.

(Signed) LEBLANC.

	YRS.	MOS.	DAYS.
Campaigns in Italy, years VIII. and IX.	2		
Ans X., XI., XII., XII., and XIV. in the army of observation on the Gironde, in the armies of Spain and Portugal, and the army of England	5		
1806 and 1807, in Prussia and in Poland	2		
Years 1808, 1809, 1810, 1811 1812, 1813, and 1814, and subsequently in Prussia, Poland, Spain, Germany, Russia, Saxony, and Poland, and in the army of the North	7		
Total of campaigns	16		

Legionary, the 25 Prairial, year XII. (June 14, 1804).

RECAPITULATION.

	YRS.	MOS.	DAYS.
Effective services	16	2	4
War campaigns	16		
General total of services up to and including the 31st of October, 1815	32	2	4

A True Copy:

The Sub-Inspector of the reviews,

(Signed)   LUCET.

DECEMBER 2, 1816.

www.ingramcontent.com/pod-product-compliance
Lightning Source LLC
Chambersburg PA
CBHW031426230426
43668CB00007B/452